SAYONARA AMERIKA, SAYONARA NIPPON

ASIA PERSPECTIVES: HISTORY, SOCIETY, AND CULTURE

ASIA PERSPECTIVES: HISTORY, SOCIETY, AND CULTURE

A Series of the Weatherhead East Asian Institute, Columbia University

CAROL GLUCK, EDITOR

Comfort Women: Sexual Slavery in the Japanese Military During World War II,
by Yoshimi Yoshiaki, trans. Suzanne O'Brien

The World Turned Upside Down: Medieval Japanese Society,
by Pierre François Souyri, trans. Kathe Roth

Yoshimasa and the Silver Pavilion: The Creation of the Soul of Japan,
by Donald Keene

*Geisha, Harlot, Strangler, Star: The Story of a Woman, Sex, and Moral Values
in Modern Japan*, by William Johnston

Frog in the Well: Portraits of Japan by Watanabe Kazan, 1793–1841,
by Donald Keene

The Modern Murasaki: Writing by Women of Meiji Japan,
edited and translated by Rebecca L. Copeland and Melek Ortabasi

So Lovely a Country Will Never Perish: Wartime Diaries of Japanese Writers,
by Donald Keene

SAYONARA AMERIKA, SAYONARA NIPPON

A GEOPOLITICAL PREHISTORY OF

J-POP

MICHAEL K. BOURDAGHS

Columbia University Press

New York

Columbia University Press wishes to express its appreciation for assistance given by the Northeast Asia Council of the Association for Asian Studies toward the cost of publishing this book.

COLUMBIA UNIVERSITY PRESS
Publishers Since 1893
New York   Chichester, West Sussex

cup.columbia.edu

Library of Congress Cataloging-in-Publication Data
Bourdaghs, Michael K.
  Sayonara Amerika, sayonara Nippon : a geopolitical prehistory of J-pop /
Michael K. Bourdaghs.
     p. cm. —(Asia perspectives)
  Includes bibliographical references and index.
  ISBN 978-0-231-15874-9 (cloth : alk. paper)
  ISBN 978-0-231-15875-6 (pbk. : alk. paper)
  ISBN 978-0-231-53026-2 (e-book)
  1. Popular music—Japan—History and criticism.   I. Title.
  ML3501.B69 2012
  781.630952—dc23

                                                      2011029162

FOR RONALD BOURDAGHS (1937–2010)

CONTENTS

ACKNOWLEDGMENTS

This book took fourteen years to write. It was only after I had already been working on it for several years that I even realized I was writing a book on Japanese pop. As a result of this unnaturally prolonged gestation, the project became so entangled with the threads of my life that it is difficult now to trace its chapters back to clearly defined starting points. This makes providing adequate acknowledgments here a challenging task. In a very real sense, everyone who has been a part of my life the past decade and a half deserves a share in the credit: thank you.

In part, the book began with a panel I organized on Japanese popular music for the 1997 Association for Asian Studies (AAS) annual meeting. My fellow panelists—Mark Anderson, Leo Ching, Brett de Bary, Joanne Izbicki, and the late Miriam Silverberg—shared their insights on popular music and gave me valuable feedback on my own work. My paper for the panel was based on research funded in part by grants from the UCLA Center for Japanese Studies and the AAS Northeast Asia Council. Thanks to Barbara Claire Freeman, that paper appeared as "The Japan That Can 'Say Yes': Bubblegum Music in a Post-Bubble Economy," *Literature and Psychology* 44, no. 4 (1998): 61–86. A revised version is included here as chapter 6.

Mark Anderson's paper at that AAS panel introduced me to the music of Happy End and started me down a pathway that eventually led to another section of this book. It began with a paper I presented at the International Conference on Monuments and Memory

Making in Japan at the National University of Singapore in 2002. I am grateful to my fellow participants for their helpful suggestions, and I in particular thank Beng Choo Lim for talking her colleagues into allowing me to sneak the Kinks into an academic event where they had no rightful place. My conference paper was published as "What It Sounds Like to Lose an Empire: Happy End and the Kinks," in *Perspectives on Social Memory in Japan*, edited by Tsu Yun Hui, Jan Van Bremen, and Eyal Ben-Ari (London: Global Oriental, 2005), and revised portions of it are included here in chapter 5.

Chapter 3 began in an e-mail exchange with Joseph Murphy, who pointed out what an interesting translation the song title "Sukiyaki" presented. I delved into the problem of translation and Sakamoto Kyū's rockabilly as a member of the University of California Multicampus Research Group on Transnational and Transcolonial Studies, organized by Shu-mei Shih and Françoise Lionnet. Early versions of that chapter appeared as "Mystery Plane: Sakamoto Kyū and the Translations of Rockabilly," *Proceedings of the Association for Japanese Literary Studies* 3 (2002): 38–50, and as "The Calm Beauty of Japan at Almost the Speed of Sound: Sakamoto Kyū and the Translations of Rockabilly," in *Minor Transnationalism*, edited by Françoise Lionnet and Shu-mei Shih (Durham, N.C.: Duke University Press, 2005). I received capable research assistance on this chapter from Theresa Orth.

The earliest version of chapter 1 was presented at the Nikkei Bruin Conference on Japanese Popular Music at UCLA in 2004. I received many helpful comments from the other participants, including E. Taylor Atkins, Loren Kajikawa, Susan McClary, Michael Molasky, Robert Walser, and Christine Yano. Material from the chapter was also presented in talks at Yale University, Nagano Prefectural College, and Nishō Gakusha University. Material from chapter 2 was first presented in talks at Macalester College and Josai International University. I thank all those who organized and attended these talks; they gave me many good questions to think over. I received capable research assistance on this and other chapters from Loren Kajikawa.

A research trip to Japan to collect material for chapter 4 was made possible by another grant from the UCLA Center for Japanese Studies. I first presented my ideas about Group Sounds in a 2007 talk at the Asia Forum at International Christian University (ICU). Among others, John Maher, Ken Robinson, and William Steele provided helpful comments. While at ICU, I was given the opportunity to join a student research trip to Okinawa led by Tanaka Yasuhiro. There, I had the distinct pleasure of having Kattchan, former leader of the legendary Okinawan rock band Condition Orange, dedicate his performance of Led Zeppelin's "Stairway to Heaven" to me. The fact that that number is my least favorite song in the universe hardly distracted from my enjoyment of the moment.

I am grateful for a 2004/2005 University of California President's Research Fellowship in the Humanities, as well as for a year of research leave from the University of Chicago, both of which provided me with the time needed to do the listening, thinking, reading, and writing required to finish the book. My colleagues and students at UCLA, ICU, and Chicago have contributed, often intentionally, sometimes by accident, to this book. Specific thanks for specific favors over the past decade are due to Sarah Arehart, Mariko Bird, James Dorsey, the surviving members of the Golden Cups, Hosokawa Shūhei, Reginald Jackson, Karatani Kōjin, Seiji Lippit, Masui Shōji, Alan Merrill, Satō Nobuhiro, Michael Raine, Cheryl Silverman, Jordan Smith, Takahashi Akinori, Teranishi Takatomo, Mina Yang, Yoshida Junji, and Judith Zeitlin. Japanese popular music is not usually high on the priority list for American research libraries, but I have been blessed with very capable and tolerant librarians, in particular Toshie Marra at UCLA and Eizaburo Okuizumi at Chicago. Kathryn Tanaka kindly prepared the index for this book.

Jennifer Crewe at Columbia University Press patiently waited year after year for my manuscript, and once it was finally in her hands she guided it through the submissions and editing process with her usual grace and good sense. I am also grateful to Carol Gluck at Columbia University's Weatherhead East Asian Institute and to two anonymous referees for the press, whose suggestions made this a better book.

Over the years, several students have handed me mix tapes of their favorite Japanese music. I learned a great deal by listening to those and by talking with the students about what attracted them to these songs. My wife, Satoko, has, as always, contributed in countless ways, big and small—helping me work out an obscure lyric, identifying a formerly popular singer, pointing out a subtle allusion—and in general providing the sort of insider's knowledge that only one who grew up as a teenager listening to this music can have. My children, Walter and Sonia, endured a great deal of strange music over the past ten years and can now hum along to any number of songs by Kasagi Shizuko, Misora Hibari, and Sakamoto Kyū. I hope the experience hasn't warped them too badly.

Perhaps the starting point of the starting point to this project came in my childhood. When I was in grade school, my father, Ronald Bourdaghs, used to bring home the oddest records for us to play on our living room stereo: Library of Congress field recordings of rural southern blues, Taj Mahal, Buffy Sainte-Marie, and others. He taught me from an early age that music comes in all sorts of patterns, colors, and sizes, and that I shouldn't be frightened of melodies and rhythms that at first sounded queer. It was one of many important lessons he taught me over the years. I only wish he had lived to see this book's completion. His unexpected death, three weeks before I signed the publishing contract, robbed me of the chance to tell him in person that the book is dedicated to him.

A NOTE ON NAMES
AND THE TRANSLATION

Japanese personal names are rendered in their original order—that is, family name first and given name second—except in citations from English-language sources, in which the order has been reversed, or in cases where the persons have established professional names using the English order. All translations from Japanese-language materials are my own, except where a translator is otherwise noted.

SAYONARA AMERIKA, SAYONARA NIPPON

n October 1984, I traveled to Japan for the first time. I was an undergraduate with little previous exposure to Japan; my trip across the Pacific had come about through a series of fortunate accidents. Thanks to them, I would be spending a year at Miyagi University of Education in Sendai, a city about 180 miles up the Pacific coast from Tokyo. I arrived in a daze, and my immediate submersion into the everyday life of the men's dormitory that became my new home threw me even further off balance. My roommate H and the other dorm residents could not have been friendlier, and yet everything was so different from life back home in Minnesota—the food, etiquette, language, even the toilets.

I quickly discovered one point of commonality with my new friends: music. I had brought a handful of cassette tapes with me to Japan, and they went up on the shelf next to H's own more extensive collection of self-recorded cassettes. As was the fashion in Japan, his tape cases were more elaborately decorated than mine, with rub-off lettering and cutout illustrations giving his homemade compilations a professional look.[1] H loved all the genres that I did: punk, new wave, funk, power pop, even old-time rock and roll. Yet we collected entirely different artists. I listened to Prince, while H listened to Sano Motoharu. I liked Brian Wilson and the Beach Boys; he liked Yamashita Tatsurō. I loved the Clash and the Sex Pistols; he, the Stalins and the Mods. We both were into Bruce Springsteen, but H was into Hamada Shōgo even more. In fact, we had a large Hamada

Shōgo poster hanging on our dorm room wall, the singer's eyes concealed behind a pair of jet-black Ray-Bans.

There was an asymmetrical quality to our respective musical knowledges, an asymmetry that was the product of historical processes. While H didn't collect the Western artists that formed the core of my library, he at least knew about them from the radio and the music magazines he regularly imbibed (in particular, he was a devoted reader of the monthly *Rockin' On*). To borrow the words of historian Harry Harootunian, H, like other Japanese rock fans, had little choice but to listen "comparatively."[2] To me, however, H's music library was entirely unknown. Nonetheless, it was oddly familiar. The sounds and styles were known to me, but the names and faces were alien. I felt a bit like a character in a science fiction novel who wakes up in an alternative universe where everything is the same, yet different. Just as with H's listening habits, my own seemingly natural feelings of both estrangement and familiarity were the products of historical processes of which I was only dimly aware. Without knowing it, I was living in a domain that had already been mapped out for me, with musicians from some geographical regions highlighted, and those from others largely erased from view.

I fell in love with a great deal of the new music I heard in Sendai that year. H and I listened together regularly to late-night radio shows that featured new releases from up-and-coming rock bands. We attended live concerts by such artists as Sano Motoharu and Bakufu Slump. I made my own mix tapes of highlights from H's music collection to bring back to Minnesota at the end of my year. I was excited to introduce my new discoveries to my friends back home. Their response, though, was disheartening. Under no obligation to listen comparatively, my American friends for the most part resisted this music: something held them back from allowing it to permeate their bodies. To their ears, it sounded derivative, the English lyrics were laughably mispronounced, and most of all, I think, they lacked any framework by which they could open themselves up to enjoy the music.

Ultimately, I think, they couldn't locate the tunes on their imaginary maps of the domain of popular music. Maps are a necessity of life: without them, we would have a hard time navigating the spaces (both physical and mental) of the world. But we need to remember that maps are also inherently selective: they include certain spaces and thereby exclude others, and even in representing the included spaces they highlight some features and ignore others. This necessary process of selection can have problematic consequences: when we come to internalize certain maps as second nature, we tend to assume that things not shown on them don't matter. In other words, maps are often ideological: they lead us to accept as natural and inevitable situations that are actually the results of historical contingency.

My inability to interest my Minnesota friends in the music I brought back from Japan provided one of the motivations that led me to write this book. It left me with a desire to introduce a vast body of terrific music to English-language readers, as well as to provide some sort of initial mode for enjoying it—a map. Another motivation was more selfish. Writing this book allowed me to spend a number of years exploring more widely in that alternative universe I first encountered in 1984, to understand its history and the ways that history was intertwined with the forces that shaped me as a music lover in North America. At least in terms of that second motivation, the book is an unmitigated success. I've learned a great deal more about Japanese popular music since 1945, though there remain whole galaxies out there waiting for me, unexplored.

It's an enormous canon, and I've managed to present only a tiny sliver of it here. In other words, my map is as selective as any other. For both practical and historical reasons, I've limited myself to the period lasting from the end of World War II to the beginning of the recession that followed the collapse of the economic bubble in 1990. I must note, however, that Japan's modern popular music industry didn't begin suddenly with the American Occupation in 1945. There is a commonsense notion floating around the English-speaking world that it was only defeat in World War II that moved Japan forward into the modern world, including its mass media and consumer culture. That view is utterly wrongheaded. In fact, it was only because of Japan's advanced mass media and consumer culture, including popular music, that it was able to mount and sustain its massive military campaigns of the 1930s and early 1940s.[3] Many of the personalities and institutions that would shape postwar popular music in Japan were products of that earlier period. Nonetheless, the American Occupation of Japan (1945–1952) and the subsequent rebuilding of Japan's economic and cultural spheres do mark a significant turning point in terms of popular music styles, the structure of the music industry, the geopolitical environment that shaped artistic practice (notably, the Cold War), and the ways people in Japan used popular music in their everyday lives.

The ending of my story around 1990 is likewise in part arbitrary but also in some ways historically justified. In practical terms, the lack of any historical distance makes it hard to tell the story of the remarkably diverse spectrum of popular music produced and consumed in Japan since 1990—though I sketch in some of the recent developments in the book's conclusion. Moreover, something new seems to have emerged around that point: people started speaking about "J-pop" in the early 1990s. To put things somewhat too schematically, J-pop exists in a different historical moment from the popular music I discuss in this book: it names a new kind of map. It isn't so much that musical style changed radically after 1990 (though, of course, new styles and genres continued to arise) or that an entirely different generation of artists took over. In fact, many of the musicians mentioned in the latter half of this book continued to enjoy success beyond 1990, often with songs clearly similar to music they had recorded in earlier decades. But from around 1990, there was a change in how popular music was used in Japan, in the distribution routes and technological media through which it circulated, and in the meanings and kinds of pleasures people derived from it. The dominant geopolitical imaginary that had served most Japanese since 1945, a mental mapping of the world centered on the U.S.–Japan relation, gave way with the end of the Cold War and of a period of almost uninterrupted economic growth in Japan to a new, still emerging geopolitical framework in which Japan is increasingly conceived through a more complex imaginary global map, one in which Asia reemerges as central and in which continuous economic expansion is no longer the basic assumption guiding people's understanding of their place in the world. Something new began around 1990, something quite important and fascinating, but something beyond the range of this book.

Hence my subtitle, *A Geopolitical Prehistory of J-Pop*. Please note the use of the indefinite, rather than definite, article: this is "a geopolitical history" rather than "the geopolitical history" of postwar pop. British musician Julian Cope in his invaluable and passionate (but occasionally unreliable) survey of Japanese rock writes sarcastically about "elite Westerners whose experience of Japanese culture" causes them to set themselves up "as oracles of a kind," grounded in their ability to speak and read the language. They "have a vested interest in keeping the mystery to themselves, enabling them to magnify the talents of their own particular favourite artists simply by not referencing those that fall outside their own personal taste."[4]

Guilty as charged. That is one reason I call this "a history" rather than "the history" of postwar Japanese popular music. Literally hundreds of important artists and whole genres are left out here, in part by necessity and in part by fiat. I've chosen to focus on artists and music that interest me. Moreover, although I'm pretending to be a kind of historian here, I utilize mainly the training and skills I have acquired in my home discipline of literary studies. Instead of providing a widespread survey, I tend to focus intensely on a few key artists and songs, carrying out thick analyses that help bring out the complexity of their creations. The book may lack the breadth of coverage that a "real" history might boast, but I hope my approach avoids some of the excessive simplifications and generalizations that can mar a broadly historical approach.

In addition to not being a historian, I am also not a musician or a musicologist. I've tried to include at least some basic analysis of structure and form of the music discussed here, but anyone with a musical background will quickly spot the limits of my abilities in that direction. I have taken up primarily a kind of cultural studies approach here, thinking of music and the pleasures it provides in terms of their ideological functions: how they help make certain historical forms seem natural and inevitable, how they cause people to answer to certain identities without resistance and to reject others, how they guide us to understand and feel the realities we live. Clearly, this is not the only or perhaps even the best way to understand music. But music shapes us politically and socially: to enjoy music, whether as a performer or as a listener, is to allow it to mold our bodies and sensibilities, to accept certain patterns as pleasurable and to disdain others as unnatural. It is to accept a certain model of what is right and proper in ourselves and in our communities.

As Jacques Attali argues, there is a political economy of music: "The entire history of tonal music, like that of classical political economy, amounts to an attempt to make people believe in a consensual representation of the world . . . to stamp upon spectators the faith that there is harmony in order."[5] I also borrow from musicologist Christopher Small, who attempts to rethink the object of his study from the noun *music* to the verb *to musick*. Musicking is a complex social activity that involves not only musicians but also everyone involved in the performance: audiences, promoters, critics, investors, and so on:

> The act of musicking establishes in the place where it is happening a set of relationships, and it is in those relationships that the meaning of the act lies. They are to be found not only between those organized sounds which are conventionally thought of as being the stuff of musical meaning but also between the people who are taking part, in whatever capacity, in the performance; and they model, or stand as metaphor for, ideal relationships as the participants in the performance imagine them to be: relationships between person and person, between individual and society, between humanity and the natural world and even perhaps the supernatural world.[6]

In discussing the ideologies produced and reproduced through music, it's also important to recognize that the field on which they operate is uneven, open-ended, and conflicted. Multiple ideologies compete for dominance and interact with other levels of reality in complex ways. There isn't a single ideological order that is then reflected in music, even as some forms in fact achieve wider sway than others. I try to recognize some of the messiness and complexity of ideology in music, including moments when music is used to imagine an alternative world—a revolution.

Another goal I had in writing this book relates to that nebulous ghost known as theory. When I was trained as a graduate student in the 1980s and 1990s, it was fashionable to mobilize one's knowledge of abstract literary and critical theory, the denser the better: largely (but not entirely) French theorists such as Derrida, Foucault, and Lacan became the new coin of the realm. As I finish this book at the end of the first decade of the twenty-first century, the worm has turned. It is now quite faddish for academics (as well as for the mass media, always eager to leap onto an anti-intellectual bandwagon) to decry "theory." In both cases, oddly, the currently fashionable stance is often justified in the name of an equally nebulous entity: "politics." Theory-heads in the 1990s believed that theory provided a better way to carry out politics, or micropolitics, at the level of everyday life: older forms of macropolitics were shown to replicate the very structures of domination they were ostensibly trying to replace. Today's anti-theory-heads, on the contrary, argue that theory cynically moved the focus of politics away from the real world. They argue that theory shifted our focus away from organizing actual human beings to resist material oppression and toward harmless cultural realms, transforming "politics" into a harmless game of chasing words around in circles on the page.

I am suspicious of both sets of claims. This is in part because of my location in the field of Japan studies, where the historical circumstances under which "theory" was introduced differ somewhat from those in English and other fields in the humanities and social sciences. I can't recount that history in any detail here, but to put it quite schematically, early Western studies of Japanese culture tended to stress the aesthetic beauty of Japanese art and literature, to the neglect of its intellectual or political content. Politics and abstract theory were supposed to be the domains of Western modernity; Japan was assigned the task of producing pretty pictures and lyrical poems. (This is related to the question discussed in chapter 3: why Sakamoto Kyū could succeed in the West as the singer of sentimental ballads but not as a singer of rockabilly rave ups). This version of Japanese studies was created largely in the early Cold War period and was complicit with the need in the United States to transform the image of Japan from that of a treacherous enemy to a benevolent Asian ally, a problem I return to repeatedly in the book.

This model came under increasing pressure in the 1970s and 1980s. The generation of scholars that rejected it did so in the context of their opposition to the Vietnam War and to the role academic Asian studies had played in providing the ideological justifications for American Cold War policy in East Asia. These scholars introduced theory into Japan studies. In doing so, they worked closely with a new generation of Japanese scholars and critics who found in structuralist and poststructuralist theory powerful tools for critiquing Japan's own cultural modernity. Moreover, they faced and still face enormous resistance from mainstream scholars in the field.

This history makes me perhaps more disposed to use theory than is fashionable these days. More important, I think theory can provide powerful tools, giving us new ways to imagine our relation to the world and thereby providing potential openings for us to act in novel modes to change that world: theory at its best allows us to question the mental maps that have become our unspoken common sense. But I think it is true that scholars engaged in theoretical work have often failed to carry out the necessary work of explaining that theory to nonspecialist readers. One of the goals of this book is to attempt to do so. The reader will find chapters here on such topics as liberation and ideology, translation and identity, noise and revolution, and melodrama and gender. In each case, I rely on theoretical notions to carry out my analysis. I do my best, however, to explain the conceptual frameworks I am using as clearly as I can in language that I hope is accessible to nonspecialists. In the chapters that follow, I strive to meet the reader halfway. I hope that my readers will do likewise, and if we're lucky it will turn out that we have been traveling along the same road.

Whether or how this makes my work "political" is for someone else to decide. My analyses of popular music look at how songs are shaped by and in turn shape the geopolitical situations in which Japanese musicians and fans operated during the Cold War era, a situation that transcends the boundaries of the place known as Japan. The music unfolded within and left its mark on a political environment, but the political charge of the songs was not necessarily or solely something inherent to their musical form. Rather, it was a question of what people *did* with the songs in a specific situation. The same pop song can be reactionary or revolutionary, depending on how and where it is enjoyed. Theory works, I think, in a similar manner, albeit in a less glamorous and smaller market. As a tool, it allows us to analyze a given problem in a novel and unconventional manner, to step past the blinders of common sense and to frame it in a new way that might allow us to *do* something unexpected. As with pop songs, though, this is more a matter of what people *do* with the theory than some sort of magical genetic code buried in the structure of the theory itself.

As I've noted, I come to this book as neither a historian nor a musicologist. I am a specialist in literature and also in what is called area studies, specifically Japan studies. As noted, the institution of area studies that was put together in the United States early in the Cold War era has come under much criticism in recent years for its ideological roles, a critique with which I largely sympathize.[7] But area studies may not have entirely outlived its usefulness: at its best, it allows for interdisciplinary study of objects that can range across the humanities, the social sciences, even the natural sciences. In many ways, area studies provides the only possible justification for a scholarly book on Japanese popular music by someone with no formal training in musicology or ethnomusicology. One of my other goals in writing this book is to see what might be possible now in area studies: Is there some more creative, useful way to apply the knowledge and techniques developed in Asian studies? In part, this means using knowledge about Japan to think critically about ideologies and structures of power here at home in North America. Naoki Sakai has argued trenchantly that any critique of Japan studies as an institution must simultaneously also be a critique of the West, which constructs its own identity through the mirror image of others, like Japan, that it projects onto the world.[8] I've tried in the book to carry out this sort of dual-focused engagement.

In the chapters that follow, the reader will encounter jazz singers, mournful *enka* divas, rockabilly sensations, manufactured rock-and-roll idols straining to become rock rebels, protest folk balladeers, new-music innovators, and techno-pop computer geeks. I've added my own ideas about how all this musicking interacts with the culture and politics of the Cold War era in ways that I hope readers will find stimulating. And if my readers find themselves feeling an urge to track down and listen to some of the songs I discuss, to engage in creative acts of musicking with them, allowing the rhythms and melodies to gain sway over their bodies and connect them to new and old forms of pleasure, and if those dancing bodies begin to think and rethink their own locations on various maps of the world, then the trap I have tried to set in the following pages will have done its work. Reader, proceed with caution.

1

THE MUSIC WILL SET YOU FREE

KUROSAWA AKIRA, KASAGI SHIZUKO, AND THE ROAD
TO FREEDOM IN OCCUPIED JAPAN

He [Kurosawa Akira] listened to all kinds of music, mainly classical, but he couldn't stand Japanese-style popular songs [*kayōkyoku*]—especially *enka*. He called them "unhealthy."

KUROSAWA KAZUKO (AKIRA'S DAUGHTER)

The Japanese people shall be encouraged to develop a desire for individual liberties and respect for fundamental human rights, particularly the freedoms of religion, assembly, speech, and the press.

SUPREME COMMANDER FOR ALLIED POWERS, "BASIC INITIAL POST-SURRENDER DIRECTIVE"

The music came to an abrupt halt on August 15, 1945. It gave way first of all to a spoken-word recording: the airing over the NHK network of a prerecorded message in which Emperor Hirohito spoke over the radio for the first time, announcing Japan's surrender. The broadcast shocked many, but it also confirmed what everybody already knew: that the nation had plunged into catastrophic failure. Japan's cities lay in ruins, millions of its citizens were dead or dying, and Japan's own actions had transformed it into a pariah nation. Moreover, it was on the verge of military occupation—an unprecedented condition that provoked dread and anxiety. Music, at least momentarily, seemed out of place. What song could possibly mark this turning point? The melodies that had been on everyone's lips over the past decade now bore an indelible taint. Whether it was the inspiring brass fanfares of *gunka* (military songs) such as Kirishima Noboru and Fujiyama Ichirō's "Burning Sky" (Moyuru ōzora, 1940) or seductive love ballads sung by the faux Chinese superstar Ri Kōran proclaiming Asian fondness for Japan, all now fell into disrepute.

A short, mournful silence followed—very short. The dark moment of surrender quickly led to the unleashing of a powerful sense of liberation, one that in the minds of many Japanese was intimately bound up with song. NHK resumed popular music programming on September 9, barely ten days after General Douglas MacArthur landed in Yokohama to take charge of the Occupation of Japan.[1] Four months later, the Shōchiku film studio released the bubbly *Grand Show 1946* (*Gurando shō 1946-nen*; dir. Makino Masahiro), a compendium of staged musical numbers tacked onto the flimsiest of boy-meets-girl narratives. This resurgence in pop music provided the sound track for a series of important social developments that also seemed to promise liberation: the end to state suppression of dissident thought, the seemingly real possibility of democratic revolution, and—despite an overwhelming reality of poverty, malnourishment, and material shortages—a renewed dedication to consumption and leisure as ideals, replacing the grim wartime insistence on production and self-sacrifice in support of the war effort.[2] The human body, with all its pleasures and desires, emerged as one locus of the new freedom. The first major hit of the postwar period, "The Apple Song" (Ringo no uta, 1945; performed by Namiki Michiko and Kirishima Noboru, released January 1946), with its bouncy rhythm and cheerful melody—and its lyrics focusing on food!—seemed to enact this emancipation.[3]

On the day the war ended, film director Kurosawa Akira (1910–1998) was at the Tōhō studios in suburban Tokyo, shooting his fourth feature film. Production halted briefly after the crew listened to the emperor's radio broadcast, but filming resumed within days. Completed a few weeks later, the brilliant *Men Who Tread on the Tiger's Tail* (*Tora no o o fumu otokotachi*, 1945) would later be heralded as Kurosawa's sole musical: an adaptation of the oft-told tale of the loyal warrior Benkei, it features a sound track that combined such diverse genres as Noh chanting, Kabuki music, and Western-style choral and orchestral pieces.[4] Ironically, the American Occupation authorities instantly banned the film, and it would not be seen publicly until 1952. Nonetheless, for Kurosawa, who had clashed repeatedly with Japanese military censors, the end of the war meant liberation. As he would write in his autobiography, "Having lived through an age that had no respect for creation, I recognized for the first time that freedom of creation can exist."[5] In his subsequent films, including his first postwar production, *No Regrets for Our Youth* (*Waga seishun ni kui nashi*, 1946), music would provide Kurosawa with one of his most powerful tools for expressing this liberation.

Hattori Ryōichi (1907–1993), Japan's premier jazz composer and arranger, found himself stuck in China at war's end. Mobilized by the Japanese military, he was living in Shanghai, the city that since the late 1920s had served as the jazz Mecca of Asia. There, Hattori staged propaganda musical revues promoting Chinese-Japanese friendship. In the summer of 1945, for example, he mounted *Ye Lai Xiang Rhapsody* at the Shanghai Grand Theater, a musical spectacular built around a famous Chinese pop song and featuring the glamorous Ri Kōran backed by the Shanghai Symphony Orchestra.[6] In the looser atmosphere that prevailed in occupied China, Hattori was able to slip traces of boogie-woogie sound, his latest musical passion, into his new compositions for the show. Hattori spent the evening of August 15 drinking with Chinese songwriting friends, who told him that the end of the war meant they could now engage openly in music collaborations. Hattori's biographer imaginatively reports the toast offered that night by Li Jinguang, composer of "Ye lai xiang" (Fragrance of the Night): "From now on, we can carry out our musical activities in freedom."[7]

At the time of the emperor's radio broadcast, Kasagi Shizuko (1914–1981) was ten days shy of her thirty-first birthday. A popular jazz singer since the mid-1930s, she spent the war years fronting her own orchestra, contributing to the war effort with morale-boosting performances for the troops and for workers on the home front. Ironically, Kasagi would look back on the closing months of the war as a time of personal happiness. After the May 25, 1945, air raids over Tokyo burned down her own residence, she secretly shared a home with the great love of her life, Yoshimoto Eisuke, the only time the two lived together before his untimely death in 1947.[8] But otherwise, the wartime was a disaster for Kasagi. She found it increasingly difficult to perform in public after jazz had been banned as the enemy's music following Pearl Harbor. Singled out by the authorities for special harassment, she was ordered to stop her wild dance movements on stage and was once even rounded up off the street for the offense of wearing false eyelashes.[9] She would later write, "Those five years of the war, the blank in my career, were hell for me."[10] But with the surrender, Kasagi wasted no time in reclaiming her career. When Hattori finally managed to return to Japan from China in December 1945, on his very first day back in Tokyo he visited the Nichigeki Theater, which was advertising *Highlight Show*, a new musical revue that featured Kasagi.[11] She was free to perform again: "You can't imagine how happy I was then," she would write.[12] In short order, she would transform herself into an omnipresent force on the hit parade, the Japanese queen of boogie.

Kurosawa, Hattori, and Kasagi celebrated the end of the war as a kind of emancipation. For each, music provided a crucial vehicle for living out the new freedom. Each, however, defined liberation in starkly different terms. In their works from the period of the U.S. Occupation (1945–1952), these three giants of Japanese postwar culture adopted distinct, and often mutually contradictory, stances toward emancipation, and especially toward the versions of liberation that centered on the fleshly body. The tension between these different stances, a tension that often centered on questions of sex, pleasure, and consumption, is the theme I explore in this chapter. Kasagi's numerous boogie-woogie hits, composed and arranged by Hattori, were themselves popular commodities meant to be enjoyed through the body. Moreover, their lyrics and their musical form explicitly celebrated consumerism and bodily pleasure as forms of liberation—even if Kasagi in performing the songs at times seemed to stand back from the image that her male songwriters and producers constructed for her.

Kurosawa's films were no less commodities. Despite the hagiography that since the 1950s has constructed the image of Kurosawa as an auteur, a unique genius who bears single-handed responsibility for his works, his early postwar films were of course the products of corporate entities that bankrolled and then distributed them into a rapidly expanding market for mass culture. Despite this entanglement with the "culture industry"—or perhaps because of it—Kurosawa's films frequently depict mass culture not as a site of liberation but as a form of enslavement, especially for men. This rejection of mass culture is the direct theme of his film *Scandal* (*Sukyandaru*, 1950), starring none other than singer Yamaguchi Yoshiko (the former Ri Kōran), and it forms a dark undercurrent in many of his works from this period. As one critic has noted, in these films the "fruits of conspicuous consumption are toxic to the social body."[13] Moreover, Kurosawa frequently situates popular dance music as the primary representative of the new postwar consumerism. In his films, popular music defines the road not to freedom but to slavery.

In sum, early postwar popular music in Japan involved the working out of new questions about freedom in relation to an exploding market in mass culture. The universally celebrated goal was liberation, but freedom from what and for what? Did popular dance music (known universally in Japan at the time as jazz, regardless of genre) in and of itself enact emancipation, or was it a femme fatale whose siren call lured men away from the path to authentic freedom? And did freedom for women lead to freedom for men—or the opposite?

These struggles were one of the ways people lived out immense shifts in geopolitical formations that occurred in the years following surrender. The fall of the Greater East Asia Co-Prosperity Sphere and the militarist Japanese state meant the collapse of one set of political institutions and its attendant ideological worldviews. With the onset of the Occupation and its democratizing reforms, everything was supposed to change. For a time, it seemed that real liberation was possible, genuine across-the-board emancipation: freedom of political expression, sexual freedom, freedom from hunger and poverty, freedom from gender inequality, freedom of thought and belief. For a brief time, Communists, socialists, liberals, and moderates all joined hands. Kurosawa's *No Regrets for Our Youth* is an eloquent expression of this fleeting belief that a single, shared liberation was possible for all.

This intoxicating optimism passed quickly. As historian John Dower has noted, "Japan remained under the control of fundamentally military regimes from the early 1930s straight through to 1952."[14] Japanese military censorship was abolished—and American military censorship introduced. The ironies of this became more blatantly apparent with the onset of the "reverse course" in Occupation policies around 1947. With the flaring up of the Cold War, the United States now showed less interest in democratizing Japan and more instead in building up a strategic ally to bolster its security policies across Asia. A new ideological map of the world was emerging. Under its worldview, certain kinds of freedom suddenly became dangerous, while others were shifted to center stage. From around 1949, disgraced wartime elites, banned from public life early in the Occupation, started returning to positions of authority and influence. Everything had changed, and nothing had changed. The same record labels that had flourished in the wartime era—Nippon Columbia, Nippon Victor, Teichiku, King—still dominated hit charts during the Occupation. Even the very singers who had produced wartime incitements to victory remained shining idols in the postwar period: Kirishima Noboru, Ri Kōran/Yamaguchi Yoshiko, Watanabe Hamako, Fujiyama Ichirō, among others.

In this fluid and often treacherous environment, what could liberation mean? How did music relate to it? No single answer could suffice. The now-classic works produced in the late 1940s and early 1950s by Kurosawa, Hattori, and Kasagi have a great deal to tell us about the complex interweaving of music, liberation, and the ways we live in and against social and political structures. And it is likely that the tension between their contrasting ideas about freedom has the most to teach us.

*　　*　　*

The career paths of Kurosawa, Hattori, and Kasagi crossed more than once, most notably in *Drunken Angel* (*Yoidore tenshi*, 1948).[15] Often called Kurosawa's breakthrough film, *Drunken Angel* also provided the first major role for Mifune Toshirō, who would go on to star in many of Kurosawa's pictures.[16] The story is set in a gritty urban neighborhood in early postwar Japan, a world characterized by *panpan* streetwalkers, a thriving black market, and seedy dance halls; in fact, U.S. Occupation censors were concerned that the script excessively foregrounded negative elements.[17] The most memorable image from the film is the swamplike garbage pit that occupies the center of the neighborhood; its bubbling, contaminated surface is the first image we see in the film, and it subsequently reappears repeatedly, clearly functioning as a metaphor for the corruption of the surrounding neighborhood. Mifune plays Matsunaga, the hoodlum boss of the neighborhood who learns that he has tuberculosis. Shimura Takashi, another actor whom Kurosawa used repeatedly, plays Sanada, an alcoholic doctor who reluctantly treats Matsunaga, trying both to cure his tuberculosis and to make a better man out of him.

The film boasts an effective, if conventional, sound track composed by Hayasaka Fumio (1914–1955), whom Kurosawa identified as his best friend and right-hand man in creating many of his early masterpieces. The *Drunken Angel* sound track employs Western-style orchestration and Western instruments throughout—Kurosawa specifically requested music in the style of Debussy's "Clair de lune."[18] The film uses background music to heighten emotional tension, to provide continuity between shots, to create a sense of spatial depth for the flat images on the screen, and to establish musical motifs associated with the various characters: a sweet, ethereal melody played on strings that is used nine times in the film and is associated with the doctor and his good influence, for example, or a darker, ominous theme played largely on woodwinds that is used seven times through the film (including over the opening credits) and is associated with the dark side of Matsunaga's character.[19] Alongside this sound track, the film also frequently uses diegetic music—that is, music that arises from within the visually depicted world and that is presumably audible to the characters in the film—including a performance by Kasagi Shizuko of "Jungle Boogie," with music composed by Hattori Ryōichi.[20]

By 1948, Kurosawa had developed a sophisticated theory for using diegetic sound, based in part on his exposure to Soviet film practices. He aimed to use diegetic music in counterpoint to the visual image, thereby creating a kind of tension, a dialectical relationship between image and sound. Kurosawa expressed this with a mathematical formula: the goal was not simply to achieve image + sound, but to achieve an exponential effect of image × sound, to produce an effect greater than the mere sum of the two parts.[21] This innovative technique is one of the things that make Kurosawa's films so effective, and it also, particularly when we contrast this ironic, contrapuntal use of diegetic music to Kurosawa's more conventional use of nondiegetic sound-track music, provides an entryway for exploring how Kurosawa reacted to his historical moment—how he understood the problem of liberation.

Drunken Angel is one of Kurosawa's earliest films to employ this contrapuntal technique. Diegetic music in the film is used consistently to register the presence of a threat. It functions as a kind of miasma permeating the neighborhood, the aural equivalent of the pestilent miasma that wafts off the surface of the garbage sump. In the film, even when characters are in a relatively safe place, the sound of music reaches out to touch them and remind them of the danger that threatens them. Inside the doctor's clinic at night, for example, the characters repeatedly hear—and comment on—the sound of a man outside playing a guitar: the music is part of the corrupt world that surrounds them, and it is capable of penetrating even into the sanctuary of the clinic. This effect is intensified midway through the film when music is used to signal the return of Okada (Yamamoto Reisaburō), the evil former boss of the neighborhood gang who has just been released from prison. The doctor is sheltering a young woman who used to be Okada's lover but who now wants to break with him and go straight. Okada's return to the neighborhood is announced to the woman when the gangster borrows the guitarist's instrument and plays an old song he knew before going to jail, a song that the woman instantly recognizes: again, diegetic music signifies the threat of the corrupt neighborhood.[22]

Kasagi Shizuko makes her appearance a few minutes later. Her performance helps specify the nature of the threat that music, especially popular music, poses to the film's characters. Up to this point, Matsunaga (Mifune) has been trying to follow the doctor's orders to lead a healthier and more ethical lifestyle, but when his old boss Okada returns from jail, Matsunaga finds himself falling back into his old ways. He ends up out on the town carousing with Okada. This is the beginning of the end for Matsunaga: although he was the boss of the gang during Okada's absence, he now finds himself being displaced by Okada. Not only is Okada again taking control over the gang, but he is also moving in on Nanae (Kogure Michiyo), Matsunaga's girlfriend.

The film depicts a night of drinking to celebrate Okada's return. The gang ends up at the nightclub where Nanae works as a hostess. At first we see Okada dancing with Nanae as the orchestra plays "Nighttime on the Station Platform" (Yoru no purattohōmu), another Hattori composition—and itself a symbol of postwar liberation: the song had first been released in a version sung by Awaya Noriko in 1939 but was banned by wartime censors because its mournful lyrics about a sad parting on a train platform seemed ill-suited to wartime propaganda needs. The ban was lifted in 1945, and the song became an enormous hit in 1947 when it was re-recorded by Futaba Akiko.[23]

It is during this nightclub scene that Kasagi Shizuko makes her appearance in the film. She delivers a remarkable, over-the-top performance of "Jungle Boogie" as villain Okada dances with Nanae—and Matsunaga with another dance-hall girl, he clearly intoxicated by both alcohol and the music. The pounding music builds to a climax, ending with a powerful shriek by Kasagi—whereupon the film cuts abruptly to the doctor's clinic as the doctor slaps Matsunaga for disobeying orders and getting drunk. Matsunaga subsequently enters a downward spiral, meeting a tragic death at the film's climax. Sanada's project to reform Matsunaga ultimately fails, but the good doctor does not abandon hope. The film closes with him in the company of a pure young schoolgirl in whom his cure has apparently succeeded as the bright string-based theme associated with the doctor plays over the end credits.

*　　*　　*

Critics have sometimes dismissed the "Jungle Boogie" sequence in *Drunken Angel*.[24] In the context of both the film's thematic content and its formal structure, however, it seems quite significant. Repeatedly through the film, we are told that times have changed: the old ways of hierarchy and the old models of masculinity that went with them—as represented by gangster boss Okada—are no longer valid. In this new world, Dr. Sanada vows to make a man out of Matsunaga, a man in the way that masculinity is understood in the new postwar world, where irrational violence and militaristic hierarchies are rejected. As in so many of Kurosawa's films, Shimura Takashi plays a kind of father figure to Mifune Toshirō's character. Matsunaga even calls the doctor Oyaji, a term of endearment that implies a father–son relationship between the two. In a sense, Dr. Sanada represents the paternal superego, Okada represents the unrestrained id, and the question that drives the film's narrative is whether or not Matsunaga will be able to emerge as a new masculine ego.[25] Seen from this perspective, the film clearly participates in the ongoing debates among early postwar Japanese intellectuals over subjectivity and the meaning of authentic freedom—a debate that implicitly, and sometimes explicitly, involved assumptions about gender. Did liberation mean primarily a passive (and therefore supposedly feminine) freedom *from* all restraints, an unleashing of the desires of the body from all strictures, or did it mean an active (and therefore supposedly masculine) freedom *for* something, a process of self-disciplining that would make possible a world governed by individual responsibility rather than state authority?[26]

In the nightclub scene, Kasagi's performance of "Jungle Boogie" posits a threat: it invokes the unrestrained, destructive impulses that threaten to unman Matsunaga. Quite literally, his girl is being stolen before his eyes, and he is powerless to stop it. The scene echoes the anxieties about emasculation that permeate Kurosawa's early postwar films and much Japanese postwar culture. Imagery and language suggesting that the Occupation amounted to national castration were common during the period, especially in works produced by men. The writer Takami Jun, for example, would jot down in his diary in late 1945 that "the Japanese, in a sense, have been castrated."[27] Postwar popular culture and music, in particular, were closely associated with this emasculating American Occupation, and so their very presence in *Drunken Angel* functions as an allusion to the apparent loss of authority by Japanese men.

This figuring of the Occupation as castration was widespread at the time but also quite problematic. By situating Japanese males as the primary victims of 1945, the trope functioned ideologically. Among other things, it cloaked the very real patriarchy and gender hierarchies that existed within Japan, both during and after the war. Images of castration appear much less frequently in works of popular culture produced by Japanese women. In fact, for women in Japan, the Occupation could sometimes signify liberation. Occupation legal reforms, for example, gave women the right to vote, and the postwar constitution imposed on Japan by the Occupation even included a clause guaranteeing gender equality. Moreover, the renewed stress on consumption, an activity often identified as feminine, signaled new possibilities for active agency by women—agency that was often seen as threatening by males. The very same popular dance music that for Kurosawa threatened enslavement might help open the way to new, more liberated lifestyles for female producers and consumers.

In other words, the castration imagery used in *Drunken Angel* presents us with a gendered schism on what liberation meant in occupied Japan. Matsunaga's tuberculosis is repeatedly described in the film with a remarkable trope: he has a "hole" in him, we're told—a hole that leaks blood. Dr. Sanada will try to cure him both of the disease and of the implicit castration that this hole portends. Note that the threat of castration here arises not from the father figure but from the realm of the feminine, associated closely with popular music—in the film, it is the song "Jungle Boogie" that literally makes Mat-sunaga sick. In the nightclub scene, both Kasagi and her listeners sway their bodies to the rhythms of the music, and the camera work overtly foregrounds the female body (of both Kasagi and Nanae, Matsunaga's girlfriend). Popular dance music is portrayed as a swamp in which one surrenders to the irrational passions of the flesh—particularly the female body. As an interviewer would comment to Kasagi years later, "Those old boogie-woogie songs of yours, you really had to use your body in performing them."[28] This association is not unique to Kurosawa or Kasagi; it is a commonplace in Western music criti-cism, where as one musicologist notes the "mind / body–masculine / feminine problem places dance decisively on the side of the 'feminine' body rather than with the objective 'masculine' intellect."[29] Kasagi's performance of "Jungle Boogie" in the film marks the point where Dr. Sanada's treatment begins to fail and where Matsunaga begins to surrender to irrational desires inconsis-tent with the new postwar version of masculinity and the "reason" (*risei*) that the doctor argues is the most crucial medicine, not just for TB but for all that ails humankind (on some prints of the film, the subtitles translate *risei* as "willpower.").

The realm of dance music is also charged with racial imagery. The music that Hattori composed for "Jungle Boogie" is in a minor key but sprinkled with flattened "blue notes," associated closely with certain idioms of African American jazz and blues, including Duke Ellington's "hot jazz" and "jungle sound" compositions of the 1920s.[30] Moreover, there is a strong primitiv-ist and orientalist feel to the composition, given the pounding drums, the absence of harmonic development, and its use of a pentatonic scale, especially in the song's bridge. As Kasagi sings the slinky, exotic melody, her voice rises and falls in lockstep with a clarinet that sounds for all the world like a snake-charmer's flute. The all-male orchestra and chorus then follow Kasagi's lead, musically repeating her sung lines after her as if enchanted by her voice (this call-and-response tendency is more pronounced in the full recorded version of the song than in the abbreviated version used in the film). The lyrics to "Jungle Boogie" were written by Kurosawa himself—albeit with some nego-tiation, as we will see later. They situate the singer as a woman living on a South Sea island and who burns with a bestial passion. The music and words present Kasagi as a sexual aggressor, a self-described "leopardess" howling with desire, an imagery that is reinforced musically as the song crescendos to a final orgasmic climax in the vocal shriek on which it ends.[31] The song features Kasagi's characteristic over-the-top "natural voice" (*jigoe*) singing style, which Hattori identified as one of the innovations that he and Kasagi worked out beginning with their first recording session in 1939.[32]

Here, as elsewhere in *Drunken Angel,* diegetic popular music is associated with the lure of the feminine, and especially the feminine as representing the possibility of unmanning. This pattern is repeated later in the film in a famous scene that provides an instance of the contrapuntal use of diegetic music. Matsunaga, now utterly humiliated, walks through the neighborhood market to the strains of the absurdly cheerful "Cuckoo Waltz" being played over loudspeakers.[33] For Kurosawa, popular music represents not subjectivity or liberation but enslavement. It is part of the sticky web of commodified culture that Kurosawa repeatedly portrays as a threat to the fragile male ego, a threat that referred implicitly back to the U.S. Occupation and the changes it was bringing to Japan. As one historian has noted, Kurosawa "locates jazz in sleazy, filthy ghettos populated with swaggering gangsters, coquettish taxi dancers, prostitutes, black marketers and gamblers," allowing him to express "the continuing apprehension that many Japanese felt toward the music and the wholesale cultural transformation it portended."[34] When we consider the association of jazz with the United States, and the Occupation censorship's ban on direct portrayals of the Occupation itself in Japanese film, it is tempting to speculate that Kurosawa's portrayals of the permeation of jazz into Japanese daily life functioned in part as displaced commentary on the presence of the American military.[35]

This suspicion of mass culture in general, and of popular music in particular, is one of the tendencies that allow us to identify Kurosawa as a modernist director.[36] A suspicion of music in film has been shared by many modernist film critics and directors—whether it be the critical theorist Theodor Adorno writing in the 1940s or the more recent Dogme 95 school of directors, all of whom condemn the use of music in film as a symptom of commodification and of the manipulation of audience desires.

For Adorno, sound-track music in film operates as a kind of archaic and irrational magic. It functions as an ideological device that soothes spectators over the shock of the ghostly mechanical reproduction of images on the screen, thereby restoring belief in the reality of those images and eliciting emotional identification with them. It provides a false form of emotional depth to mask the lack of genuine emotion that commodity culture produces.[37] Moreover, it manipulates the audience to produce a sense of shared community, thereby erasing the traces of conflict and contradiction that mark social reality under capitalism. Music's apparently rational structure and its retention of traits from precapitalist communal feelings render it a particularly effective ideological tool for masking the irrational alienation and fake communality of modern society: "It is," Adorno wrote, "*par excellence* the medium in which irrationality can be practiced rationally."[38] In the typical nondiegetic sound track, "music removes barriers to belief; it bonds spectator to spectacle, it envelops spectator and spectacle in a harmonious space. Like hypnosis, it silences the spectator's censor. It is suggestive; if it's working right, it makes us a little less critical and a little more prone to dream."[39] For Adorno, music and other forms of art are supposed to sharpen our critical faculties and point the way toward genuine freedom. But once they are commodified, they instead function to dull those faculties and render us passive consumers, unable and unwilling to question the power structures of our societies. Rather than have us confront our social reality, the music causes us to "delight in the process of killing time."[40] In sum, nondiegetic film music plays on spectators' emotions to blunt their rationality, and it makes them more likely to identify with, rather than critically question, the commodities produced by the culture industry.

Moreover, for Adorno the threat to the rational ego that mass culture poses is perceived of not only as feminine but also specifically as a form of castration. Adorno's description of jazz music, which he condemned as fiercely as he did sound-track music, is instructive: "The aim of jazz is the mechanical reproduction of a regressive moment, a castration symbolism, 'Give up your masculinity, let yourself be castrated,' the eunuchlike sound of the jazz band both mocks and proclaims, 'and you will be rewarded, accepted into a fraternity which shares the mystery of impotence with you, a mystery revealed at the moment of the initiation rite.'"[41] Adorno is carrying on a line of thought here that can be traced back to the origins of modernism with, for example, Flaubert and Nietzsche, who repeatedly describe women as a dangerous source of corruption for the male artist.[42]

Kurosawa largely shares this stance toward mass culture and especially toward commodified music. There is an interesting twist, however. When Adorno and the Dogme 95 school condemn the use of music in films, they have in mind primarily the nondiegetic sound track. The Dogme 95 group's "Vow of Chastity" contains ten clauses that its adherents vow to obey in order to produce a purer form of cinema. The second clause relates to music: "The sound must never be produced apart from the images and vice versa. (Music must not be used unless it occurs where the scene is being shot)."[43] Note that this is not a blanket condemnation of music in film but only of nondiegetic music—that is, of background sound-track music. Hence, there is no contradiction when the director Lars von Trier, one of the founders of the group, makes a musical, such as *Dancer in the Dark* (2000), since all the music in it is diegetically motivated. Similarly, Adorno sees hope for the use of diegetic songs in musical comedies because while these "may be of little musical merit . . . they have never served to create the illusion of a unity of the two media [visual image and sound track] or to camouflage the illusionary character of the whole," so that in them the "alienation of the media from each other reflects a society alienated from itself."[44]

Like Adorno and the Dogme 95 group, Kurosawa is concerned with the corrupting influence of music in film. But unlike them, for Kurosawa the threat of mass culture does not arrive via the nondiegetic sound track—at least not at this stage in his career: his stance seems to change in later works.[45] In the early postwar films, Kurosawa is often brilliantly creative in his use of the sound track, but he basically follows the rules laid down for sound track in the most commercial of films: like any Hollywood director since the late 1930s, Kurosawa uses sound-track music to intensify emotions, to provide commentary on actions, to anchor the meaning of the visual image and guide spectators to a correct reading of it, and to ensure continuity between shots. For Kurosawa, as we have seen, the threat of mass culture in film comes not from the sound track but by way of diegetic music, especially popular dance music.

This tendency to use diegetic popular music to mark a threat against masculine subjectivity recurs in nearly all of Kurosawa's early postwar films. The film that perhaps most blatantly demonstrates this tendency is the masterpiece *Stray Dog* (*Nora inu*, 1949). In this drama, also set in the gritty streets of occupied Tokyo, we again encounter Shimura Takashi playing a quasi father figure to Mifune Toshirō, trying to make a man out of his younger counterpart in the changed world of masculinity that the end of the war has brought. Here, the theme of castration is brought forward unmistakably: Mifune plays Murakami, a police detective whose gun has been stolen, and the plot consists of his desperate efforts, aided by the older and wiser detective Satō (Shimura), to get his gun back.[46] The film contains a famous nine-minute montage sequence set in the seedy streets of lower-town Tokyo, in its cheap gin joints and amusement centers. Here, as in *Drunken Angel*, popular music is omnipresent like a miasma, usually in diegetic form. Even when the direct source of the music remains invisible, the music is played back in a filtered, distorted form, so that we understand that we are hearing it via a loudspeaker located somewhere in the depicted world. The montage sequence includes snippets of twelve different popular songs, including an orchestral version of Kasagi Shizuko's best-known hit, "Tokyo Boogie Woogie," another Hattori composition, as well as another song associated with Hattori, "Ye lai xiang," which reappeared on Japanese hit charts in 1949 in a new version arranged by Hattori and sung by Yamaguchi Yoshiko (the former Ri Kōran).[47]

In *Stray Dog*, as in other films from this period, Kurosawa sets into motion a dialectical tension between different kinds of music: popular and classical. Two parallel but contrasting scenes help us pinpoint the way the film distinguishes between musical genres. The first scene occurs rather late in the film. Satō has tracked the villain down to a hotel and tries to telephone back to Murakami to alert his junior partner and summon help. Murakami is at the apartment of the villain's girlfriend (Awaji Keiko), keeping an eye on her. There is at first some confusion about whom Satō is trying to call, though, and Murakami initially believes that the phone call might be from the villain Yusa (Kimura Isao) trying to contact his girlfriend. As Satō desperately tries to get Murakami on the phone, we see a female hotel employee turn on a radio, which is playing a popular arrangement of Sebastián de Iradier's "La Paloma." The male hotel owner (who is married) steps into the shot and starts flirting with the woman, not his wife. The way the hotel man and his employee sway their bodies to the song removes all doubt that what we are listening to is dance music. Here a popular song is used once again to signal moral corruption: the music is linked to an adulterous affair that the hotel man is apparently having with one of his employees. Satō visibly winces in annoyance at the sound. Moreover, to Murakami's ears on the other end of the telephone line, the sound of the music is linked to evil—he presumes that the sound means that the phone call is from the villain, probably calling from a nightclub. The net result of these misunderstandings is that Satō, the father figure, ends up being shot by the villain—who is using Murakami's stolen gun. The Oedipal implications are deliciously complicated, but what I want to stress here is the way that popular dance music in the scene is linked to the threat of unmanning. The scene ends with the hotel employees gathered in shock around the prone body of Satō as "La Paloma" continues to play in the background.

The second scene comes near the end of the film and again features diegetic music. Satō is in the hospital, and Murakami has tracked down the villain to a train station, in a sequence that involves voice-overs demonstrating that Murakami is learning to conquer his emotions and master the rationality that characterizes the wiser Satō. Murakami has no gun, and he knows that the villain carrying his own stolen Colt has three bullets left. Yusa and Murakami recognize each other, and Yusa bolts from the station. Murakami gives chase, and they end up running through the woods. In the background, we hear a piece of classical piano, played by an amateur: the first movement of Friedrich Kuhlau's Piano Sonata no. 1. Shortly thereafter, the camera cuts away to a shot of a woman practicing piano at a nearby home. The film cuts back to the chase—now Yusa fires at Murakami and hits him in the hand. The piano music stops, and we cut to a shot of the woman standing at her open window, looking out to see the source of the commotion. We cut back to see the chase resume—just as the piano music resumes.[48] Yusa fires wildly twice, hitting trees rather than Murakami. The piano music stops again. Yusa pulls the trigger once more, but there are no bullets left. In desperation, he throws the pistol and then turns and runs. Murakami recovers the stolen gun. Within a few more seconds, he has tackled and handcuffed Yusa. The two men, both exhausted, look up at the sky and at the leaves and blossoms above them, and the unmanly "mad dog" Yusa breaks into a pathetic wailing.[49]

In this second sequence, diegetic music is again used in counterpoint to a shooting, with the threat of unmanning, but here the music is identifiably classical music. In other words, the music used in this sequence is not a commodified product of mass culture but a work of high art. Not coincidentally, the threat of castration is overcome here: Mifune is only slightly wounded and recovers possession of his pistol. He is able to conquer the unrestrained mad dog villain: the ego masters the id. If popular dance music presents the threat of castration, classical music signifies the restoration of masculine subjectivity. Freedom is achieved through a process of self-disciplining.[50]

Classical music, then, is the music that plays when autonomous masculine subjectivity is restored, whereas popular music, especially dance music, initiates the threat to unman the same male subject.[51] This contrast is perhaps most apparent in *One Wonderful Sunday* (*Subarashiki nichiyōbi*, 1947), for which Hattori Tadashi served as music director, a film that depicts two impoverished lovers desperately trying to enjoy their Sunday afternoon together in early postwar Tokyo. The hero faces several moments of humiliation linked to music. In one scene, for example, he visits a cabaret owned by an old war buddy in hopes that his connection will get them admitted for free so that he can show his fiancée a good time. After being kept waiting backstage through several dance numbers played by the club's orchestra, he finally finds himself snubbed by the club owner in a particularly humiliating manner. Again, diegetic popular dance music accompanies the threat to the hero's masculine pride.

As he gradually recovers his masculinity toward the end of the film, the hero engages in a fanciful scene in which he and his fiancée fantasize about the coffee shop they hope to open one day. It will have a phonograph record, he muses—but no popular songs (*ryūkōka*). She demurs that they will have to have at least a copy of "The Apple Song" (Namiki Michiko and Kirishima Noboru's massive 1946 hit, mentioned earlier), a tune that in fact provided the diegetic music heard in one of the earlier scenes of masculine humiliation. At the film's climax, the hero is resurrected as a man when he conducts an imaginary orchestra in Schubert's "Unfinished Symphony." At first, he cannot hear the music and again feels a failure, but then his girlfriend turns to the camera and directly addresses the audience, asking for the audience to applaud so that her man can go on. He tries again, and this time both the characters and the film audience can hear the symphony as he heroically conducts the swelling music. In essence, the characters demand that they be permitted to hear the film's classical music sound track—the symphony that they have unsuccessfully been trying to encounter all through the day (but that the film's audience has all along been able to hear on the nondiegetic sound track). Here again, unmanning is associated with popular song and the recovery of the masculine ego signified by classical music.[52]

Kurosawa has been accused of choosing the Schubert work for the film primarily for the connotations of its title—a sound-track selection practice that Theodor Adorno and Hanns Eisler specifically condemned as something that "is retained only in cheap pictures."[53] Yet the formal construction of Schubert's symphony suggests a thematic narrative in consonance with the film's narrative of liberation achieved through bolstering masculine subjectivity. In the first movement of the symphony, the second theme, traditionally identified as the feminine, meets a particularly brutal disciplining at the hands of the primary, "masculine" theme, which reasserts its authority in the triumphant climax.[54] In other words, the implicit story told by the piece's formal structure mirrors the narrative of Kurosawa's film. In this, we find unintended echoes behind a comment that Kurosawa wrote in his autobiography: "A good structure for a screenplay is that of the symphony."[55]

Throughout his career, the sound tracks of Kurosawa's films repeatedly paid homage to works from the canon of Western classical music.[56] In the early postwar films in particular, classical music is a device by which the film distances itself from the threatening world of popular culture and associates cinema with the world of high art. Usually, the classical music appears on the sound track, while the popular dance music arises from within the visually depicted world. As the films reach their narrative climaxes, usually involving the restoration of masculine subjectivity and the overcoming of the feminine threat of castration, the classical music sound track takes over. *Record of a Living Being*, the last film score credited to Hayasaka, uses no nondiegetic sound during the film itself but contains a somber musical theme over the closing credits, a theme that continues to play for nearly two minutes after the screen goes black following the end credit. This was in part an elegy to Hayasaka, who died shortly before filming began. But it was also a strategic gesture: it meant that movie theaters could not play popular music as their patrons filed out after the film, which Kurosawa feared would destroy the artistic effect the film had created.[57] To borrow musicologist Susan McClary's

terminology, in Kurosawa diegetic popular dance music is coded as a dangerous feminine excess, while nondiegetic classical music functions as a frame
that captures and domesticates that excess, submitting it to the dictates of
masculine reason.[58] The music in Kurosawa's films, that is, enacts at a formal
level the same narrative of liberation that the film story lines trace.

*   *   *

Since the acclaim that greeted his masterpiece, *Rashōmon* (1950), Kurosawa
has needed no introduction in the West. Kasagi Shizuko and Hattori Ryōichi,
though, are not as well known outside Japan. Their careers began in the lively
jazz scene of 1920s Osaka, where Kasagi debuted as a chorus girl in 1927 and
Hattori worked first as an oboeist, then as a saxophonist, but increasingly
as a musical arranger, composer, and bandleader.[59] In 1933, Hattori moved
to Tokyo, where he joined Nippon Columbia Records as a songwriter and
arranger; he also began to compose film music around this time. Kasagi made
her recording debut in 1934, and four years later she moved to Tokyo, where
she performed in a number of popular musical revues. It was in Tokyo that
Hattori first linked up with Kasagi. They made their first records together in
1939, and Hattori would go on to compose and arrange the vast majority of
Kasagi's recordings—including all the songs discussed here.

Hattori in the 1930s was one of the first Japanese musicians to attempt to
translate indigenous Japanese and Asian music genres into the jazz vocabulary. He wrote a number of "Japanese blues" songs in the mid-1930s, in which
his reference point was the internationally popular "classic blues" sound represented by, for example, Bessie Smith's 1925 recording of W. C. Handy's "St.
Louis Blues." Most notable among Hattori's compositions in this genre is
"Farewell Blues" (Wakare no burūsu, 1937), performed by Awaya Noriko.[60]
The song is built around variations on a typical I-IV-V chord progression,
albeit with a twenty-four-bar structure closer to Tin Pan Alley than Memphis; its melody uses the sort of minor scale that characterizes many popular
compositions from the period, such as Koga Masao's "Is Sake a Teardrop or
a Sigh?" (Sake wa namida ka tameiki ka; recorded by Fujiyama Ichirō, 1931).[61]
Like many hit songs from this time, the melody of "Farewell Blues" shifts
between a Japanese-sounding pentatonic scale and a Western minor scale,

but what made it particularly novel was Hattori's blending in of flattened "blue notes" into the piece, giving it a jazzy feel.[62] Also striking was the two-octave range that Awaya, a classically trained soprano, had to cover—the singer herself expressed reservations to Hattori about the low G she had to hit in the song's opening. "Farewell Blues" first became a success on the Asian continent—Nanri Fumio, the great Japanese trumpeter, featured it in his live performances at nightclubs in the puppet state of Manchukuo—and then subsequently won popularity back in Japan.

After his success with "Japanese blues," Hattori expanded into "Chinese blues" numbers. Kasagi's 1940 recording of Hattori's "Hot China" (Hotto Chaina), for example, participated in Hattori's "China period," in which he experimented with hybrid forms that combined elements of American jazz with elements from Chinese musical traditions (and with Tin Pan Alley versions of musical orientalism) to produce a form of "Asianified jazz" that was more palatable to censors and audiences, especially after full-scale war with China broke out in 1937 and the state became increasingly eager to promote an image of pan-Asianism.[63]

Like many jazz musicians in Japan, Kasagi was largely silenced by the prohibitions on jazz that were enforced after Pearl Harbor. She made no recordings between 1941 and 1945, and she was on at least one occasion subjected to police questioning, although she continued to perform, especially for the troops.[64] Hattori, however, is famous for having managed to continue work all through the war, though he too faced censorship problems. He remained active in film music, among other fields, in both Japan and Manchukuo—he was, for example, music director for the film *China Nights* (*Shina no yoru*, 1940; dir. Fushimizu Osamu, starring Ri Kōran), for which he composed the hit song "Suzhou Serenade" (Soshū yakyoku) for Watanabe Hamako. Hattori visited China frequently to entertain Japanese troops, and a number of his songs became hits in Manchukuo, Shanghai, and elsewhere on the continent. As noted, Hattori was based in Shanghai in August 1945, when the war ended.

Whatever difficulties they faced during the war years, Kasagi and Hattori reemerged with a vengeance soon after 1945, when restrictions on jazz and popular dance music were lifted. Kasagi's appearance in the early postwar musical revue *Highlight*, and then especially in the musical revue *Jazz Carmen*

(1947; composed by Hattori), brought her back to national popularity. *Jazz Carmen* was one of many attempts by Hattori to merge Western classical and popular musical genres. Recordings of the show do not survive, but it seems significant that its story was based on Bizet's opera, another work in which both the narrative and the musical structure revolve around the taming of a highly sexualized and racialized female figure, the eponymous seductress.[65]

Above all, it was Kasagi's hit "Tokyo Boogie Woogie" (1947; composed and arranged by Hattori) that transformed her into an icon of Occupation-period culture. In the depressed circumstances of postwar Japan, Hattori would later recall, he realized that the melancholic "blues" pieces he had specialized in during the 1930s were no long appropriate; what was needed now was a brighter sound.[66] No doubt commercial considerations as well as an awareness of current fashions in American dance music also contributed to his thinking. He had been experimenting with boogie-woogie for several years, after encountering sheet music for the Andrews Sisters' hit song "Boogie Woogie Bugle Boy" in wartime Shanghai. As this anecdote indicates, for Hattori "boogie-woogie" meant not so much the rapid-fire piano style developed by such players as Pine Top Smith and Meade "Lux" Lewis in the 1920s and 1930s as the more commercial adaptation of the form by American big-band orchestras that achieved popularity in the late 1930s and early 1940s.

Hattori got the direct inspiration for "Tokyo Boogie Woogie" while riding the Chūō Line train in Tokyo, listening to the rhythm of the rails and the afterbeat of the overhead hand straps slapping in response: they seemed to emulate the "eight-to-the-bar" rhythm of the boogie-woogie style. When he got off the train at Nishi Ogikubo, Hattori raced to a nearby café and jotted down the tune on a napkin.[67] The lyrics were subsequently written by Suzuki Masaru (son of the famous Buddhist philosopher Suzuki Daisetsu), albeit with help from Hattori. The tune begins with a somewhat lumbering introduction, as if its engine has to warm up before lurching into motion—but once the main theme kicks in, Kasagi's powerful performance and Hattori's eight-beat rhythm surge forward with an unstoppable force. The melody is in the cheerful key of B-flat major, with the flattened blue notes that Hattori had mastered since the 1930s; it does not utilize the pentatonic scale that characterizes many other Japanese songs from this period. The song's lyrics stress the transnational, global success of boogie-woogie music. They also make it clear that you were not supposed to sit passively when you listened—this is self-avowed dance music:

> Tokyo boogie-woogie, happy rhythm
> hearts throbbing, exciting sounds
> what reverberates across the ocean: Tokyo boogie-woogie
> the boogie dance is the world's dance

Kasagi debuted "Tokyo Boogie Woogie" in an Osaka stage show in October 1947 and two months later recorded it with Nippon Columbia's in-house orchestra. Supposedly, U.S. soldiers, both black and white, flooded into the recording studio to listen as the track was laid down and erupted in spontaneous cheers when the song finished. The recording was used in the film *Spring Feast* (*Haru no kyōen*; dir. Yamamoto Kajirō, Kurosawa's primary mentor), released late that month, just in time for the New Year holiday season.[68] By March 1948, when Kasagi opened a new musical revue at the Tokyo Nichigeki Theater called *Tokyo Boogie Woogie*, the song was a nationwide sensation. Shortly after this, Kurosawa approached Kasagi and Hattori to request that she perform "Jungle Boogie" in his upcoming film, *Drunken Angel*. That song likewise would soar up the popular music charts.

Kasagi's string of hits continued through the early 1950s. "Shopping Boogie" (Kaimono bugi, 1950), a Hattori composition that blends a boogie-woogie minor melody with lines closer to a Japanese *miyako bushi* scale, featured Kasagi singing in Osaka dialect. It is said to have sold 450,000 copies—an astonishing figure given the still-depressed state of the Japanese economy.[69] Also in 1950, she and Hattori toured the United States, performing concerts in Hawaii, California, and New York (figure 1). After returning to Japan later that year, she performed in a musical revue written by Hattori titled *Honolulu, Hollywood, New York*, in which she performed the song "Los Angeles Shopping" (Rosuanzerusu no kaimono). "Home Run Boogie" became another enormous hit for Kasagi and Hattori: in January 1953, Kasagi was chosen to sing it as the finale number for the third annual *Kōhaku uta gassen*, the NHK network's annual New Year musical extravaganza. In 1955, however, Kasagi announced her retirement from the music business. She subsequently refused many offers to resume singing—though she remained active as an actress in film, television, and commercials through the 1970s.

FIGURE 1 Kasagi Shizuko and Hattori Ryōichi about to depart Tokyo's Haneda Airport for their American concert tour, 1950. (Courtesy Mainichi Photo Bank, Tokyo, Japan)

One Japanese critic has spoken of "Tokyo Boogie Woogie" in terms of the "explosive sense of liberation" (*bakuhatsu suru yō na kaihōkan*) that the song unleashed.[70] If Kurosawa's films portray mass culture and popular music as threats to masculine subjectivity, the version of freedom that Kasagi's songs present sees material scarcity as the chief threat: the main hindrance to liberation, her lyrics suggest, is that there aren't enough goods available for Japanese consumers to purchase, or enough money to buy them with. The popularity of these songs during the Occupation contrasts sharply with the wartime period, when the simple mention of contemporary material shortages could lead to a song being banned—the fate of Hattori's humorous ditty "The Shortage Song" (Tarinai songu, 1940; performed by the Rhythm Boys).[71]

Consequently, many of the postwar numbers that Hattori wrote and Kasagi performed present a fantasy of unlimited consumption as the realization of a realm of freedom. The lyrics to "Shopping Boogie" consist largely of a catalog of things that the singer might buy—the recorded version goes on for slightly more than three minutes, but in live stage performances, the musical shopping list continued for more than six minutes. If Kurosawa's films use jazz music as a stand-in for the invisible figure of the U.S. Occupation and the threat it posed for Japanese masculinity, Kasagi's recording of "Los Angeles Shopping" completely reverses the image, presenting the United States as a paradise of consumption, as a place where a Japanese woman can finally be free to enjoy life. For the woman speaker of the song's lyrics, the Occupation turns out to have been a good thing, a moment of liberation.

Kasagi's hits contributed to the newly revived leisure and entertainment industries in Occupied Japan, be it in the movies, dance halls, stage shows, or radio. Even in the hardscrabble early postwar years, when millions of Japanese lacked the basic necessities of life and when economic production ground nearly to a halt, the poorest of the poor could still consume pop music and enjoy the pleasures it offered. As we have seen, the lyrics to Kasagi's songs often hinge around encouragements to consumption. Moreover, the records themselves were increasingly important commodities: production figures for records pressed during the immediate postwar years show remarkable growth.[72] The very act of listening to these songs meant engaging in consumption, whether one purchased records, bought tickets to a movie or concert, danced to them at one of the dance halls and nightclubs that sprouted up in postwar urban centers, or simply whistled the melodies while walking down the street. With Kasagi's hits, we are in the heart of what Adorno would condemn as "the culture industry," and one of the ideological messages conveyed by the songs seems to be that postwar liberation can be achieved through the act of consumption.

Moreover, listening to these songs was a physical, fleshly act. You were not meant to hold still while listening to this music, but to enjoy it through your body. We find here, that is, a stress on the body as an avenue for liberation, a tendency widely seen in early Japanese postwar culture. Kasagi's music marks an attempt "to rescue the body from the tyranny of institutionalized reason" in which "the dancing body is romanticized as what is left over when the burdens of reason and civilization have been flung away."[73] The aggressive female sexual desire voiced in a song like "Jungle Boogie" also suggested emancipation from wartime patriarchy and its insistence on subjugating individual pleasures, especially feminine pleasures, to the national good. A useful comparison can be made with Angela Davis's argument that explicit celebrations of female sexuality by such women blues singers as Ma Rainey and Bessie Smith carried on a tradition in African American communities after 1865, where sexuality was "one of the most tangible domains in which emancipation was acted upon." For former slaves, the promised political and economic liberation never arrived, but the freedom to choose one's own sexual partners continued to mark "an important divide between life during slavery and life after emancipation" and remained a domain in which the performers insisted on gender equality.[74] The historical circumstances are quite different, but in the Occupation-era jazz hits of Kasagi Shizuko, we find a similar celebration of the deliverance of female sexuality from wartime state regulation. Perhaps this helps account for Kasagi's legendary popularity among *panpan* girls, the omnipresent streetwalkers who were perceived as a threat to public morality in late 1940s Japan.

It is also important to remember, however, that Kasagi was performing music composed by a man, Hattori, and that she was singing lyrics written for her by men—including Kurosawa. A tension exists between Kasagi's own position as a female subject and the male-authored versions of femininity that she was performing so successfully. In this instance, at least, we need to try to tell the dancer from the dance.

*   *   *

Kurosawa, Hattori, and Kasagi present us with radically different versions of what freedom meant in postwar Japan. Each of the three models is relatively easy to pick apart on its own: each is baldly ideological, promoting a tendentious imaginary relationship to social reality and simultaneously erasing from view certain inconvenient facts. A more interesting and productive question lies in their interrelationship: Why did these three figures need one another? Why would Kurosawa ask Hattori and Kasagi to participate in his films, and why would they accept?

Let me begin with Kurosawa. Why did he seek popular musicians for his films? In fact, media crossover had been a strong feature of the Japanese film industry dating back to the silent era. For example, the explosive success of the hit jazz song "Tokyo March" (Tōkyō kōshinkyoku, 1929; music by Nakayama Shinpei, lyrics by Saijō Yaso, performed by Satō Chiyako) prompted the Nikkatsu studio to release a silent film of the same title, under the direction of Mizoguchi Kenji. The advent of talkies in Japan—the first was *The Madame and the Wife* (*Madamu to nyōbō*, 1931; dir. Gosho Heinosuke), which features several performances by a jazz orchestra—made this sort of crossover between the film and record industries even more common. This integration is depicted brilliantly in the final montage sequence of the film *Tokyo Rhapsody* (1936; dir. Fushimizu Osamu), starring Fujiyama Ichirō and based on the latter's hit song of the same title, composed by Koga Masao. The montage traces the rapidly proliferating popularity of the song through the cityscape of Tokyo, as it is conveyed alternately by means of a radio broadcast, a nightclub dance band performance, a phonograph recording in a café, and people from various walks of life singing the tune as they stroll along the streets of the city.

Kurosawa served as third assistant director on *Tokyo Rhapsody*. He was, in other words, from early in his career made aware of the commercial possibilities that popular songs presented to the film industry. Kurosawa's apprenticeship as assistant director took place at PCL Studios, one of the leaders in introducing talkies and musical comedies in 1930s Japan: one critic has suggested that this early training helps explain Kurosawa's skillful use of music in his later films.[75]

But this offers at best a partial explanation for his decision to use Kasagi Shizuko in *Drunken Angel*. At the same time that he was exploiting the commercial potential of popular culture, Kurosawa was also trying to distance himself from it. I have argued that Kurosawa's films are examples of cinematic modernism. High modernism in order to become high modernism needs to distinguish itself from its lowly others, most prominently popular culture. To emerge as the leading auteur director of postwar Japan, Kurosawa needed to invoke the scandal of popular culture precisely in order to distinguish himself from it. In literary critic Andreas Huyssen's formulation, the long-held antagonism between high modernist art and mass culture "may lead one to conclude that perhaps neither of the two combatants can do without the other, that their much heralded mutual exclusiveness is really a sign of their secret interdependence. . . . Or, to put it differently, as modernism hides its envy for the broad appeal of mass culture behind a screen of condescension and contempt, mass culture, saddled as it is with pangs of guilt, yearns for the dignity of serious culture which forever eludes it."[76]

But the relationship between high art and popular culture goes beyond that general mutual interdependence. In setting up the dialectical opposition between classical music and popular dance music that I have described, I think Kurosawa was trying to construct a coherent statement about what freedom might mean in the specific geopolitical context of Occupied Japan. Like political theorist Maruyama Masao in his famous essay "From Carnal Literature to Carnal Politics" (1949), it seems that Kurosawa was reacting against the widespread notion that the fleshly body provided the gateway to liberation and authentic subjectivity.[77] Hence, for Kurosawa, classical music on the sound track was crucial, because in both Japan and the West, it was ideologically situated as a medium that denied the fleshly, erotic body in favor of a lofty, disembodied spirituality and rationality.[78] Conversely, the targets of Kurosawa's scorn in these films are popular songs, especially dance music: music that is meant to be enjoyed through the body. As the doctor in *Drunken Angel* proclaims, only (disembodied) reason will lead us to authentic freedom—even as Kurosawa cannot help but acknowledge the visceral excitement generated by and through the body, as enacted in the film by Kasagi Shizuko and Mifune Toshirō, whose performance as the tubercular gangster steals the picture.

Furthermore, the form of liberation that Kurosawa advocated depended precisely on maintaining differences. In the wartime period, all distinctions were in danger of disappearing under the emergency situation in which only one difference was permitted to remain meaningful: the opposition between Japan and its enemies. In music, this meant that all genres were lumped together into one of two categories: good music, and the enemy's music. This tendency persisted in altered form even after 1945, as both the U.S. Occupation and Japanese intellectuals developed elaborate theories of "Japaneseness," a quality always defined in contrast to its opposite, the West (and increasingly, the United States). Within this overarching opposition, all subtle differences—all the diversity and heterogeneity internal to both Japan and the United States—stood in danger of erasure. The singularity of individual difference was at risk of disappearing behind the mask of cultural homogeneity. It was this erasure of small differences that Kurosawa perceived as the real threat to freedom in postwar Japan. Authentic freedom meant attending to the differences that persisted on both sides of the geopolitical divide, internal differences that troubled any attempt to reduce the world to a stark opposition between "us" and "them."

Kurosawa's films display an almost obsessive concern with the need to draw distinctions and observe minute gradations. Kurosawa does not simply draw an opposition, for example, between masculinity and femininity but differentiates between multiple forms of masculinity and femininity. Not content merely to oppose cowards and heroes, he is compelled to draw subtle distinctions between different kinds of bravery and cowardice, different kinds of high and low. This insistence on respecting small differences, this refusal to collapse small distinctions into overarching oppositions, is why, I think, we get seven samurai instead of only two, or why we are presented so many different versions of the story in *Rashōmon*.

A crucial part of this political and aesthetic commitment lies with Kurosawa's refusal to collapse sound and image—his insistence on holding them apart. Moreover, we characteristically find him distinguishing between multiple forms of sound and vision on each side of this opposition, including, as I have argued, distinctions between popular and classical music, as well as between diegetic and nondiegetic sound track. In both the wartime and postwar historical situations, the overwhelming power of the opposition between Japan and the West (which increasingly meant the United States) threatened to erase the distinctions between genres of music: it was all Western music, or it was all Japanese music, regardless of genre.[79] But liberation for Kurosawa requires us to respect the generic boundaries and distinctions between kinds of music: classical and popular, as well as everything in between. In this sense, Kurosawa again resembles Adorno in the latter's concern for maintaining aesthetic distinctions as a form of resistance against the homogenizing influence of the culture industry. For them, respecting the differences between musical genres is one practice by which we maintain a measure of freedom in an otherwise corrupt world.

For Kurosawa, only the preservation of these sorts of distinctions and differentiations makes choice possible—which is to say, they make what Kurosawa understood to be authentic individual subjectivity possible. It was here that Kurosawa's own self-image arose—"Kurosawa the risk-taker, Kurosawa the free agent" who "places his hope in the extraordinary individual who can exceed structural limits by sheer willpower and earnestness."[80]

We can, of course, criticize this model of freedom—noting, for example, that genre distinctions are hardly innocent or neutral but in fact function ideologically to legitimate other hierarchies of, for example, class, race, and gender. The notions of taste and distinction are crucial mechanisms for the establishment and reproduction of power relationships in our societies. Moreover, the rise of a global mass medium like cinema challenged the old modernist definition of "culture" as being "those places where the commodity does not yet rule": in the new world that emerged after 1945, it became increasingly impossible to deny that "culture was itself an economic realm."[81] Despite these problems, though, I doubt that we can do without this model of liberation. It underlies our very basic distinctions between good and bad music, between art and trash, between music that leads toward liberation and music that imposes enslavement. To enjoy any sense of liberation from music, we have to make distinctions between music that dulls us and music that awakens us, even if we recognize that these distinctions are always provisional.

*　　*　　*

Hattori Ryōichi presents a remarkable contrast, because the goal of Hattori's lifework as a composer was to erase the very boundaries that were so crucial to Kurosawa. "My philosophy," Hattori writes in his autobiography, "is that in music, there is no fundamental distinction between classical or popular, which derived from my wish simply to bring to the masses good music. This philosophy has remained unchanged through my entire life."[82] Hattori was first trained as a musician in 1920s Japan, where there was little distinction drawn between so-called classical music and popular music; it was all simply Western music. Hattori himself played saxophone not only in jazz bands and dance-hall orchestras, but also with the Osaka Philharmonic Orchestra, whose maestro, Emmanuel Metter (1884–1941), became his primary mentor in music theory:[83] "For me, who sees no distinction in music between popular music and elite music [kōkyū ongaku], the object of my struggles with the music theory and techniques I was studying then was to bring them to life in the worlds of jazz and popular song [*kayōkyoku*]."[84] His lifelong dream was to follow the path blazed in the United States by Paul Whiteman: Hattori wanted to achieve "symphonic jazz," a merging of classical and jazz, ever since he heard about the 1933 "Symphonic Jazz Recital" at the Hibiya Kōkaidō concert hall in Tokyo, which had included the Japanese premiere of Gershwin's "Rhapsody in Blue."[85]

This belief in the fundamental similarity of all musical genres arises from Hattori's belief in the directly embodied experience that music provides:

> Music is a sweet sound bestowed on us by heaven; a song is something that can only be bestowed upon us by the gods. Compared to this, painting, sculpture and the other arts are not as readily able to move us directly or to draw out tears from us. Herein lies the difference between a static art like painting and the dynamic arts, as represented best by music.
>
> Truly, nothing touches the heart of people more than the mystical quality [*shinpisei*] of music. . . . In this, there is no difference between so-called Art Music [*jun ongaku*] and popular music.[86]

This mystical ability of music to provide embodied pleasure is for Hattori universal: "Music transcends the barriers of language and is understandable throughout the world."[87] Following this line of thought, emancipation means to tear down the artificial boundaries that separate genres of music, to return to the authentic pleasures of the body that had been repressed both by wartime fascist ideologies and by bourgeois ideologies of taste that insisted on rigidly distinguishing between high and low forms of musical art.

Hattori was also interested in crossing ethnic and racial boundaries. In his autobiography, he recounts a conversation he had in the early 1930s in which he declared to a friend, "I don't think there is any need for the blues to be monopolized by blacks, like William Handy's 'St. Louis Blues.' Don't you think there should be a Japanese blues, an Oriental blues in Japan?"[88] As we have seen, Hattori went on to compose numerous Japanese and then Chinese blues numbers, and he would continue after 1945 to produce hybrid compositions that combined Latin dance rhythms, Asian melodies, Italian opera arias, African American chord progressions, and so forth. The libratory aspect of music as something experienced through the body transcends parochial boundaries of language, culture, and race: as the lyrics of "Tokyo Boogie Woogie" proclaimed (and as the music demonstrated), "what reverberates across the ocean: Tokyo boogie-woogie; the boogie dance is the world's dance." Postwar liberation meant rejoining the world in a great surge of bodily pleasure.

Note, however, that there is also a notion here of an essential Japaneseness. "Jazz is jazz," Hattori would write of his prewar "jazz chorus" music, "but I think I was successful because I aimed at producing Japanese jazz."[89] Or again: "My dream was to use symphonic music to compose a folk *poesie*, a poem of the unique beauty of the soul of Japan [*Nihon tokuyū no utsukushii tamashii no shi*]."[90] The universal that is music requires the particularity of Japan. Where Kurosawa seems determined to hold off the erasure of small distinctions between genres that are under threat of being swallowed up by the overarching distinction between Japan and the foreign, Hattori conversely wants to erase the small distinctions but maintain that fundamental distinction between Japan and the outside world. Again, it is relatively easy to critique Hattori's model of liberation: to start with, it ignores the tremendous diversity of Japanese musical practices, ancient and modern. Yet the notions of music as something closely linked to bodily pleasure, as something capable of crossing cultural and ethnic boundaries, and of music as being linked in complicated ways to distinct cultural traditions—these are not positions that we can easily abandon. In certain situations, they can provide the only handy tools for resistance against oppressive norms of official culture. In certain situations, they may provide the only path to liberation.

*   *   *

Finally, let me turn to Kasagi Shizuko, who is in many ways the hardest of the three for me to explicate. How did Kasagi define liberation in the postwar situation? Kasagi is the trickiest to pin down because I am faced with the basic problem of how I might locate her voice—an ironic difficulty, given that she was such a distinctive singer, as well as the proud bearer of a pronounced Osaka accent. Japanese musicologist Hosokawa Shūhei describes her natural-voice singing as being unique among her generation of performers, marked by her skill "in adapting herself well to the rhythmic malleability of American singers" and by the way the "sound and meaning of the words were neatly integrated to express her emotion as if it had been her own nature."[91]

Kasagi's voice is indelible, and yet she was, after all, singing words and notes written for her by men. Present-day female *enka* singers in Japan similarly find themselves caught up in a genre that "molds female singers, songs and subjectivities in its own male-dominant image. As a result, the discourse and performance of femaleness are determined by the men who control the genre rather than by the women who people it."[92] Is there any room for agency in Kasagi's performances? How do we hear the voice of this subaltern?

As we have seen, in her interaction with Kurosawa and Hattori, Kasagi was often positioned to perform the role of the body, a figure that was simultaneously attractive and threatening. She became, in other words, an icon of bodily pleasure and material consumption. This is consistent with the positive view of human flesh that emerged in the wake of the postwar disillusionment with abstract ideals in Japan: in a world where abstract ideology seemed to have failed massively, leading to national ruin, the body in its pleasures, pains, and desires was widely perceived as the only reliable truth, and hence the best avenue for liberation. The body, in the end, is the grounding of all human existence. Kasagi would stress this herself: as she wrote in 1951, "I recently went to America and realized that one sings differently depending on one's physical condition; I realized that Japanese people have a way of singing that is defined by the Japanese blood that flows through them." In the same article, she tells about meeting the American actress Mary Martin, who told her about the time Helen Keller visited and asked permission to touch with her hands the body of the great artist. Martin held out her hand to shake, but was surprised to find Keller's fingers reached out to touch her breasts, her shoulders, her arms, a sensation that, Kasagi writes, "was like being bathed in holy water." "To tell the truth," Kasagi writes, "it made me feel so jealous of Miss Martin!"[93] Kasagi's fans in Japan, too, identified her performance with the body and her "gestural overstatement."[94] Novelist Hayashi Fumiko wrote in 1948 that she liked singers Watanabe Hamako and Awaya Noriko, but that they couldn't match the way Kasagi "dances with her whole body and sings with her whole body."[95]

Yet to perform the role of the body is for female singers also to fall into a trap: that body is not only an ethnic body, or only the body of an artist, but also a sexual and gendered body. As Susan McClary has argued, "Women musicians have usually been assumed to be publicly available, have had to fight hard against pressures to yield, or have accepted the granting of sexual favors as one of the prices of having a career. . . . Women on the stage are viewed as sexual commodities regardless of their appearance or seriousness."[96] It didn't help that Kasagi spent much of her career as an unmarried mother, after her fiancé tragically died young during their potentially scandalous affair. Perhaps this is why Hattori in his autobiography goes out of his way to describe how Kasagi's personal life was marked by moral rectitude, quite in contrast to her loud public persona—even as he notes her popularity among streetwalkers.[97]

This theme is particularly foregrounded in the film musical *Ginza Cancan Girls* (*Ginza kankan musume*, 1949; dir. Shima Kōji). Kasagi Shizuko and Takamine Hideko star as young women who try to raise money for a needy old friend by becoming wandering singers who work for tips in Tokyo's Ginza nightlife district. A pun is embedded in the song title from which the film takes its name, another Hattori composition: it really should be "Ginza *panpan* girls." The plot revolves around the question of whether there is any distinction between women cancan performers on nightclub stages and the *panpan* prostitutes who sit in the audience alongside their customers. The film itself enacts this problematic by repeatedly having its actresses risk indecent exposure—including one sly sequence in which they start to undress, then realize the camera is watching, and conceal themselves behind a blanket.[98] Here, as elsewhere in her early postwar career, Kasagi's singing celebrates dancing, consumption, and bodily pleasure as means to liberation, but we also find those values set in tension with an insistence on her self-discipline, probity, and prohibition.

In other words, even as she enacted the desired sexual body of the female singer, Kasagi also refused the role. A male critic writing in 1950 about Kasagi's "big mouth" performance style expresses an almost vexed irritation with her lack of sexual allure:

Carmen Miranda, the "Queen of Seduction" (Copacabana) not only is a talented artist but also has an untamed allure about her. She has a sexiness that really delights the men who watch her. If someone were to compare this actress with Kasagi Shizuko, well, I think it would make Carmen Miranda break down and cry. That's how difficult it is to compare the Japanese queen of boogie-woogie to what should be her counterparts among Western actresses and singers. Most regrettable is that Kasagi's body lacks all Western-style sexiness. She also lacks any talent worthy of the name talent. On top of that, her neck is too skinny, which makes her voice sound pained, as if it were being wrung out of her.[99]

The closest counterpart the critic, who elsewhere praises Kasagi's indomitable spirit and tireless energy, can find in Hollywood is the comedienne Martha Raye.

Kasagi's performance style comes out more clearly when we contrast her "Los Angeles Shopping" with another Hattori composition used in the same musical revue that celebrated her and Hattori's 1950 American tour. The song "American Souvenir" (Amerika miyage) was performed by Hattori's sister, Hattori Tomiko, who also performed on that tour. In the lyrics, Tomiko effuses about how wonderful her trip to America was, but concludes quite primly:

> But for me
> after all, I love Japan the best
> and that is the story of my travels.

She goes on to sing that Western-style dresses and high-heel shoes are nice, but she prefers kimono, just as she will take *ochazuke* (rice steeped in tea) over champagne and cocktails.[100] In contrast, Kasagi in her "Los Angeles Shopping" plays the fool, infatuated with all things American and tripped up by her own ignorance: the souvenirs she brings back from Los Angeles turn out, much to her self-mocking dismay, to bear a "Made in Japan" label. Yet Kasagi enjoys the laugh on herself as much as everyone.

The humor seems central. Even as Kasagi repeatedly plays the sexual body in her songs, we also sense that she is standing back from the role and laughing at it. Kasagi's parodic performance of "Tokyo Boogie Woogie" in the film *Singing Enoken's Detective Story* (*Utau Enoken torimonochō*, 1948; dir. Watanabe Kunio), for example, transforms her signature number into a silly ode to housekeeping. Here and elsewhere, Kasagi is both performing the assigned role and standing back to enjoy it. It is reminiscent of the manner in which Billie Holiday appropriated the trite—and often offensive—lyrics of Tin Pan Alley songs, using her musical performance to transform them into something else, unleashing a "capacity to speak the unspeakable, to convey meanings that differed from and sometimes contradicted the particular terms employed to express them," thereby establishing "an almost magical control of the tired words, revitalizing them and pushing them toward a criticism of the very cultural context out of which they were born."[101] Kasagi's performances are more playful, her irony more humorous, and yet the effect is similar: even as she performs the role that males have written for her as the liberated and liberating female body, she stands back from the role, winking at the audience not to take it too seriously. The incongruous grin that remains on her face throughout her performance of "Jungle Boogie" in Kurosawa's *Drunken Angel* is paradigmatic.

Accordingly, one place where we can seek Kasagi's voice is, not surprisingly, in her singing: in the ways that her vocalization of the lyrics opens up a subtle gap between the implicit meaning of her performance and the explicit meaning of the lyrics. We should also note that Kasagi wrote some of the lyrics to her songs, even though she was not granted official songwriting credit. Some of her improvised scatting phrases were incorporated into Hattori's lyrics for "Shopping Boogie," for example.[102]

Ironically, however, perhaps the best place to locate Kasagi's voice is in moments of silence and refusal to speak. We know, for example, that she refused to perform the original lyrics that Kurosawa submitted to Hattori for "Jungle Boogie." Kurosawa's first draft stressed physical love, and Kasagi refused to record the song until Hattori toned down the words.[103] And, as I've already noted, in 1955 Kasagi chose silence: she ended her career as a singer. There were probably numerous reasons for this sudden retirement: the waning of the boogie-woogie craze, for example, and the ascendancy of new genres such as the mambo, cha-cha, and early rhythm and blues.[104] In an interview given around the time of her retirement, however, Kasagi goes out of her way once again to stress that "what gets on my nerves more than anything else are things that might harm public morals [*fūkijō*]. . . . I make it an absolute condition that whatever I perform must be something that even children and old ladies can watch. When a script has something wrong in it, I come right out and say, 'I won't do it, let's cut it out.'"[105] In other words, her self-silencing seems at least in part due to her discomfort with the role she was assigned to play. In the world of Japanese popular music, this kind of retirement is not an unusual gesture, especially for female singers. The case of super idol Yamaguchi Momoe, who retired abruptly at the peak of her popularity in the late 1970s and who had a similarly problematic relationship with the suggestive lyrics to some of her hits, comes to mind.

I don't want to project a definite meaning behind Kasagi's self-imposed silence, which was likely the result of complex factors. But it at least seems possible to say that one model of liberation is the right to remain silent, the right to refuse to voice lines that have been scripted for one. Again, we can easily take issue with this version of liberation: silence in its passivity can fall complicit with the very tendencies it refuses to speak. Nonetheless, the right to refuse to speak or sing, the right to say no or to say nothing at all, seems part of the complicated puzzle here. I return to this problem in a later chapter, discussing the reaction of Asian fans to the music of Chage & Aska in the 1990s.

* * *

This chapter began in a moment of silence, and it ends in one. Like ourselves, the musicians and music fans of early postwar Japan lived out a contradictory reality, with multiple fantasies of liberation competing for dominance. It was precisely an inability to distinguish between different models of liberation that undermined Adorno's often brilliant attempt to account for the ways that music served, or resisted, the enslavement of our imagination. Adorno understood liberation via a dialectical model, in which each individual responded to the demands of the totality to which it belonged, yet in which the totality also shifted in response to each individual member—a model under which real historical change was possible. The uniqueness of each individual was permitted, and yet a social totality based on a synthesis of all the different parts was also constructed. A change in one note, a single change in rhythm or tone, led to a corresponding change in the structure of an entire musical piece. Rather than reiterate a preexisting musical law until they reached some preordained conclusion, individual parts possessed freedom to create something new and unprecedented. In Adorno's words, "The detail virtually contains the whole and leads to the exposition of the whole, while at the same time, it is produced out of the conception of the whole."[106] He found the perfect model for such an ideal state in Western classical music, above all Beethoven.

Conversely, for Adorno popular music represented a trap. Seeming to promise liberation, instead it captured its listeners' desires for freedom and locked them into a static, unchanging world, in which interchangeability trumped individuality. Individual elements, whether human subjects or musical phrases, were subjected to the discipline of the unyielding totality—that is, to "the fundamental characteristic of popular music: standardization."[107] Musical elements in a popular song are only so many "cogs in a machine."[108] The creation of something new is forbidden, and the only pleasure permitted under such conditions is that of recognition of the preexisting. Rather than pointing the way out from slavery, such music serves to blunt our critical capacities and numbs us into servile acceptance of our lot.

We ignore Adorno's critique of the cultural industry at our own peril: mass culture's techniques for manipulating consumer desire have, if anything, only become more sophisticated since Adorno wrote these words. We live in a world where the most rebellious forms of popular music are used as sound tracks for television commercials, selling us the message that freedom can be ours if only we purchase a certain brand name. Popular music becomes one of the ways we not merely accept but come actively to desire our own domination.

The problem, though, is that Adorno could see only one kind of political domination and hence could imagine only one road to freedom. While his work remains of crucial importance in helping us understand how the culture industry functions ideologically to make us accept as natural the hierarchies that structure our societies, it needs to be supplemented and challenged by other versions. Adorno's model of liberation, for example, requires us to accept as natural the domination of the masculine over the feminine, whether in society as a whole or in a single musical composition. Moreover, it requires us to accept the normative preeminence of one musical tradition over others: Adorno presumes a specific form of musical composition, one in which melodic and harmonic development is central (as in the Western classical canon), whereas other features such as rhythm, timbre, and connotation are secondary.[109] This bias causes Adorno to use the yardstick of Western classical music to measure the worth of other forms of music—and, not surprisingly, they come up short. This also blinds Adorno to tremendous differences existing between various popular music genres, as well as to the ways in which the pleasures of recognition might serve as a means toward identifying, rather than submitting to, forms of social domination—among, for example, members of ethnic or cultural minorities for whom recognition is a matter of survival.

In the complex geopolitical situation in which Japanese musicians and listeners found themselves after August 1945, how could any one model of liberation possibly have worked for everyone? A much more complicated map was needed. The enemies of freedom, both actual and potential, existed in all directions: the remnants of wartime fascism with its imperialism, thought control, and denial of individual pleasures; the changing but still fundamental hierarchies of gender; the resurgent culture industry that was only too eager to sculpt and commodify the desires of Japanese consumers; the all-too-helpful U.S. Occupation with its promises of freedom and a model of liberation that brooked no questioning of the basic meaning of liberation, especially after the outbreak of the Cold War. To seek liberation as a Japanese intellectual—or musician or listener—meant confronting power in any number of guises and understanding one's own roles as both victim and victimizer. Situated in different positions across this complex field, it is hardly surprising that Kurosawa, Hattori, and Kasagi would sing different tunes.

Music often does promise a sense of liberation: this is one reason it provides pleasure. We achieve that pleasure in part by surrendering to the music, allowing the rhythms and melodies free sway over our persons. To steal a phrase from historian John Dower, to enjoy music is to embrace defeat, to actively live out our surrender. This puts us on dangerous ground: to achieve liberation, we let ourselves be captured. We live in a different historical moment today from that of Kurosawa Akira, Hattori Ryōichi, and Kasagi Shizuko, and yet they have something crucial to teach us—if we are able to hear the moments of both harmony and dissonance among them.

2

MAPPING MISORA HIBARI

WHERE HAVE ALL THE ASIANS GONE?

I am a woman in whom Japanese blood flows. I intend to continue singing the songs of Japan, bringing their spirit to life in a manner befitting
a Japanese.

MISORA HIBARI, *HIBARI JIDEN: WATASHI TO KAGE*

When we take pleasure (or, for that matter, displea-
sure) in music, it often arrives through an imaginary process of mapping. We say, for example,
that a given tune sounds French or Brazilian or Chinese, so that in
enjoying the piece we are in fact enjoying a certain notion we have
about life in France, Brazil, or China. This is true even for people
who happen to be French, Brazilian, or Chinese—in fact, it is often
especially true for them. National and ethnic cultures are primary
codes by which we organize the experience of musicking and decide
whether to imbibe or resist the pleasures offered. Such codes also
make possible playful crossings: slipping a step-dance melody or a
samisen into a hip-hop song, for example. Such crossings exploit a
certain portability inherent in the codes, yet they do not undermine
them: in order to provide their playful pleasure, such crossings must
in fact reinforce the identification of the particular musical element
employed as being Irish or Japanese.

These filters are not simply a matter of idle enjoyment. Musicologist Christopher Small has argued that to engage in musicking

is a crucial "part of the survival equipment of every human being," because it is "an activity by which we learn what are our ideal social relationships."[1] Music realigns our bodies and minds to provide us with an ideal orientation in the world, just as at the same time we use our own imaginary maps of the world to organize our experience of music. In this back-and-forth process, our imaginary maps undergo constant revision as we engage with music and as we live out the specifics of our own ever-shifting historical situation.

If we were to sketch in the imaginary geopolitical map through which early postwar Japanese performers and audiences oriented their acts of musicking, we could safely locate the heroine of chapter 1 at one pole. Kasagi Shizuko's music sounded inexorably American. To jitterbug to "Tokyo Boogie Woogie" in Japan in 1948 was to allow one's body and its pleasures to be reorganized into a certain kind of intimate relationship with the occupying power—it was a prime instance of what historian John Dower has called "embracing defeat."[2] Both contemporary and later accounts identify this tendency in Kasagi's music. A flippant 1948 article on the Japanese boogie-woogie craze in *Time* took up her best-known hit in terms of its indelible Yankee taint:

Tokyo, too, was suffering from a contagious American disease: the boogie. Blaring forth in Tokyo's tawdry nightclubs, and even from loudspeakers in the streets last week, was a song that went:

Tokyo boogie-woogie
Rhythm ookie-ookie [floats]
Kokoro zookie-zookie [heart pounds]
Waku-waku [thump-thump]

After he finishes his next one, a baseball boogie, Tunesmith Ryoichi Hattori intends to go on to higher things, like the kind of music Gershwin wrote.[3]

Likewise, cultural critic Isoda Kōichi in his landmark study *Tokyo as Intellectual History* (1978) would hear in Kasagi's music the infiltration of Americanness into the everyday life of the metropolis. "Tokyo Boogie Woogie," which Isoda describes as "an epochal work of postwar popular music history," symbolized the way Tokyo had shifted from being an "imperial metropole" (*teito*) to being an "American metropolis" (*beito*). The assertion in the song's lyrics that boogie-woogie was simultaneously "the song of the world" and the song of Tokyo created a "linguistic conjunction" that "was probably unprecedented and would not subsequently be repeated. Tokyo, previously the 'imperial metropole,' by becoming an 'American metropolis' was now conceptualized as a center of universal values that were valid throughout the 'world.'" All this ideological freight was carried along on the boogie-woogie rhythm that Isoda thought was indelibly American.[4]

In sum, despite her enormous popularity among postwar Japanese audiences, there was something foreign about Kasagi, a foreignness that everyone identified with the Occupation and the United States. She represented a kind of colonization of Japanese popular music by a foreign power, and to accept the pleasures her music offered was, for better or worse, to embrace a certain geopolitical arrangement of the world.

If Kasagi Shizuko occupies the pole labeled America on the imaginary geopolitical map of postwar Japanese pop songs, who sits at the antipode? The answer to this question gets a bit trickier for reasons I explore subsequently, but at least in terms of how the period is remembered today, this second pole can be identified with another female singer, Misora Hibari (1937–1989). We can label this pole Japan.

Just as country music is frequently proclaimed the sound of the American heartland, *enka* is the genre of pop music believed today to be most authentically Japanese, and Misora Hibari is the undisputed queen of *enka*—even though, as we will see, her repertoire included diverse musical genres. Like many other superstars, she is usually referred to using only her given name, and for decades Hibari has been celebrated as the most Japanese of singers. Film director Suzuki Noribumi wrote in 1992 that "over the past forty years for those of us living in the Japanese archipelago, the sign 'Misora Hibari' has provided an apt keyword for those seeking the prototype of the Japanese 'nation' and the Japanese 'ethnos.'"[5] Entire books are devoted to exploring Hibari's music and career as archetypes of Japanese cultural identity. Religious studies scholar Yamaori Tetsuo, for example, finds in Hibari the paragon of such supposed hallmarks of an essential Japaneseness as *amae* ("emotional dependency," a favorite buzzword of pop theorists of Japaneseness since the

1970s), a maternalistic family structure, pilgrimage and other religious rituals, the cultures of rice cultivation and sake fermentation, and an overall tendency toward the dark and melancholic.[6]

For musical and historical reasons we will explore in the following, Hibari's songs do sound indelibly "Japanese" to both her fans and her detractors. To enjoy her music (or to reject it, as many did) was to situate oneself in a specific kind of relationship to the thing known as Japan, understood in terms of a particular mapping of the geopolitical order of the Cold War world. For her fans, Hibari's hit records provided pleasures of resistance: resistance against social elites who found the singer an embarrassment and resistance against the foreign, especially the American. To shiver in enjoyment to Hibari's dramatic vibrato runs, to feel goose bumps at the sight of a single tear trickling down her cheek as she sang, was to imbibe in the fleshly pleasures of being Japanese. Hibari herself helped create this aura. In her 1971 autobiography, she wrote, "I have always believed that I am singing the songs of Japan. I am a Japanese. Because of this, I must sing the songs of Japan. To do so, I must have a good understanding of the Japanese language. Even when I am approached by nisei [the descendants of Japanese emigrants from overseas], I tell them, 'If you are really my fan, then please speak in Japanese.' That's how it should be."[7]

Not surprising, novelist Mishima Yukio, that ultimate defender of Japanese tradition, was a big fan.[8] Today, Hibari's Japaneseness is as much a matter of common sense as is the Americanness of Chuck Berry, Johnny Cash, and the Beach Boys.

What's curious about all this is that Hibari began her career in the late 1940s as a boogie-woogie singer. More specifically, she debuted as a child performer famed above all for her uncanny ability to mimic Kasagi Shizuko, that most American of singers. One contemporary observer even had it that imitator Hibari was the superior boogie-woogie stylist.[9] The magnetic poles on our imaginary geopolitical map seem mysteriously to have swapped places.

How was this pint-size boogie-woogie singer retooled to become the most Japanese of singers? How was the geopolitical map of popular music redrawn through this process? What sorts of images and memories were left off the map, and where did those repressed memories and images go? These are questions I explore here as I trace the remarkable career of Misora Hibari, the most important figure in postwar Japanese popular music, and one of the world's most talented singers of the twentieth century. Hibari recorded hit songs in virtually every pop music genre discussed in this book, and my decision to end my historical narrative in 1990, the year after Hibari's death, is not coincidental: in many ways, the story I am telling in this book begins and ends with her. No other single person so fully embodies the entirety of postwar Japanese song. And while many previous critics have sought in Hibari the archetypes of a national essence, I am more interested in exploring what her putative Japaneseness tells us about the geopolitical imagination of popular music during this period—about the pleasures that the Cold War opened up for Japanese music lovers, as well as those that it closed off.

*   *   *

Searching for Western counterparts to describe Japanese singers is a dubious undertaking at best. Yet it is a persistent practice, both inside and outside Japan: as we will see in subsequent chapters, there are any number of claimants to being the Japanese Elvis, Beatles, or Dylan. It's hard, though, to find a single counterpart who summons up adequately the significance of Hibari. When trying to explain her to non-Japanese (no explanation is needed for Japanese, of course), I often describe her as a combination of Judy Garland, Frank Sinatra, and Elvis Presley. Like Garland, she made the transition from child novelty act to adult singer, appearing along the way in numerous films—Hibari had 160 screen credits to Garland's 32. Like Sinatra, she appeared on the hit charts with classic singles in every decade from the 1940s to the 1980s, including a late-career renaissance: her final singles "Tangled Hair" (Midaregami, 1988) and "As the River Flows" (Kawa no nagare no yō ni, 1989) are among her most acclaimed and popular recordings. She also shared Sinatra's history of being dogged throughout her career by rumors of involvement with underworld figures—entirely true in Hibari's case. Finally, like Presley, she had a penchant for gaudy stage costumes and inspired an almost religious devotion among her fans—one critic has described the "shaman-like aura" she acquired.[10] She also shares with Elvis a legendary comeback concert: her 1988 "Phoenix Concert" at the Tokyo Dome is in many ways homologous to Elvis's spectacular 1968 NBC special.

Hibari was born Katō Kazue in 1937 in the cosmopolitan port city of Yokohama, the oldest child in the family of a poor fishmonger.[11] Her father played the guitar and led an amateur dance band on the side. He no doubt influenced Hibari's musical upbringing, but it was her mother who became the driving force behind the daughter's career, acting indirectly and often directly as her manager. A child prodigy, Hibari began singing at neighborhood events during the war years, including a 1943 party to send her father off to war. There are a handful of legends about her childhood that are included in all the hagiographies: for example, she memorized ninety-five of the hundred classical *waka* poems used in the popular *Hyakunin isshu* game by the age of three. In 1946, she made her professional debut at the age of nine, singing under the name Misora Kazue at a local theater in Yokohama. In 1947, she joined a concert tour of the southern island of Shikoku—and was nearly killed when the tour bus collided with a truck. Another myth sprouted from this accident: when she had recovered sufficiently to leave her hospital bed, Hibari made a pilgrimage to the nearby site of a famed two-thousand-year-old cedar tree, one that legend had it was planted by Shinto deities. She vowed to the tree that she would become the biggest singer in the nation. Biographer Honda Yasuharu has compared this legend with those that surround the founders of Japanese New Religions, aptly capturing the aura that surrounds Hibari.[12]

With or without divine aid, Hibari made good on her vow. She quickly became a national sensation, famous for singing adult songs, in particular risqué boogie-woogie tunes, despite being a child. Cultured elites despised her music and performing style as vulgar, yet despite this (more likely, because of it) nonelite audiences found an idol in the young girl. As she would admit in her autobiography, Hibari was basically a Kasagi Shizuko imitator at this stage in her career.[13] One of Hibari's biographers reminds us that her hometown, Yokohama, was at the time a center of the U.S. Occupation, its residents living "under miserable conditions, like those of a colonized land."[14] It's hardly surprising that she would sing "American" songs. In a 1948 engagement at the Yokohama Kokusai Gekijō theater, where she was now using the stage name Misora Hibari, her featured number was the song "Second-Hand Girl" (Sekohan musume), one of Kasagi's early postwar hits, and her stage makeup and costumes were also modeled after Kasagi's.[15] In fact, Kasagi shortly thereafter shared a bill with Hibari and apparently was quite taken with the eleven-year-old girl. She frequently played in the green room with Hibari between performances during this joint engagement.

Hibari's fame exploded after this. In 1949, she moved up to bigger theaters in Tokyo proper. In her performances there, she again featured her imitations of Kasagi, including the songs "Hey Hey Boogie" and "Tokyo Boogie Woogie." Hibari signed a contract with Nippon Columbia and released her first record in 1949, a song called "Kappa Boogie Woogie" that, as the title suggests, was in the Kasagi Shizuko mode, including Hibari's take on Kasagi's patented technique of using yelps and growls to punctuate the ends of lines.[16] A number of her other early records also referenced Kasagi's style, including "Pistol Boogie" (Kenjū bugī, 1950), "Disgusted Boogie" (Akireta bugi, 1950), and "Mud Boogie" (Doronko bugi, 1951).[17] In 1949, she also appeared in her first starring role in a movie: *Mournful Whistling* (*Kanashiki kuchibue*; dir. Ieki Miyoji), in which she performed yet another boogie-woogie number, "Carried Away by Boogie" (Bugi ni ukarete). The film took its title from her second single, a bluesy vamp with a slow, pounding beat that is vaguely reminiscent of "St. James Infirmary Blues"; it provided twelve-year-old Hibari's first major hit. The single "Mournful Whistling" (music by Manjōme Tadashi, lyrics by Fujiura Kō) sold 500,000 copies, breaking the postwar record for sales.[18] Hibari's performance of the song at the film's climax, appearing before a nightclub audience dressed in top hat and tails, provided one of the iconic images by which she would always be remembered. It also provided an early instance of Hibari's cross-dressing; throughout her career, she frequently appeared in male costumes, and many of her songs feature her singing in a deep, masculine voice.

By the late 1940s, Hibari was also a media sensation. Early press coverage was often unfavorable. In part, this was because Hibari represented a troubling new trend in postwar popular culture, a breaking down of the boundary between the cultures of adults and children.[19] One newspaper columnist avoided using Hibari's name, but his target was obvious: he declared child boogie-woogie singers to be "monstrous" and said that they made him want to vomit.[20] Entertainer Tokugawa Musei lamented in an NHK broadcast that Hibari's songs were the "music of a ruined nation," proof that Japan was an "inferior race."[21] Likewise, an article in the October 1949 issue of *Fujin Asahi*, a women's magazine, explicitly links Hibari to Kasagi's "corrupt adult" music, asserting, "That those boogie-woogie numbers shouted through a wide-open mouth would touch people's hearts is no doubt a technique that arises from the postwar sense of liberation, but when we encounter a wicked boogie-woogie number skillfully sung and danced by an innocent young singer, it only reinforces our sense of being a defeated nation."[22] A sense of shameful colonization is palpable, as are accusations (repeated elsewhere in the media) that the minor Hibari was being immorally exploited by her adult managers. An investigation was even launched to determine if her handlers were violating the new postwar child labor laws.[23]

It was around this time that Kasagi Shizuko stopped seeing Hibari's imitations as a form of flattery and started seeing them as a professional threat. In several widely publicized incidents, Kasagi demanded that Hibari stop performing her material. Hibari's management responded coolly: as of late 1949, Hibari had only two original numbers that she could call her own, so the bulk of her live act was made up of her versions of hits by others, most notably Kasagi. If Hibari dropped the Kasagi impressions from her repertoire, she really would not have any live act to perform.[24]

In early 1950, Hibari announced that she would be traveling to the United States to appear in concert. Kasagi Shizuko seems to have panicked. Kasagi was planning her own American concert tour for later the same year. If Hibari appeared before American audiences prior to Kasagi, she feared that American audiences would not be able to tell who was the real thing and who the imitator. Kasagi arranged to have the Japanese Composers Copyright League issue a cease-and-desist order to Hibari, demanding that she not perform any Hattori Ryōichi compositions during her American performances. In fact, this order had no legal standing, since, as Hibari's managers quickly pointed out, they were carrying out their only real legal obligation—to pay royalties for their use of the songs. But the mass media went into a frenzy over this dispute between two popular celebrities.[25] Hibari's invitation to appear in Hawaii came from former members of the famous Japanese American 100th Infantry Battalion and 442nd Regimental Combat Team, who wanted her to headline a charity show. Hibari's manager announced that she herself hoped to refrain from singing Hattori's numbers in America, but that if the veterans who invited her were themselves to insist that she sing those songs, then she would have no choice because, he claimed, refusing such a request would provoke an international incident. Once Hibari got to Hawaii, of course her sponsors obliged her by issuing a formal request that Hibari sing boogie-woogie numbers, distributing written copies to the Japanese press, and of course Hibari gave in and performed those numbers at her shows in Honolulu—though she apparently avoided Kasagi's repertoire (figure 2). The Hawaii shows were a sensation, and Hibari received full superstar treatment there, including a police escort to her hotel upon arrival. She and her mentor, Kawada Haruhisa, toured the Hawaiian Islands for several weeks, enjoying success wherever they performed, appearing on local radio programs, and even encountering a young Japanese American Hawaiian girl who was a skilled Hibari imitator.[26]

FIGURE 2 Misora Hibari on stage in Honolulu, 1950. (© Hibari Productions. Used by permission)

From Hawaii, Hibari traveled to the West Coast of the American mainland. Together with Kawada and her mother, she visited Sacramento, Portland, Spokane, Seattle, San Jose, Los Angeles, Monterey, and San Francisco. In California, she made at least one appearance on American television, performed several concerts, and met a number of Hollywood stars, including Bob Hope, Margaret O'Brien, and Spencer Tracy. Nonetheless, the West Coast tour seems to have been somewhat disappointing to Hibari in terms of the size and nature of the halls she played there and in terms of her overall reception. Recently unearthed private recordings from Hibari's June 24 and 25 performances in Sacramento confirm that she did indeed sing some of Kasagi Shizuko's numbers in the United States, including "Hey Hey Boogie," as well as songs associated with the postwar queen of swing, Ike Mariko.[27]

Hibari was in the United States from May through July 1950. Kasagi Shizuko's journey to America took place shortly thereafter, from July through October. Joined by her mentor Hattori Ryōichi and others, Kasagi performed concerts in Honolulu, Los Angeles, and New York. The shows were apparently well received, although Kasagi seems not to have been quite the sensation in Hawaii that Hibari was. While in the United States, Kasagi and Hattori hung out with such jazz luminaries as Lionel Hampton and visited live clubs to hear the latest sound: bebop.

The two 1950 American tours helped mark a turning point in Japanese popular musicians' overseas activities. Since surrender in 1945, economic and legal barriers had prevented Japanese performers from traveling abroad. But in 1950, the actress Tanaka Kinuyo made a celebrated trip to the United States, as did the singers Kirishima Noboru, Futaba Akiko, Watanabe Hamako, Ichimaru, Kouta Katsutarō, and Yamaguchi Yoshiko (the former Ri Kōran). Traveling to the United States had become an attractive possibility for Japanese musicians. Their American appearances were also clearly helpful in promoting the image change for Japan that U.S. Cold War policy required, especially after the Chinese Revolution in 1949 and the outbreak of the Korean War in 1950. Japan was no longer to be depicted as a bloodthirsty enemy but as a friendly ally in the anti-Communist bloc. The successful attempt by the United States to arrange a "separate peace" with Japan in the Treaty of San Francisco (1952), signed by neither the Soviet Union nor the People's Republic of China, symbolized this new era. Elite and popular discourse in both the United States and Japan spun a new version of Japan's recent past. Under modernization theory, the historical philosophy that increasingly held sway in American foreign policy during the 1950s and 1960s, Japan was depicted as a nation that was continuously becoming more modern—which is to say, more like the United States. World War II was reconfigured as primarily a struggle between the United States and Japan (erasing from memory Japan's military conflict with China and other Asian nations), a melodramatic story that led to an ultimately happy ending. As historian Yoshikuni Igarashi has written, "This narrative cast Japan's defeat as a drama of rescue and conversion: the United States rescued Japan from the menace of its militarists, and Japan was converted into a peaceful, democratic country under U.S. tutelage."[28]

Postwar performances in America by Japanese singers, especially female singers, helped promote this new, softer image. For example, Eri Chiemi, who would later become part of the celebrated Three Girls (Sannin Musume) trio along with Misora Hibari and Yukimura Izumi, traveled to the United States in 1953. While there, she appeared in a charity concert with the Harry James Orchestra in Los Angeles, recorded the orientalist song "Gomen nasai" and performed it on the popular *Jukebox* radio show, and sought out personal singing lessons from Kaye Starr, Rosemary Clooney, and Ella Fitzgerald. In all these activities, she was embodying the new image assigned to Japan: a place of fun and romance, a docile and cultured land that was eager to learn from the United States.

Such mimetic performances helped reinforce American Cold War culture's bifurcated view of the world. On the one hand, it focused on containing Communism (hence the widespread military bases in Japan and Okinawa), a policy that stressed absolute difference. On the other, that same culture focused on integrating capitalist allies like Japan into a single family of nations, a tendency that stressed similarity and shared values. This new intimacy was produced in part through popular culture, which provided a sentimental education for American audiences, teaching them how to overcome racist bigotry and accept Asia as an exotic friend. The American tours by Japanese singers in the 1950s helped produce this new cultural terrain, as did such Broadway musicals as *South Pacific* and *The King and I* or the Asia-Pacific novels of James Michener, all of which generated compelling narratives of love overcoming racial and ethnic segregation. Exoticism in such works functioned not so much to hold Asian nations like Japan at a distance as to generate an emotional thrill that could be achieved only by crossing the boundary that separated East from West.[29]

That message was aimed primarily at white American audiences. A second set of messages was delivered to the primarily Japanese American audiences that packed the halls for Hibari's and Kasagi's American concerts (all stage dialogue in the recently discovered tapes of their 1950 Sacramento concerts is in Japanese). Their ties to Japan were now something to be celebrated rather than condemned as they negotiated their own reintegration into American society following the wartime interment camps. In the recording of Hibari's Sacramento concert, we hear her mentor and costar, Kawada Haruhisa, expressing his admiration at how much Japanese Americans have accomplished in the city. He promises after returning home to Japan to report to his countrymen on the achievements of their "brothers" (*dōhō*) in California, news that he says will encourage Japan to move ahead in its recovery.[30]

A third set of messages was directed at Japanese consumers. After returning home in 1950, both Hibari and Kasagi went about making sure that Japanese fans could consume the spectacle of their American tours. As we saw in chapter 1, Kasagi mounted a new musical revue in Tokyo: *Honolulu, Hollywood, New York*. It featured a number of new America-themed compositions by Hattori—for example, "Los Angeles Shopping," a humorous paean to America as a shopping paradise for a young Japanese woman. She sings, for example, about gingerly approaching a young man to ask a question, shy about her ability to speak English. It turns out, however, that the young man speaks perfect Japanese: he is a veteran who spent time in Japan. The refrain to the song declares, "Ah, America is a great country, a great country, la la la la!"

Hibari also leveraged the publicity surrounding her American tour for maximum impact in the Japanese market. Her return to Tokyo was celebrated with a parade through the streets of the city, and in August 1950 she celebrated her American success by mounting *Paramount Show: Amerika Chindōchū*, a stage revue with Kawada Haruhisa at the Asakusa Kokusai theater (figure 3). Many of the songs she recorded around this time use American slang in their titles or lyrics. For example, the sunny hit "My Boyfriend" (Watashi no bōifurendo, 1950) is built around the hook of having Hibari count to four in English at the start of each chorus. The first major work that

FIGURE 3 The poster for Misora Hibari and Kawada Haruhisa's post–American tour musical revue in Tokyo, 1950. (© Hibari Productions, © Okamura Kazue. Used by permission)

Hibari undertook after returning to Japan following her American tour was the film *Tokyo Kid* (1950; dir. Saitō Torajirō), in which she stars and sings the title song, another enormous hit featuring lyrics sprinkled with English colloquialisms.[31] In the opening credits of the film, next to Hibari's name in the cast list there appears the phrase "Her first film since returning from America," in case anyone had missed the news.

In *Tokyo Kid*, Hibari plays a street urchin who is finally reunited with her estranged father, now a successful businessman in the United States (how a Japanese man achieved wealth in wartime America remains unexplained). The film includes a striking dream sequence. In the rented room of the street musician who has temporarily adopted her (played by Kawada Haruhisa),

Hibari drifts off to sleep. The room in which she sleeps is a kind of dream factory: its walls are lined with travel posters depicting America, reflecting the street musician's burning desire to visit the United States. The dream sequence itself consists of footage of Hibari in Hawaii, shot by Kawada during the concert tour earlier that year: Hibari visiting a statue of King Kamehameha, Hibari doing a hula dance, Hibari frolicking on Waikiki Beach, and so on.[32] The climax of the film arrives with a shot of Hibari, happily reunited with her father, boarding an airplane bound for America.[33] As in so many of her early postwar films, Hibari here manages to reunite the Japanese family that has been sundered by the war—though in terms resonant more with the American Occupation's celebration of the virtues of democracy and equality than with the wartime ideology of a hierarchical national family.[34]

Perhaps the most striking linkage between Hibari and America came with another film, *Girls Hand in Hand* (*Futari no hitomi*, 1952; dir. Nakaki Shigeo), released in Japan a few months after the formal end of the American Occupation and in the United States the following year. The film costars Hollywood child star Margaret O'Brien, whom Hibari had met in Los Angeles on the 1950 concert tour. Hibari again plays one of the ubiquitous street orphans who populated Japanese cities in the early postwar period. Her character is named Abe Marie, which quickly morphs into "Ave Maria," a musical cue that Hibari takes up in the film. O'Brien plays the saintly Katie McDermott, daughter of a U.S. Occupation official who comes to Japan to visit her father during summer vacation; she wears a kimono and even speaks a few lines in Japanese (O'Brien remained lifelong friends with the Japanese tutor who prepped her for the role).[35] Marie and Katie meet, and Katie launches a campaign to build an orphanage that will rescue Marie and her siblings (and their mutt) from their impoverished plight. The final scene in the film again takes place at an airport. This time, though, it is O'Brien returning home to America. As her savior's plane passes overhead, Hibari falls to her knees, tears streaming down her face, and she raises her hands toward the aircraft as if in prayer, while "Ave Maria" swells on the sound track. O'Brien would later reflect on Hibari: "Why she was such a legend . . . was that she brought Japan and America together after the war, as a goodwill gesture."[36] But Hibari's act of genuflection must have grated against the ears and eyes of Japanese who were increasingly sensitive to the semicolonial status of Japan even after the end of the formal U.S. Occupation.

*　　*　　*

Despite their shared beginnings as boogie-woogie singers, and despite their shared travel itineraries in 1950, Misora Hibari would come to be remembered as the most Japanese of postwar singers, while Kasagi Shizuko would be remembered as the most American singer from the same generation. Kasagi, that is, would remain a symbol of Japanese popular culture's colonization at the hands of the U.S. Occupation, while Hibari metamorphosed into a powerful icon of musical decolonization. In part, this has to do with an image change that Hibari underwent as she became more popular, switching from the persona of a naughty child singing risqué adult songs to that of the innocent girl role she played in many films.[37] In part, this also has to do with the kinds of songs that Hibari began recording around the end of the Occupation in 1952—during, that is, the Korean War and the economic boom that it brought Japan in its role as a staging ground for American military operations. For example, the hit "Echigo Lion Dance Song" (Echigo shishi no uta, 1950; music by Manjōme Tadashi, lyrics by Saijō Yaso) referenced both musically and lyrically traditional folk culture from the rural Echigo district. The backing orchestral instruments are all Western, but the violins are plucked to sound like samisen, Western flutes and drums mimic *shakuhachi* and *taiko*, and Hibari sings in the guise of a wandering performer of the traditional festival lion dance.

The song that most decisively marked the turning point in Hibari's image would come two years later. "Apple Oiwake" (Ringo oiwake; music by Yoneyama Masao; lyrics by Ozawa Fujio) claims in its title to be an *oiwake*, a kind of traditional folk song found primarily in northeastern Japan. Like "Echigo Lion Dance Song," its orchestration is built around standard Western instruments. But in both its lyrics and its music, the song would have a decisive impact in redefining Hibari as a distinctly Japanese singer. The mournful dirge is particularly famous for its spoken bridge, supposedly improvised by Hibari herself. In it, she adopts a strong (and, of course, fake) northeastern accent, breaking down into sobs as she recalls her dead mother, a victim apparently of wartime air raids on Tokyo. The lyrics celebrate apple blossoms and springtime, but in terms marked by a powerful sense of loss: clearly, the song's popularity was due in part to the way it mourned the traumatic experiences many Japanese suffered during the war. As was frequently the case with historical memory as represented in postwar popular culture, only Japan's role as victim of wartime violence was remembered. The celebratory yearning for America that characterized Hibari's earlier songs and films gives way here to a mournful embrace of Japanese pain and suffering. Symbolically, Hibari made her debut live performance of the song at the Kabukiza theater in Tokyo on April 27, 1952—the day the U.S. Occupation officially ended.[38] The new song must have resonated with the audience's frame of mind: the single sold some 700,000 copies, allowing Hibari to break the postwar sales record for a second time.[39]

The song does use a number of musical cues to signal Japaneseness, some of them modeled after the *oiwake* genre (although, as befits a 1950s pop song, Hibari's tune features a more clearly defined rhythmic pulse than was usual for the traditional genre: in fact, the song's pulse seems to imitate a horse's trot).[40] Yamaori Tetsuo, always eager to link Hibari to traditional Japan, traces the origins of the song's style back to *goeika*, an ancient chanting style used by Buddhist pilgrims in Japan.[41] But we might do better to look closer to home for the source of the musical markings of Japaneseness. The song displays many elements that in the 1960s would become recognized as defining the genre of *enka*: it is sung in a minor key, its melody follows a pentatonic scale, and its ornamentation is provided by Western instruments masquerading as Japanese counterparts. Moreover, Hibari in singing employs vibrato and melisma (shifting between multiple tones on a single syllable, one of the defining traits of the *oiwake* genre) to a degree rarely heard in her previous recordings. Where earlier she had imitated Kasagi's boogie-woogie numbers, now she mimics rural folk-singing styles.

The sense of a return to Japanese tradition in the song was further enhanced by the narrative of the radio drama *Girl from the Apple Orchard* (*Ringoen no shōjo*) in which it was first featured. The radio serial was subsequently adapted into a film of the same title (1952; dir. Shima Kōji); both versions starred Hibari. She plays a city orphan sent out to rural northeastern

Japan to live with her grandfather, a poor apple farmer. There, she not only becomes a singing success but also learns the true values of home and family. The film, shot on location in the Tsugaru region, features much footage of traditional rural festival dances and musical performances. In other words, the flashy values of the city and American culture give way to the supposedly unchanging values of self-sacrifice and human decency found in the Japanese countryside. Although the film ends with Hibari singing a vamped-up version of "Apple Oiwake" that references American hot jazz, her melismatic runs bordering on the realm of scat, the musical centerpiece to the film is a new composition, "Apple Festival" (Ringo matsuri). Hibari sings it in a style that clearly alludes to traditional folk music, and the accompaniment is played on native instruments, including *taiko* drums, Tsugaru-jamisen, and traditional Japanese flutes. In the film, the performance of the song provides the climax to a powerful melodrama of personal decolonization: the city girl reclaims her rural roots as city and countryside are reunited.

This "return to tradition" was also an example of sophisticated media cross-promotion. Hibari's managers skillfully constructed a highly commercial web of interlinked products using radio, live appearances, recordings, and film: success in one medium helped create momentum for success in the others. The film version was in fact Hibari's first to be financed and produced by her own management company, Shingei Pro. Hibari's career helped pioneer the dominant role that talent management agencies such as Watanabe Productions and Johnny's Jimusho would subsequently play in the Japanese popular music industry. The "Apple Oiwake" campaign also provided an instance of Hibari's characteristically aggressive exploitation of new media and technological possibilities. The radio drama helped launch an important new mass medium: it was the initial featured program broadcast by the TBS network when it took to the airwaves as Japan's first commercial network (Japan's official NHK network had begun broadcasting in 1925). For all her celebrated traditionalism, Hibari consistently rode the cutting edge of new media and technologies. She was the first Japanese singer, for example, to grasp and fully utilize the new hi-fi stereo-recording technology.[42] Likewise, in the late 1950s when the recording industry began shifting from the single to the LP format, Hibari was the first Japanese pop singer to release an album in that new, extended format.[43]

In other words, Hibari's celebrated Japaneseness was the sophisticated product of modern marketing and technology, in addition to a creative innovation in popular music styling. We should also note that even as Hibari increasingly recorded songs that signaled "Japan" musically and lyrically, she continued performing in a remarkably cosmopolitan variety of styles. The numerous singles she released in the years after "Apple Oiwake" include such titles as "Festival Mambo" (Omatsuri manbo, 1952), "Bye Bye Hawaii" (1952), "Springtime Samba" (Haru no sanba, 1953), the tango "El Choclo" (1953), the astonishing hybrid country-western novelty "Soba Song" (Charumera sobaya, 1953), "Christmas Waltz" (1953), "Hibari's Cha-Cha-Cha" (Hibari no chachacha, 1956), and "Rockabilly Swordfighting" (Rokabirī kenpō, 1958), to cite just a few. She also continued to perform jazz standards such as Hoagy Carmichael's "Stardust" and "Lover Come Back to Me" with remarkable skill, perhaps not surprising given her roots in boogie-woogie.

Despite this continued variety, it was from the mid-1950s that Hibari would undergo redefinition and emerge as the quintessentially *Japanese* singer. This was a period in which, as the philosopher Takeuchi Yoshimi noted in an influential 1951 essay, nationalism was reemerging in Japanese public discourse for the first time since 1945.[44] In political terms, this was also the era in which the so-called 1955 system was established—and in which the nature of Japan's relations with the United States in the post-Occupation Cold War era was worked out, often with great turbulence. In 1955, the Liberal and Japan Democratic parties merged to form the conservative Liberal Democratic Party, which would maintain a firm grip on the reins of government as Japan's ruling party until 1993. Building on the legacy of Prime Minister Yoshida Shigeru (in office 1946–1947 and again 1948–1954), Japan established a position as a bulwark of U.S. anti-Communist strategic policy, allowing itself to be used as a staging base for American military operations across Asia and essentially surrendering independence in foreign policy to the United States—but also resisting pressure from Washington to rearm, focusing instead on domestic economic growth achieved through aggressive trade and industrial policies, as well as expanded domestic consumption. Given the Japanese state's subservient relation to the United States in international relations, both the ruling party and the opposition sought to stress Japan's cultural independence. Put crudely, the more Japanese autonomy seemed to disappear under American Cold War strategic policy, the more crucial it became to distinguish Japan from the United States in other realms, including the cultural. It was in such a geopolitical environment that Misora Hibari became redefined as a distinctly Japanese singer, one increasingly lionized as "a powerful tool in resisting our artistic colonization."[45]

The manner in which Hibari's life and music were now read through the lens of decolonization is symbolized by her appearances in occupied Okinawa in August 1956. Okinawa was the one American-controlled territory not returned to Japanese sovereignty under the terms of the San Francisco Peace Treaty. Until its final reversion in 1972, its continued status as an occupied territory was a painful reminder of Japan's compromised autonomy, its semicolonial status, even after the end of formal occupation in the remainder of Japan in 1952. Resentment was even stronger in the Okinawan islands themselves. There, anger against American rule reached a peak in the years 1954 to 1956, remembered now as one of the darkest periods in Okinawa's postwar history. With President Eisenhower vowing that the U.S. occupation of the islands would be permanent, popular unrest against American rule exploded against the involuntary appropriation of private lands for base expansion. The murder of six-year-old Nagayama Yumiko by an American sailor in September 1955 triggered particular outrage. Just the month before Hibari's visit, a demonstration against U.S. land appropriation policies had attracted more than 100,000 protestors, at that time the largest mass gathering in Okinawa's postwar history.[46] While many Okinawans continued to resent the pre-1945 history of mainland Japanese prejudice toward Okinawans, continued undemocratic military rule in the islands made many Okinawans increasingly yearn for a reunion with mainland Japan.

Japanese popular culture offered one field for expressing this desire for decolonization. A number of Japanese talents made live appearances in Okinawa during the 1950s, including Kasagi Shizuko. Kawada Haruhisa, Hibari's partner on the 1950 American tour, appeared there in 1953 and apparently was the first to raise the possibility of Hibari's making an Okinawa tour.[47] The negotiations to bring Hibari to Okinawa were unusually long and involved, taking fully three years, but on July 24, 1956, an article in the *Okinawa Times* announced that contracts had been signed and that Hibari would be appearing in Naha the following month.[48] Her performances at the Kokueikan Theater were apparently worth the wait: the total audience for the one-week run (with three performances daily) was nearly one-tenth the entire population of Okinawa. Despite claims made in early advertising that Hibari's tight schedule made any extension of her Okinawa run impossible, in fact popular demand led to the tour being extended by an extra day, and her evening performance on August 11 was broadcast by live remote to radio listeners across occupied Okinawa.[49] The *Okinawa Times* reported that the tour had created an "unprecedented Hibari boom," with all shows sold out and some in the audience traveling from distant islands just to see the performances. The newspaper also reported large crowds gathered outside the theater at all hours in hopes of catching a glimpse of the singer, keeping police and fire departments busy.[50]

Okinawan journalist Ōshiro Asajirō, a high-school student in 1956, would later reflect on the meaning of Hibari's visit:

> For people in Okinawa, Misora Hibari was the embodiment of the fatherland Japan itself. At that time, the fatherland Japan was concluding the first stage in its postwar economic recovery and was beginning its rapid development as a newly reborn Japan. In contrast, Okinawa was still being made to undergo a variety of difficulties. It was at this time that Hibari showed up with her youth and glamour, the incredible power that only her authentic background could supply. These overlapped in the minds of the people of Okinawa with the hopes and yearnings they harbored for the fatherland Japan itself.

Ōshiro goes on to describe her as a "bridge" linking Okinawa to Japan. Symbolically, Hibari was paid in Japanese yen, rather than the B-yen U.S. military scrip normally used on the islands. To raise the enormous sum under the strict foreign currency controls enforced by the U.S. military government, the promoter had to resort to the black market.[51]

From genuflecting on the runway in reverence toward the America-bound plane carrying Margaret O'Brien, Hibari had transformed into an object of worship, one who seemed to promise salvation: through her music, marginal subjects such as those in occupied Okinawa could attain a full return to Japanese identity.

*   *   *

The sense that Hibari provided to listeners on Okinawa, in mainland Japan, and elsewhere (she continued to tour abroad to cities with large ethnically Japanese populations, such as Honolulu, Los Angeles, and São Paulo) that her singing represented a decolonized, authentically Japanese voice crystallized in her classic recordings from the mid-1960s. These songs became massive hit records, commodities that rode the explosive economic growth of the 1960s (Japanese per capita GNP more than doubled during the decade) and circulated out along the increasingly dense networks of mass media: records and radio, as in earlier decades, but now also the rising new force of television. This economic growth was accompanied by massive urbanization as rural laborers migrated to cities in search of factory jobs, and Hibari's tunes also came to speak increasingly to a nostalgic longing for rural roots and lost hometowns.

Today, the best-loved Hibari song from this era is one she first recorded in 1966, "Mournful Sake" (Kanashii sake; music by Koga Masao; lyrics by Ishimoto Miyuki). At the time, however, another Hibari record was even more popular. "Yawara" was the theme song for a television drama of the same name. The title is an alternative pronunciation for the first Chinese character in the name of the martial art judo (the song played on the sport's popularity at the 1964 Tokyo Olympics); on its own, the character means something like "supple," "soft," or "gentle." The single won Hibari the coveted Record of the Year Award (Nihon Rekōdo Taishō) for 1965 after selling 1.8 million copies.[52] Released just after Hibari had become the object of scandal for divorcing her husband, actor Kobayashi Akira, some see the song as marking another turning point in her career. Biographer Honda Yasuharu, for example, dislikes the record: he hears in it not only the moment when Hibari's singing style rigidified into a stale formula but also the moment when she stopped voicing the populist possibilities of early postwar democracy and started representing instead a passive consumerist market, the "managed society" that he fears Japan has become since the early 1960s.[53] Other critics see the song as marking the moment when *enka*'s position as the preeminent musical carrier of Japaneseness achieved the status of common sense.[54]

"Yawara" opens not with one of composer Koga Masao's signature Spanish guitar phrases but with a four-beat percussion intro on timpani and vaguely Chinese-sounding cymbals. The orchestra then establishes the main melodic theme in back-and-forth dialogue with a Japanese-style flute before Hibari enters with the first verse. In instrumental bridges throughout the song, the orchestra and solo flute continue to engage in a kind of struggle that is finally resolved in the coda as the flute surrenders its autonomy and merges into a final communal rephrasing of the melody line. The tune is constructed around a pentatonic melody in E-flat major, albeit with some glances in the direction of the relative minor key of C minor. Hibari sings much of the song in a husky voice near the bottom of her register, but both the verses and the chorus feature resolute vocal runs that take her up into her falsetto, and she ends each chorus in particular with a dramatic flourish. Sekizawa Shin'ichi's lyrics allude to the philosophy of judo, with its nonaggressive technique stressing defensive use of an opponent's strength against him, turning it into a metaphor for a certain type of masculine character. The words stress resignation, voicing the stance of a silent majority that must grin and bear it, postponing its dreams and disdaining selfish ambition in an attempt to forbear with its dignity (or "gentleness") intact. Like the characters voiced in a Loretta Lynn country tune, the singer here describes someone whose "dignity derives from their passivity."[55] The plodding timpani that recurs throughout the song echoes the manly stoicism of the lyrics.

Clearly, "Yawara" aimed to help soothe the pains of an increasingly fragmented, urbanized world in which selfish individualism seemed to threaten all communal values. A premier instance of the *enka* genre, the song evokes a powerful nostalgia for a fantasy lost world of silent, self-sacrificing men with deep emotions. Ethnomusicologist Christine Yano writes, "The enticement of enka is that it suggests a forum for collective nostalgia, which actively appropriates and shapes the past, thereby binding the group together. Enka encodes within nostalgia a historical moment of self-reflexivity, establishing a particular relationship with the temporal past that distances it from, while also placing it firmly in, the present. . . . It is nostalgia compartmentalized, assigned a place, just as 'things Japanese' are kept categorically separate from 'things Western.' "[56] Although the word *enka* has been used since the nine-teenth century to name a variety of popular music forms, the version we now recognize emerged as a coherent genre only in the 1960s as the music industry underwent a dramatic reorganization in the face of new practices characterizing the rising teen market for such genres as rock and folk. In that restructuring, long-standing practices of the mainstream Japanese music industry crumbled: in-house orchestras and songwriters under contract to record companies gave way to freelance musicians and independent compos-ers. Artists and their management firms took more direct control over their recording careers. *Enka* emerged as a distinct, somewhat marginalized genre as a result of these processes, one that retained many of the old practices and one that was largely the domain of a well-defined set of record labels devoted to its propagation.[57] In other words, *enka* is as much a business model as it is a musical genre. Despite the genre's cultural valence as the most Japa-nese of pop music forms, its sales figures pale next to those for more popular genres. *Enka* is also defined via a kind of media obsolescence: its devotees are thought to be older and less technologically savvy, so that new *enka* record-ings are often issued in media forms already obsolete in other genres—vinyl records and eight-track tapes in the age of the cassette tape, for example, and cassette tapes in the age of the compact disc and MP3.

In musicological terms, *enka* has also acquired since the 1960s well-defined parameters. Yano has identified a set of *kata* (stylized formulas) that charac-terize the genre. Some revolve around performing styles—stage costumes, for example (either traditional kimono or glamorous Western-style formal wear) and routine patterns of gesture and between-song patter. Song lyrics tend toward an exaggerated nostalgic sorrow, and tearful spoken passages (as in Hibari's "Apple Oiwake" and "Mournful Sake") are common.[58] There is a distinct vocabulary of emotionally laden words repeatedly used, referring, for instance, to mother, hometown, sake, festivals, wandering, and so on. Lyrics frequently cite rural and other peripheral locations—harbors, for example, and working-class districts. *Enka* songs are similar to American country music in the way they "symbolize the past, exude nostalgia, describe a way of life that city dwellers value more now that they don't have to live that way again."[59] The affect triggered by the words is also reflected in the music, which typically consists of midtempo ballads (though up-tempo songs, especially those invoking the excitement of local festivals, are not unknown). Instrumentation and orchestration are typically Western derived: Spanish guitar, easy-listening string sections, smooth saxophones, and Latin American rhythms are all common. Ironically, many of the musical features that found their way into 1960s *enka* were inherited from a series of proto–world music booms that swept Japan in the 1950s, when tangos, sambas, and other exotic styles enjoyed popularity (recall the list of Hibari's singles given earlier).

Nonetheless, the Japaneseness of the genre derives from the lyrics as well as from a number of *kata* that reverberate as tradition. Musically, Yano identifies some thirty-six distinct compositional and performative *kata* that add up to the *enka* formula. Among the most important of these are the use of a pentatonic *yonanuki* scale (that is, a diatonic scale missing the fourth and seventh degrees: do-re-mi-so-la-do), which emerged in early-twentieth-century Japan as a compromise form between preexisting folk musical modes and the Western chorus music that became part of the required public school curriculum in the 1880s.[60] *Enka* melodies occur frequently in an elegiac minor mode. Women's songs are frequently sung in very low registers (frequently, Hibari's lyrics seem to voice a man's point of view, just as she often appeared in films and on stage in male clothing), and both male and female songs feature singing techniques that heighten emotional drama: sudden leaps in pitch or changes in dynamics, shifts between natural voice (*jigoe*) and falsetto (*uragoe*), alterations in rhythm, as well as powerful use of vibrato, melisma, and other kinds of vocal ornamentation.[61]

*   *   *

Hibari's classic recordings from the 1960s helped define the *enka* form. With them, her transformation from boogie-woogie mimic into the most Japanese of singers was complete. This image only intensified during the years of her final comeback in the late 1980s, culminating in her posthumous receipt in 1989 of the People's Honor Award (Kokumin Eiyo Shō, similar to a Presidential Medal of Freedom), an honor never before bestowed on a popular singer— or, for that matter, a woman.[62] Her death on June 24, 1989, was announced with banner headlines, and all major television networks interrupted their programming schedules to broadcast extended tributes. Commentators spec-

ulated that Hibari's death, more so than that of Hirohito a few months earlier, brought to a close an era in Japanese history: she seemed to symbolize
the nation even better than the emperor. By this point, Hibari's origins as a
Kasagi Shizuko imitator, as an American-style singer, were largely forgotten:
she had for more than two decades served as the lodestar for Japaneseness
on the imaginary geopolitical map of popular music. In part because of this
acquired sense of authenticity, since the 1960s younger musicians had been
seeking collaborations with this living deity—rock-and-rollers Jackie Yoshikawa and the Blue Comets in the 1960s, folksinger Okabayashi Nobuyasu in
the 1970s (and again in 2010, when he released a tribute album to her), and
electro-pop maestro Sakamoto Ryūichi in the 1980s, to cite a few.

Hibari's transformation from an American-style singer into an icon of
musical Japaneseness is telling of changes in the political and social situation
of Japan in the 1950s and 1960s. But perhaps even more telling are the things
left out of this imaginary mapping of popular music. Its organization around a
bipolar opposition that organized global space around an opposition between
Japan and the United States (one that persisted, as we will see, in subsequent
decades) provided a certain orientation to enjoying Hibari's music. But it also
tended to conceal other geopolitical factors, historical ties that could have
suggested other possible modes for taking pleasure in Hibari's *enka*.

In the new geopolitical mapping that held sway in the 1950s and 1960s,
for example, the rest of Asia largely disappeared from view. This erasure was
not unique to the world of popular song. In describing the intellectual history
of Japan since 1945, political scientist Kang Sangjung asks, "What has been
excluded or concealed in this discursive space of the postwar?" His answer:
Asia, which has been reduced to the status of a "ghost" or "shadow" dog-
ging the postwar narrative of Japan's rapid development.[63] Iwabuchi Koichi, a specialist in media studies, has identified this neglect of Asia as a by-
product of the tendency to define Japan as a monolithic culture, a tendency
that requires continuous identification of "Japan" through contrast with the
"West," especially the United States. This "not only homogenizes the two
cultural entities but also directs our attention away from the doubleness of
the Japanese (post)colonial experience as a non-Western colonizer"—that is,
from Japan's own imperial past, when it was deeply enmeshed in the rest of
Asia.[64] Narratives that express alarm at Japan's "cultural subordination to the

West," that is, often have the effect of erasing Japan's own colonizing history with respect to the rest of Asia. Moreover, while U.S. regional strategy for East Asia positioned South Korea and Okinawa as front-line military bases in confronting Communist powers, with South Korea and Taiwan situated as sources of raw materials feeding into the Japanese industrial machine, it also stressed managing this hierarchical network through discreet bilateral ties with each involved nation, thereby downplaying cross-regional ties between the various nations.[65] In Japan, the resulting imaginary geopolitical map has been summed up succinctly by historian Harry Harootunian as "America's Japan/Japan's Japan," a process of identity formation through a narcissistic mirroring structure that strategically conceals from view such troubling spaces as Korea, Taiwan, China, and Vietnam.[66]

This postwar forgetting of Asia can be seen in a wide swatch of popular culture in Japan. Historian Igarashi has noted that in the melodramatic narrative of postwar historical memory in Japan, a gender swap took place. Whereas before 1945 Japanese popular culture presented Japan as a dominant male in relation to a feminine Asia, after 1945 the United States adopted the masculine role and Japan the subservient feminine role, a melodrama that "assisted in concealing Japan's historical connection with Asia."[67] Igarashi finds traces of this newly reconfigured melodrama in, for example, the increasing tendency in postwar scholarly and popular writings to stress Japanese "uniqueness"—as opposed to a pronounced tendency in pre-1945 writings to stress Japan's commonalities with Asia.[68]

The postwar erasure of Asia was especially striking in the domain of popular music. A dense network of connections between Asian and Japanese musicians had existed prior to 1945. After the Immigration Act of 1924 made it virtually impossible for Japanese to emigrate to the United States, Japanese jazz players eager to learn their chops traveled in large numbers to the dance halls of Shanghai, where they mingled with American, European, and Asian musicians.[69] Others sought jobs elsewhere in Asia, especially after wartime restrictions made it difficult to play jazz in Japan itself. For example, as we saw in chapter 1, trumpeter Nanri Fumio became a fixture in the nightclubs of semicolonial Dairen during the late 1930s, while composer Hattori Ryōichi moved back and forth between Japan and the continent, scoring films in Manchukuo and staging musical revues in Shanghai. Many others, such as the singer Fujiyama Ichirō, were drafted by the Japanese military and traveled the region, staging morale-boosting shows for Japanese troops and settlers.[70] Perhaps the best embodiment of this pattern of fluid movement by musicians from Japan across Asia was the singer Yamaguchi Yoshiko, who in the late 1930s and early 1940s was active across East Asia under the stage name Ri Kōran (Ch., Li Xianglan).[71] Pretending to be Chinese, she performed songs and movie roles that presented the image of a feminine China that wanted only to be dominated by masculine Japan.

Songs also crisscrossed the region. As we have already seen, one of Hattori Ryōichi's early hits, "Farewell Blues" (Wakare no burūsu), recorded by Awaya Noriko in 1937, received little attention when it was first released in Japan. But Nanri Fumio took a liking to the tune and began featuring it in his act in Dairen. The song became popular there, and that popularity then spread to Shanghai and other parts of China. Finally, it was imported back into Japan, where "Farewell Blues" finally became a hit.[72] Musical styles and techniques also flowed freely between Japan and continental Asia. The late 1930s and early 1940s saw numerous hit songs in Japan that referenced Asia, including a boom in a genre known as continental melodies (*tairiku merodi*).[73] Hit songs in this style presented through their lyrics and musical cues a highly exotic, desirable image of China and other Asian lands. As these tunes permeated daily life in Japan, they brought colonial and semicolonial Asia into a position of remarkable intimacy for Japanese music fans, even those who were unable to travel directly to Asia. To sway in time to a tune like singer Watanabe Hamako's hit "China Nights" (Shina no yoru, 1939) was to experience directly through one's body the pleasures of empire. This was even more true for another 1939 hit for Watanabe, "When Will You Return?" (Hōri chun tsairai), which was a Japanese-language adaptation of "Heri jun zai lai" (music by Yen Lu, lyrics by Bei Ling), originally a "yellow music" hit in China for singer Zhou Xuan.[74]

In sum, Japanese popular music up through 1945 was deeply enmeshed in the culture of the Asian continent—it was, that is, intimately entangled in Japan's experience as an imperialist power. The map through which listeners in those earlier decades organized their experience of music included the United States and Japan—but also Asia. Musicians, songs, records, and styles moved freely back and forth between Japan and the continent. Chinese and Korean melodies became Japanese hit songs, and Japanese songs became popular among listeners across Asia. Some expected that this cosmopolitanism would continue even after Japan's defeat: as we saw in chapter 1, on the night Japan's surrender was announced, Chinese composer Li Jinguang consoled Hattori Ryōichi in Shanghai, telling him, "From now on, we can carry out our musical activities in freedom."[75] But this history of dense interconnections with Asia disappeared when postwar Japanese popular music came to be understood through an imaginary geopolitical map that included only two poles: America and Japan.

It seems clear that Japanese musicians and music fans from 1945 through the early 1990s organized the world of pop music around just such a map. This new worldview was complicit with U.S. strategic needs during the Cold War: as Gavan McCormack and others have argued, the isolation of Japan from the rest of Asia formed a linchpin for American postwar hegemony in the region.[76] But Asia never completely vanished from Japan, even in postwar hit songs. Exoticism remained a constant, but after 1945 its stance shifted subtly: postwar pop music orientalism was often refracted through the prism of the United States. For example, one tune that Kasagi Shizuko performed in *Honolulu, Hollywood, New York*, the musical revue celebrating her 1950 American tour, was "Aloha Boogie." Like the Hawaiian dream sequence in Hibari's film *Tokyo Kid*, and like many songs that followed in the wake of Oka Haruo's hit song "The Road to Dreamy Hawaii" (Akogare Hawai kōro, 1948; part of Hibari's early performing repertoire; she also had a featured role in the 1950 film that took its title from the song), it invokes Hawaii as an orientalist paradise—a version of the Orient that is refracted through the gaze of America.

Many other orientalist references to Asia in Japanese postwar songs were similarly reconfigured to mimic American desire for Asia. Ri Kōran, for example, continued to record: she enjoyed considerable success in 1949 with the old Chinese yellow music hit "Ye lai xiang" (Fragrance of the Night) in a new arrangement by Hattori Ryōichi. But she now recorded under the name Yamaguchi Yoshiko, and—after her own 1950 tour of the United States—she would take on yet another new stage name, Shirley Yamaguchi, under which she would appear as the Japanese love interest for U.S. soldiers in such films as *Japanese War Bride* (1952; dir. King Vidor) and *House of Bamboo* (1955; dir. Sam Fuller). Watanabe Hamako, the queen of the continental melodies genre in the late 1930s, also continued to record China-inflected songs during the postwar period, but the title of one is emblematic of the way the orientalist yearning she voiced was now grafted onto American desire for the exotic: "San Francisco Chinatown" (1950). Likewise, Hattori Tomiko (Ryōichi's younger sister), who had one of the biggest continental melody hits with "Manchurian Girl" (Manshū musume, 1938), recorded a sequel number in 1950. In it, we again see Japan connecting to Asia by way of America, this time through the medium of English slang. The chirpy refrain of the original song, "Mr. Wang, please wait for me, okay?" (Wan-san, mattete chōdai, ne), which became a popular catchphrase in the 1930s, was updated in the 1950 version to "Hello, Mr. Wang!" (Harō, Wan-san), which also served as the title for the number. These postwar songs clearly allude to Asia, but always in a form that made it seem as if Japan had no direct ties to Asia, as if connections to the continent inevitably proceeded by way of the United States.

Moreover, even in the songs that Hibari herself performed, Asianness often remains in plain view—it simply wasn't recognized as such. When the Japaneseness of Misora Hibari is explained, as we have seen, a number of elements are routinely invoked: her preference for songs written in minor keys, her melodramatic vocal techniques such as vibrato (*yuri*), and the use of a pentatonic *yonanuki* scale in many of her best-known *enka* numbers. All of these, it is frequently noted, reflect characteristics of Japanese songs that date back many centuries. Yet these are hardly unique to Japanese music— they are widely found across Asia and elsewhere. Music critic Alex Ross, for example, has defined pentatonic melodies as "those ancient, elementary five-note scales that crop up in folk traditions all over the world, from Africa to Indonesia."[77] Other musical techniques that are thought to mark Hibari's Japaneseness can likewise be found in pop songs across much of East Asia. As Christine Yano has noted, "Enka or enka-like music can be heard on juke boxes, in karaoke, and over the broadcast airwaves in Taiwan, Korea, Hong Kong, and parts of Southeast Asia."[78] The predominance of a pentatonic scale in Japanese pop could have been the place where Japan linked up with Asia— where, as one musicologist has noted, "a common musical culture" that was "exemplified by pentatonicism" might have been produced.[79] After all, the roots of contemporary *enka* lie in part in the 1930s and early 1940s continental melodies, themselves an offshoot of the Chinese yellow music genre.

This continental link is underscored by the life of Koga Masao, the great *enka* composer who wrote "Mournful Sake," "Yawara," and many of Hibari's other signature numbers. Koga's first hits came in the 1930s with songs that Fujiyama Ichirō recorded, numbers that would subsequently provide a proto-type for the *enka* genre: "Is Sake a Teardrop or a Sigh?" (Sake wa namida ka tameiki ka, 1931) and "Yearning for a Shadow" (Kage o shitaite, 1931). Hibari first met Koga in 1947, when he judged an amateur singing contest that she had entered, and she recorded her first Koga composition—or "Koga mel-ody," as they are popularly known—in 1955. Koga's music is said to provide a paradigm of Japaneseness in music, but Koga himself was raised in colonial Korea and acknowledged that he had developed his style around the songs he heard laborers sing there.[80] Even Yamaori Tetsuo, the stalwart defender of Hibari's essential Japaneseness, acknowledges the ongoing debate over whether *enka* might not best be considered an essentially Korean, rather than Japanese, genre.[81] This shared musical tradition, with roots in the pre-1945 Japanese empire, ironically made it possible for a number of non-Japanese singers to become *enka* stars beginning in the 1970s: Teresa Ten (Taiwan), for example; Chō Yonpiru (Korea); and even I Seong-ae, who was introduced to Japanese music fans in the early 1970s as "the Korean Misora Hibari."[82]

What changed after 1945, then, was not so much the music itself but the imaginary mapping through which the music was perceived and enjoyed. Musicologist Robert Walser reminds us that,

> like genres and discourses, musical meanings are contingent but never arbi-trary. There is never any *essential* correspondence between particular musi-cal signs or processes and specific social meanings, yet such signs and pro-cesses would never circulate if they did not produce such meanings. Musical meanings are always grounded socially and historically, and they operate on an ideological field of conflicting interests, institutions, and memories. If this makes them extremely difficult to analyze, it does so by forcing analysis to confront the complexity and antagonism of culture.[83]

The Japaneseness of *enka* is not a matter of some essential musical quality; rather it is the product of a specific, complicated history of remembering and forgetting. The musical elements that after the 1960s were heard as signifying Japan could have signified Asia given a different geopolitical situation, given ears organized around a different imaginary mapping of the world. In sum, after 1945 the Asianness was still there in Japanese popular music, but it was now heard as Japanese—a Japaneseness that was defined almost exclusively through an opposition with the United States and with American popular music styles rather than through an intimacy with Asia.

The concealed past of Asianness in Japanese pop reemerged in other ways too. Like a return of the repressed, it flickered into and out of view like a ghost or a shadow, a kind of monstrous apparition. Historian Yoshikuni Igarashi finds elements of this tendency, which he calls naming the unnameable, in such postwar popular culture phenomena as the Godzilla films and the career of professional wrestler Rikidōzan.[84] Misora Hibari, too, is embedded in this phenomenon. Despite the image of Hibari as the most Japanese of postwar singers, since at least the early 1950s it has been persistently rumored that Hibari wasn't "really" Japanese at all—that she was in fact ethnically Korean, that (in the most common variant of the rumor) her father was one of the hundreds of thousands of laborers brought into mainland Japan during the period when Korea was a Japanese colony (1910–1945). The rumor persists today, not only in Japan but also in South Korea, where Hibari's Korean ethnicity is said to be a matter of popular common sense. A Japanese-language Google search on the key words "Misora Hibari" and *zainichi* (a commonly used term for the ethnically Korean residents of Japan) turned up 87,700 hits and a wide variety of theories and denials.[85] The rumor has been reported as fact in a number of English-language publications as well.

Is it true? A good deal of circumstantial evidence can be cited in its support. Although neither Hibari nor her family has done so, a number of prominent *enka* singers have acknowledged their own Korean heritage—not surprising, perhaps, given the roots of *enka* in the Korean colonial period. One such singer likes to boast that if it didn't rely on numerous *zainichi* talents, NHK could never mount its annual New Year's Eve musical extravaganza *Kōhaku uta gassen*.[86] During her lifetime, Hibari certainly befriended many *zainichi* persons, including the professional wrestler Rikidōzan. In 1979, she recorded two songs composed for her by the Korean songwriter Park Chun-seok.[87] She is said to have used a Korean term of endearment, *oppa* (older brother), as a personal nickname for a *zainichi* friend.[88] Hibari's close association throughout her career with underworld *yakuza* figures is well known, and at least in popular stereotype *yakuza* ranks are thought to be full of ethnic Koreans. Perhaps the greatest evidence on behalf of the veracity of the rumor is its persistence—and the fact that it is sometimes spread by those who claim firsthand knowledge.[89]

Following Hibari's death, the Korean press brought the rumor from the realm of hearsay to the printed page, with articles on the singer's death frequently describing her as the daughter of a Korean father. The Japanese tabloid weekly *Shūkan bunshun*, however, examined the rumors and emphatically denied them in 1989, interviewing members of Hibari's family as well as a boyhood friend of her father's.[90] Moreover, Hibari's biographers trace her family roots back to the Meiji period (1868–1912)—that is, back to a period prior to the wide-scale immigration of Korean laborers into Japan. These biographers and journalists could be victims of an elaborate hoax, but that seems uncharacteristic. A frequent target of malicious gossip during her lifetime,[91] Hibari openly acknowledged her own conduct even when it could be seen as scandalous: she was frank about her love life, her drinking, and her contacts with gangsters. When her younger brother was arrested for his involvement with a *yakuza* gang, Hibari refused to fire him from her management team, even when this resulted in NHK and public concert facilities banning her. In other words, Hibari was a woman who didn't hide from controversy, even when she faced painful consequences. Why would she lie about her ethnic heritage?

I can neither confirm nor deny the veracity of the rumor. Moreover, what difference would it make, one way or the other? I find much more interesting the rumor's stubborn persistence. Rumors are typically as evanescent as clouds—a popular saying in Japanese has it that the shelf life of a rumor is only seventy-five days. Yet this one has survived in the shadows for more than half a century, poking up through the gaps and cracks in the postwar ideological mapping of the world in which Japan was imagined primarily as a partner of the United States rather than as a part of Asia. Its survival hints that the rumor fills some sort of need for music fans in Japan, Korea, and elsewhere. When I first heard the rumor in the 1990s, I immediately believed it to be true, because there was something remarkably attractive about it. I passed it on as often as I could and even repeated it in classroom lectures as if it were a matter of fact (which I believed it to be at the time). The rumor survives and propagates because, like Hibari's music itself, it gives pleasure to those who share in it. Speaking as one who was seduced by it, it seems to me that the most interesting question here is: What makes this such an attractive rumor? Folklore scholars tell us that "rumors are brief narrative accounts that arise in ambiguous situations and, through the process of transmission—as information is leveled, sharpened, and assimilated—they become expressions of a community's collective anxieties and beliefs."[92] If that is so, then in the Hibari-is-Korean rumor, what communities are involved, and what shared anxieties and beliefs are they expressing?

Obviously, there will be wide variations in the pleasures the rumor produces. Different individuals in different places at different moments will respond to it in diverse ways. But perhaps we can make a few tentative generalizations about some of the communities involved. For South Koreans in the 1970s and 1980s, for example, the rumor may have suggested a new framework for enjoying Hibari's music: the great singer was really one of us, and her need to conceal her ethnicity made her yet another victim of Japanese colonial oppression of Korea. As one scholar who treats rumor as a form of folklore has argued, rumors can function as "counter-hegemonic discourse": "As a story passes from person to person and each one changes or adds to it, a narrative emerges that represents a more or less collaborative interpretation of events. Rumors, shaped by the historically constituted experience of a community, allow people some measure of joint control over ambiguous, stressful situations; they affect the solidarity of a group, creating a public that can then participate in collective action."[93] South Koreans in the 1970s and 1980s were burdened not only with a painful legacy of military subjection at the hands of both Japan (1910–1945) and America (1945–), but also with an authoritarian state that was in many ways complicit with those colonial and neocolonial foreign powers and that furthermore brooked no open criticism of itself. The Hibari rumor under such conditions might serve as a tactic for building a public community on a shared sense of victimhood, one mobilizing shared anger not only at Korea's past as a Japanese colony but also about its present existence as both a rival and a dependent of its wealthy neighbor Japan, not to mention as a fellow outpost for U.S. strategic policy during the Cold War. The rumor could provide an avenue for nonelites to express indirectly their anger not only at Japan and the United States but also at their own ruling elites' inability to achieve real sovereignty for the nation as a whole.[94] Mapped through this rumor, the embodied thrill that Hibari's voice summoned up in South Korean fans could be linked to a history of oppression. Hibari's triumph as an icon of postwar Japan, that is, could take on new resonances as a possible harbinger of Korean vindication.

For an American student of Japanese culture like myself, the rumor seems playfully ironic. Positioned as an outsider to Japan whose task it is to explain that place to other outsiders, the rumor seems to offer the pleasure of an insider's esoteric knowledge. Moreover, to the extent that many Japanese apparently do not possess that knowledge, it offers a seductive sense of superiority, of knowing Japan better than the Japanese. The satisfying sense of superiority is further served by the rumor's implicit undermining of an icon of Japanese authenticity: the thrill I got from exposing the "secret" of Hibari's supposedly sham Japaneseness no doubt became one way of dealing with anxieties about my own tenuous relationship to my object of study, Japan. The pleasure of Hibari's music was intensified for me by the belief that I knew the secret of her identity.

What pleasures and needs does the Hibari rumor address among her Japanese fans and detractors? Geopolitical anxieties continue even in today's Japan to be counteracted through popular rumors and gossip. Matsuyama Iwao, a scholar of the role of rumor in Japan's modern history, argues that rumors often summon up suppressed moments from the past. Feeling estranged from present-day reality, people turn to their past to find alternative possible versions of that reality.[95] In the postwar reality that mapped Japan only in relation to the United States, the pre-1945 experience of empire became a potential source of rumors by which to deal with the sense of alienation that many Japanese felt under the postwar system and the rapidly urbanizing consumer society that emerged under it. Ironically, that empire itself had been sustained in part by ugly rumors—the false reports, for example, after the Great Kantō Earthquake of 1923 that Korean immigrants were poisoning wells, a rumor that led to the massacre of thousands of persons (not all of them Korean).[96]

For many Japanese, it seems to me, the Hibari-is-Korean rumor provides one mechanism for dealing with both traumatic memories of the past and anxieties about the present. Passing it along mobilizes the repressed memories of lost empire, memories of both fraternity and domination, to challenge the dominant mapping of the present: Japan could be positioned otherwise, the rumor suggests. Moreover, the act of spreading the rumor helps create the very community that would live out that alternative reality: the act of sharing a rumor constructs a sense of intimacy in a setting characterized by anonymous anxiety. As one sociolinguist has argued, "rumor construction is a way of promulgating new schemes of coordination when we undergo a derangement in our way of life."[97] While postwar pop songs were overtly enjoyed through a mapping that defined Japan in relation to the United States, the Hibari rumor proposes an alternative map. On it, Japan's imperial past and its position within Asia obtain shadowy acknowledgement. To hear Hibari's voice through this map allows one to enjoy a ghostly overtone in the music, one that was difficult to acknowledge directly. As we will see in the final chapter of this book, the rumor foreshadows a new mapping of Japanese popular music that would emerge in the 1990s, in the years immediately following Hibari's death, when something called J-pop emerged as a genre that presumed simultaneous coexistence with counterparts across Asia: K-pop, C-pop, and all the others. If musicking provides pleasure by supplying an ideal model of our relations to the world, the Hibari rumor provided an alternative model, a seductive shadow that lingered behind the dominant mapping of the world of popular song in Japan from the 1950s through the 1980s.

*   *   *

It's something of a miracle that Hibari's last single, released just months before her death, is widely considered her greatest recording. In a 1998 poll carried out by NHK to determine the most popular one hundred songs of Japan's twentieth century, "As the River Flows" topped the list.[98] It is both gratifying and appropriate that Hibari would end her long, remarkable career on such a spectacular performance, and at least a part of the tremendous celebration of Hibari as the ultimate icon of Japaneseness that followed her death in 1989 was in response to this most recent triumph. The record went on to win several major awards.

It is a stunning performance. The lyrics, which reflect back on a life that has flowed on like a river, make the song a fitting capstone to Hibari's career. It is also perhaps fitting that there is hardly anything Japanese sounding about the composition itself. The instructions given to the composer Mitake Akira were to write a new kind of music for Hibari, one that would appeal to listeners in their thirties, a younger generation that found *enka* old-fashioned. Akimoto Yasushi's lyrics are written in Japanese, of course, but the river in question, Akimoto acknowledged, was the East River: he wrote the words while living in New York City.[99] The orchestration is fully Western, enhanced by 1980s electronic-synthesizer technology. Moreover, the tune is written in the key of D major rather than the elegiac minor keys favored in many *enka*. While its memorable melody frequently employs scale runs that skip the fourth degree (G), as would be expected in a *yonanuki* melody, it frequently hits on the seventh (C), and sometimes even on that shunned fourth.[100] In other words, while the melody invokes an *enka*-like pentatonic scale, "As the River Flows" actually employs the full range of the diatonic major scale. Perhaps this is why it is so easy for me to imagine Elvis Presley singing it as one of the show-stopping ballads that were so prominent in his later concerts.

Nonetheless, the record sounds somehow Japanese. It is as if Hibari were Queen Midas and everything she touches turns golden Japanese. The imaginary mapping through which we enjoy music causes us to hear overtones that are not included in the score. This is in some ways inevitable and even desirable: the situated historical meanings we hear in music are a source of pleasure and a tool for mapping our ideal place in the world. But historical situations change—we change them. And even as we enjoy Misora Hibari's Japaneseness, it is useful to remember that she can also be heard otherwise, even if that possibility today remains simply a rumor.

3

MYSTERY PLANE

SAKAMOTO KYŪ AND THE TRANSLATIONS OF ROCKABILLY

I'm only going to be there [America] for a very short time, but I still want
to introduce properly, in my own way, "Japan." For example, for my appearance on *The Steve Allen Show*, my costume hasn't been decided on yet,
but if they tell me to wear a *chonmage* [topknot hairstyle] or something,
I plan to turn them down flat. Because I want to show them me just as
I am, a completely ordinary visitor. In a foreign country where all they
know about Japan is Fujiyama, geisha, and sukiyaki, I'd like to use this
chance to get as many people as possible to change their way of thinking,
even if it's just a little bit.

SAKAMOTO KYŪ

Rockabilly music bubbled under the surface for a year
or two in Japan before exploding into public view in
February 1958. That month, a number of Tokyo musicians who had been performing regularly at jazz coffeehouses and
clubs on U.S. military bases appeared together at the First Nichigeki
Western Carnival, a musical revue organized by Watanabe Misa of
Watanabe Productions, a talent management agency. The results,
captured in still photographs and newsreel films, were nothing short
of sensational: wild young singers with Brill-Creamed hair slinging electric guitars, frantic teenage girls rushing the stage to grab at
the musicians' bodies—when, that is, they weren't fainting away in
their seats (figures 4 and 5). Forty-five thousand fans attended the
one-week run of the bill, and Watanabe Productions scrambled to

FIGURE 4 An excited fan rushes onto the stage at the Nichigeki Western Carnival, 1958. (Courtesy Mainichi Photo Bank, Tokyo, Japan)

FIGURE 5 Rockabilly musicians go wild at the Nichigeki Western Carnival, 1958. (Courtesy Mainichi Photo Bank, Tokyo, Japan)

organize a second, third, and fourth Nichigeki Western Carnival before the year ended.[1] A newly emergent youth culture, symbolized in the Taiyō-zoku (Sun Tribe) film genre, had found its sound track: if you were a Japanese teenager in 1958, rockabilly was it.[2] For older Japanese, however, the music was a sign of the apocalypse. Sociologist Shibusawa Hideo complained that "rockabilly singers are the preachers of a strange new faith; the low teens are the faith's blind worshippers."[3]

Like jazz before it, the Japanese version of the rockabilly genre encompassed a broader range of music than its English-language counterpart. Rockabilly in the United States refers specifically to a short-lived but influential 1950s genre that combined rhythm and blues, rock and roll, and country music. Through the early 1960s in Japan, though, rockabilly was the primary name given to all the music that was called rock and roll in the English-speaking world (even as early Japanese rockabilly singers were at first identified as jazz singers and "jazz coffeehouses" were the primary live venue for the new style). In Japanese terms, Elvis Presley and Gene Vincent (the latter toured Japan in 1959) were rockabilly—but so were Paul Anka (who toured Japan in 1958) and Little Richard. The boundaries of the new genre were quite loose, and even singers we identify today primarily with *enka* tried their hands at it. Misora Hibari, for example, released the delightful "Rockabilly Sword Fighting" (Rokabirī kenpō) in 1958. Yukimura Izumi—who, along with Eri Chiemi, was Hibari's partner in the famous Three Girls (Sannin Musume) combo—also recorded several rockabilly numbers. Yukimura's ferocious Japanese-language takes on "Be-Bop-A-Lula," "Fujiyama Mama," and "Great Balls of Fire" are mind-boggling to anyone who knows her primarily as a singer of orchestral pops.

But as rockabilly, and then rock, became increasingly identified with a specific kind of youth culture, the boundaries around the genre grew more distinct. As we saw in chapter 2, a reorganization of the Japanese music industry and its recording and marketing practices led by the late 1960s to an increasingly rigid divide between *enka* and other popular genres aimed at the youth market, including rock. *Enka* singers lay on one side, and rock singers on the other, of a generational and aesthetic boundary that would only grow sharper in subsequent decades.

This chapter is largely about boundaries and how they get crossed. I explore one of the most puzzling features of post-1945 geopolitics: the ways in which new technologies that promise to transcend boundaries end up redrawing the very borderlines they claim to erase. Often, those boundaries separate domains of unequal power: they map hierarchies between center and periphery. As I trace the remarkable history of Japanese rockabilly, I focus primarily on two very different border-crossing technologies: translation and air travel. Each promised to dissolve limits and to release us from the hierarchies that bind us, liberating us into a new equality and unity. Yet even after we unleash these technologies, we still find ourselves hedged in by the very borders we are supposed to have transcended: the new map looks suspiciously like the old one. As I trace how songs traveled back and forth between languages, and how musicians flew back and forth between continents, I try to explicate this odd phenomenon. It is one of the keys to understanding social reproduction under the conditions of global capitalism. Cultural studies theorist George Lipsitz writes that "in its most utopian moments, popular culture offers a promise of reconciliation to groups divided by differences in power, opportunity, and experience." It brings together people from wildly divergent cultures and provides a shared space in which they might form new kinds of community. "But," he cautions, "inter-culture communication can also create new sources of misunderstanding, misreading, and misappropriation that exacerbate rather than remedy social divisions."[4]

Translated Japanese rockabilly produced both division and unity: it brought people together even as it held them apart. It redrew the map, yet in the end its translations and its flight paths ended up reinforcing many of the same boundaries that had existed all along.

* * *

To begin with, where does rockabilly belong on the geopolitical map of the postwar world? One influential answer is provided by Greil Marcus's classic study *Mystery Train: Images of America in Rock 'n' Roll Music*. Marcus borrowed his title not only from Elvis Presley's last single for Sun Records but also from a whole tradition of American studies scholarship that saw in the train a leitmotif of national imagination. The train motif bolsters Marcus's thesis that popular music forms—blues, country, rockabilly, and others—fit the mainstream historical narrative of American studies as well as, perhaps even better than, the literary works conventionally used in the field. He supplied new contents for the classic liberal narrative of democratic cultural nationalism but left unaltered its basic structure and dominant motifs, even its pontificating tone. In a sense, that was the whole point: Marcus was appropriating the authority of the national narrative in order to elevate the work of artists he admired.[5]

Although *Mystery Train* remains a fundamental text in popular music criticism, this narrative framework now seems problematic. Marcus's desire to judge "authenticity" against the touchstone of national culture, along with his eagerness to assimilate widely variant cultural strains into a single homogeneous whole, and his presumption of American exceptionalism—all seem suspect. Moreover, when Marcus describes what he sees as the unique characteristics of the United States, his language suggests not so much the singularity of national culture as it does the leveling force of global capitalism. The struggles of musicians that he depicts as battles with the contradictions of American culture are more persuasively explained as resistance against commodification in an increasingly global market, and they are hardly the exclusive birthright of artists who carry U.S. passports.

Paul Gilroy does not cite Marcus in his highly influential *The Black Atlantic: Modernity and Double Consciousness*, a critique of the nationalism pervading recent cultural studies. But in his attempt to address the historical reality of racism without conceiving of the culture produced in response to that history as an unchanging national essence, Gilroy suggests a productive way to refigure the music of the African diaspora. Although he notes the importance of trains, in particular Pullmans, to African American culture, he chooses an alternative central image in his desire to construct "a theory that was less intimidated by and respectful of the boundaries and integrity of modern nation states": "I have settled on the image of ships in motion across the spaces between Europe, America, Africa, and the Caribbean as a central organizing symbol for this enterprise and as my starting point. . . . Ships immediately focus attention on the middle passage, on the various projects for redemptive return to an African homeland, on the circulation of ideas and activists as well as the movement of key cultural and political artifacts:

tracts, books, gramophone records, and choirs."[6] This image launches Gilroy's rereading of black music as an ever-changing "tradition," one that performs into existence a transatlantic cultural network linking those who live simultaneously inside and outside Western modernity.

Likewise, if we want to understand rockabilly as a (potentially) transnational culture, one that crossed boundaries of all kinds, it seems that yet another switch in vehicles is in order. If we want to understand how this genre crossed racial boundaries and yet was simultaneously defined as white, how it rode the transnational flows of commodity culture to become a global phenomenon even as it was defined as essentially American, we need a faster, more intensely capitalized vehicle. Transnational rockabilly provides us with an avenue to explore one of the central features of modern capitalism: the way it redraws the very lines it promises to erase. We cannot rely on just trains or ships if we want to understand how capitalism reproduces boundaries of nation, race, gender, and class even as it claims to render them meaningless, or how it captures revolutionary desires to transgress boundaries and transforms them into engines of conservative social reproduction. To catch up with this problem, we need an airplane—preferably a supersonic jet.[7]

Planes are, of course, as much a part of the rock-and-roll legacy as are trains. Think of the crash that killed Buddy Holly in 1959, or the opening notes of the Beatles' "Back in the USSR." Or Japan Airlines (JAL) Flight 123, a Boeing 747SR that crashed in rural Japan on August 12, 1985, killing 520 persons, including the singer Sakamoto Kyū. The rise of rock and roll and rockabilly as global phenomena is unthinkable in the absence of increasingly multinational record companies like Capitol (American corporate home to both Sakamoto and the Beatles) and RCA (corporate home to Elvis), able to place their product in the hands of teenagers around the globe with unprecedented speed. But rock and roll as a global phenomenon also required air transport and the corporate networks and capital investment that made it possible: from the Pan American jet that delivered Sakamoto Kyū to several thousand screaming fans at Los Angeles International Airport in August 1963 for his first (and only) appearance on *The Steve Allen Show*, to the other Pan American jet that five months later would deliver the Beatles to their hysterical fans at Kennedy Airport in New York City for their appearance on *The Ed Sullivan Show*. Or, for that matter, the JAL jet that delivered the Beatles to Tokyo's Haneda Airport in the summer of 1966.

At the dawn of its invention, the airplane would, it was widely believed, once and for all liberate the human race from its shackles: spatial distance, national boundaries, class conflict, even—the Italian futurist poet F. T. Marinetti declared in 1912—the constraints of syntax.[8] And yet the rise of air travel led not to the erasure of national boundaries but to their intensification. The first decades of the twentieth century gave birth to both the airplane and the modern passport-visa system, a new technology by which nation-states regulated border crossings. Under the latter, a temporary wartime measure that became permanent in the 1920s, the relatively porous borders and informal paperwork of nineteenth-century migration were replaced with a highly systematic bureaucratic procedure. The spatial boundaries that commercial air travel deterritorialized were simultaneously reterritorialized by the nation-state, with its penchant for "monopolizing the legitimate means of movement."[9] Although the rockabilly music of Elvis Presley traveled around the world at nearly the speed of sound in the 1950s, Elvis himself never appeared in concerts overseas, both because he was apparently afraid to fly and because his manager, Colonel Tom Parker, was an illegal immigrant. Parker did not have a passport and hence could not leave U.S. territory for fear that he would not be permitted to return.[10]

The airplane also made war between nations possible on a scale previously unimaginable. The attack on Pearl Harbor (two days before the birth of Sakamoto Kyū) and the atomic bombings of Hiroshima and Nagasaki are prominent examples of how air power simultaneously linked and divided nations. Sakamoto belonged to a generation of Japanese who grew up during the war, able to distinguish B-29 bombers and other makes of aircraft as they flew overhead.[11] Later, during the Cold War, air power provided the strategic key to American hegemony in Asia, a strategy that centered largely on U.S. air bases in Japan and Okinawa. It was at an enlisted men's club on one such base in Tachikawa, a suburb of Tokyo, in April 1958 that sixteen-year-old Sakamoto Kyū made his public debut, singing a cover version of Elvis's "Hound Dog," apparently to great response from the American soldiers in his audience.[12] Without air power, that audience in Tachikawa would not have existed; without air power, American Armed Forces Radio could not have provided Sakamoto's generation of Japanese teenagers with up-to-the-minute access to the latest in American pop.[13] Without air power, Sakamoto's career would likely never have gotten off the ground.

Sakamoto's global success is cited as a symbol of Japan's postwar recovery. But air travel and air cargo made that economic growth possible. In civilian aviation, JAL became both a symbol of and a key player in Japan's postwar prosperity. Founded in 1951 as a private corporation, two years later it became part of the wave of post-Occupation counterreforms, in which the central government, no longer inhibited by U.S. Occupation reform policies, reasserted its authority. The Japan Air Lines Law of 1953 made JAL a semigovernmental corporation with a monopoly on international flights among Japanese carriers. JAL began transpacific service to San Francisco in 1954 and in 1959 added a Tokyo–Los Angeles route; by the mid-1960s it was recognized as one of the world's leading airlines.[14] It became a centerpiece in the government–industry cooperative relationship that came to be known as Japan, Inc. The corrupt underbelly of that alliance surfaced to view in 1976, when former prime minister Tanaka Kakuei was arrested for having accepted bribes to influence All Nippon Airways, Japan's second largest carrier, to purchase Lockheed jets.

Despite that scandal and the sporadic crashes that bedeviled the Japanese airline industry in the 1950s and 1960s, positions as pilots or flight attendants were among the most glamorous jobs to which young Japanese could aspire. It is hardly surprising that a sixth-grader Sakamoto, when asked to record his dream for the future, wrote that he hoped someday to become an airline pilot.[15] By 1963, the peak of Sakamoto's global fame, JAL had developed an international reputation for offering top-class service to its globe-trotting clientele—the transnational jet set. Yet the border-crossing commodity that JAL offered for sale was, at least in part, national culture in a highly feminized form. JAL ads in American media from the early 1960s, for example, invariably feature kimono-clad women and frequently present biographical sketches of female flight attendants, identified primarily by their given names and their embodiment of Japanese "tradition." The copy in these ads repeatedly stresses both border crossing and distinct national culture; it overlaps transnational and national spaces. The point is made explicitly in an ad from the March 13, 1961, issue of *Newsweek*:

> You inhabit two different worlds at the same time on the DC-8C Jet Couriers of Japan Air Lines. On the one hand, you're reclining at ease in a sleek giant of a jet, flying high over the Pacific at almost ten miles a minute. Then there's your other world, the restful, tranquil world of Japan. Aboard your new Jet Courier you're surrounded by an atmosphere which is delightfully Japanese. There are shoji screens, tatami carpets, chrysanthemum designs . . . everywhere the taste and restraint of Japan.

The air passenger transcends all national boundaries—only to find himself back in "traditional" Japan. The ad invokes what by the late 1950s had become a standard mode of "Cold War orientalism," in which an emotional bond of intimacy is produced paradoxically by stressing cultural difference—thereby generating an intense thrill when the cultural divide is crossed and a relationship is established with the exotic other.[16]

The emergence of the flight attendant as a sex symbol in the 1950s and 1960s in Japan and elsewhere was an ironic instance of reterritorialization in another sense. Whereas in the 1930s, women in the United States and Europe had to fight to cross the gender line and win positions in the previously all-male world of flight attendants, by the 1950s the gender line had been redrawn to fulfill a new function: stewardesses were now sex symbols, as well as icons of corporate and national identity.[17] Commodity culture, that is, found a way to re-create the very gender line that had supposedly been erased.

*   *   *

Rockabilly spread across the world via the technology of air travel. The genre's global circulation was also a problem of translation, another modern technology promising to transcend boundaries. In a brilliant theorization of translation, Naoki Sakai has argued that in the eighteenth century Japanese intellectuals reached a previously unknown epistemological relation to the language they used: they discovered that they were using a hybrid language, one composed of both Chinese and Japanese elements.[18] With this discovery, a movement arose to separate the elements of this seemingly hybrid tongue into distinct national languages. It was no longer legitimate to read Chinese texts according to Japanese grammar and pronunciation, as had long been the practice; instead, one should read Chinese texts in Chinese, and—if there was a need to read them to a Japanese-speaking audience—they should be properly translated into Japanese first. That is to say, what now appears as a heterogeneous linguistic realm was separated into two distinct realms; what Sakai calls the schema of cofiguration was introduced, in which the discovery of a stable image of an other—in this case, China—enabled the simultaneous discovery of an image of the self, Japan.

When two languages are separated in this way, the only permissible contact between them occurs by way of a certain representation of translation. Translation in this guise claims to serve as a technique for crossing a boundary, for linking two previously distinct realms, but in fact what this representation of translation actually achieves is the drawing of that boundary, the remapping of messy, heteroglossic reality into distinct national languages. In Sakai's words, "Strictly speaking, it is not because two different language unities are given that we have to translate (or interpret) one text into another; it is because translation *articulates* languages so that we may postulate the two unities of the translating and the translated languages as if they were autonomous and closed entities through *a certain representation of translation*."[19] This new image of translation helped produce the notion of a homogeneous national language shared by all the members of the national community—the fiction, that is, of a medium in which we are supposedly able to share transparent communication.

Such a representation of translation obscured the fact that all communication occurs by way of translation; no linguistic community enjoys transparent language. Linguistic meaning is produced dialogically, in response to specific historical and social situations, so that the phrase "Be-Bop-A-Lula" might mean one thing to Gene Vincent, another thing to a teenage listener, and yet another to Yukimura Izumi (and even to them, different things at different times). We are always in some sense unknowable to one another, even when we share what is supposed to be a single language. The irreducible presence of incoherent noise disrupts all linguistic exchanges, but it gets concealed by the schema of cofiguration: we are trained ideologically to ignore it. Under this schema, we lose sight of the heterogeneous world in which we actually live; it instead produces the fantasy of a national community grounded in a single, homogeneous language and untroubled by internal difference. The schema produces the ideological illusion that "we" are all the same, and that those who are somehow different must be foreign.

The eighteenth- and nineteenth-century Japanese scholars who celebrated their newly discovered national language faced a particular difficulty. The shared national vernacular that all Japanese supposedly spoke in fact did not exist: as Sakai notes, it arrived stillborn. The dominant governing strategy in pre-1868 Japan had been divide and conquer: the ruling structure was based on maintaining hierarchical distinctions between the different groups occupying the archipelago, distinctions that were in part linguistically marked. The notion of a single, unified Japanese nation, one that shared a single, homogeneous language, arose with a small group of ideologues in the late eighteenth century (the same people who discovered, to their consternation, the hybrid status of contemporary Japanese linguistic usage), and it didn't become ruling doctrine until after 1868. Only then could Ueda Kazutoshi and other linguistic scholars in late-nineteenth-century Japan bemoan the diversity of dialects—based on such factors as region, class, profession, and gender—that threatened the very possibility of the nationwide communication they thought was essential to the process of building a modern nation. Massive institutional and ideological policies were enacted during the Meiji period (1868–1912) to bring into existence the national language that was supposedly already the birthright of every Japanese citizen. As a result, a standardized language did emerge, based on upper-middle-class speech from the Yamanote district of Tokyo, and it became the basis for the national education system, the publishing industry, and the other commercial and bureaucratic institutions of the modern capitalist nation. In the first half of the twentieth century, it also became the lingua franca in Japan's growing overseas empire: in Taiwan, Korea, and elsewhere.[20]

Other existing forms of speech in Japan—that of, for example, laborers in Osaka or women from Okinawa—simultaneously became nonstandard dialects: they were different from the new, hegemonic national standard, and yet they were not foreign to the Japanese language. They became a kind of domesticated otherness that had to be regulated but did not pose the same threat of foreignness that a competing national language such as Chinese did. Properly managed, they might even prove a beneficial resource to the nation. Although a Tokyo speaker might not understand all the words spoken by a rural farmer, according to the schema of cofiguration, no translation was needed: they were both speaking Japanese, after all.

Here, to understand Sakamoto's rockabilly, I explore the role translation plays in producing two kinds of otherness: first, the way that translation, according to the schema of configuration, establishes a boundary between two supposedly distinct languages, and second, the way that the supposedly homogeneous language community produced through this translation includes various marginalized dialects, forms of language that are exotic yet belong to the interior of the speech community—the otherness, for example, of Korea and Taiwan, on the one hand, and of Okinawa and Hokkaido, on the other, as they have been conceptualized in Japan since 1945. In the first instance, interlingual translation represents a certain text as belonging to a foreign language (and simultaneously establishes the translator and his or her readers as belonging to a single, homogeneous linguistic community, thereby concealing the failures of communication within that community). If that is so, what techniques are used in the second instance, to establish a dialect as a kind of peripheral culture but one that is still located within the boundaries of the speech community? What is the relationship between these two sets of techniques? How and when does the boundary between foreign and peripheral shift? And, most important, what opportunities are created within this fluidity for troubling the existing power relationships, for seeking a way out from the various boundaries that would limit us and our desires? All these questions become crucial for understanding the often contradictory position that Japan occupied in the geopolitical map that emerged in the 1950s and 1960s as exotic Other yet as intimate ally of the United States in the explosive East Asia region.

Sakamoto Kyū's translation of rockabilly music presents a good field for exploring this problematic because as we trace through it, we see the boundary between foreign and peripheral undergo fluid permutations. We see repeated instances of translation, as well as deliberate decisions made not to translate, as well as other instances that challenge the possibility of defining what translation is. We begin to see, that is, the tremendous diversity that the schema of cofiguration would conceal from view. Even Japan's bullet trains, the new high-speed-rail technology introduced in 1964, don't move fast enough to keep up with this phenomenon: we'll need to rely on jet planes to catch up with it.

*　　*　　*

As I trace connections between airplanes, translation, and rockabilly, I deal primarily with two songs that were central to Sakamoto's career. The first is an Elvis Presley song, "G.I Blues." Released in late 1960, shortly after Presley's stint in the army, during which he was stationed in Germany, it was the theme song for a film of the same name. The single was a minor hit in the United States but seems to have achieved greater popularity elsewhere around the world—including Japan. The song, written for Elvis by Sid Tepper and Roy C. Bennet, is a sort of translation, as was all of rockabilly.[21] It claims in its title to reproduce an African American musical genre, and it in fact does follow the traditional twelve-bar blues format, with lyrics structured around the usual call-and-response pattern. Yet the song is clearly hybrid, mixing a variety of musical genres into its blues framework: the melody vaguely recalls the bugle call from the Andrews Sisters' hit "Boogie Woogie Bugle Boy," while the song's rhythm invokes tension between a military march cadence that would discipline Elvis and the swinging blues syncopation that tries to set him free.[22] The film sound track as a whole is similarly hybrid, including lullabies, romantic ballads, straight-ahead rockabilly numbers (including another train song, "Frankfort Special"), and even a song adapted from German folk music ("Wooden Heart") that includes lyrics sung in German by Elvis.[23]

The translation that Elvis achieved in "G.I. Blues" and earlier singles seemed to erase a preexisting boundary: a minority cultural form, the blues, was brought to the center of mainstream popular culture. In the words of producer Sam Phillips, "I went out into this no-man's-land, and I knocked the shit out of the color line," a crossing that he credited at least in part to Presley himself, since "Elvis Presley knew what it was like to be poor, but that damn sure didn't make him prejudiced. *He didn't draw any lines.*"[24] Elvis's performances in fact did blur boundaries—not just racial ones but also those of class, gender, and sexuality. These transgressions provoked the sharply negative reactions to his early television appearances, accusations of vulgarity, of grinding like a striptease artist, of simulating sex acts on stage. Behind these accusations, too, lay perceived violations of racial boundaries: Elvis was problematically citing a "highly developed aesthetic of *public* sexuality" that had characterized black music for decades, in contrast to the family-oriented nature of white Tin Pan Alley pop songs.[25]

When Elvis appeared on Steve Allen's television program, the host attempted to defuse these criticisms by dressing Elvis in formal evening attire and having him perform "Hound Dog" (a song originally made famous by the female R&B singer Big Mama Thornton) in the face of a real live basset. The incident is usually interpreted as a ridiculing of Presley, and perhaps this caused the wariness that Sakamoto Kyū expresses in the epigraph to this chapter as he prepared to appear on the same program a few years later. But what strikes me as particularly interesting is the tactic used to marginalize Presley and the song. We find here not translation, at least in the ordinary sense, but a completely literal reading of the song's lyrics. The poetics of metaphor are denied to the song: it is ridiculed by making it literally into a song about a hound dog. There is an insistence that no translation is necessary. Literal reading is used to push the song away and put it in its place, to render it into something marginal, even as it is undeniably sung in the shared language of English.[26]

Accordingly, much of mainstream society rejected Elvis because of the way he seemed to cross boundaries. Yet we cannot ignore how Elvis's various crossings also redrew lines. More precisely, they showed that the crossing could occur only in certain directions. To get Elvis's early singles played on the radio and to secure concert bookings across the South, Phillips repeatedly had to assure skeptical music industry figures that his new singing sensation was in fact white.

In early 1961, Sakamoto Kyū released a cover version of "G.I. Blues," with the lyrics translated into Japanese by Minami Kazumi. The song was one of the last gasps in the rockabilly boom that had begun in 1958 with the First Nichigeki Western Carnival. Later that year, the Third Nichigeki Western Carnival provided Sakamoto with his first taste of the national spotlight. In his performance there, as well as throughout his early career, Sakamoto was closely identified with Elvis: he was one of more than twenty singers who attempted to lay claim to the title of being "the Japanese Elvis."[27] Sakamoto had already enjoyed several hits in Japan before "G.I. Blues," but this was the first single released under his own name rather than that of Danny Iida and the Paradise Kings (although they continued to back him on the record), the band he had joined in 1958 at the behest of his management, Watanabe Productions. "G.I. Blues" seems to have had a special impact on its Japanese audience. A feature on recent "Music Fashions" in the May 1961 issue of *Heibon*, a popular magazine, included a full-page spread on the "G.I. Blues" look. At least three other Japanese rockabilly singers—Kamayatsu Hiroshi, Sasaki Isao, and Mickey Curtis—also released cover versions of the song (photographs of the latter two in military uniforms were featured in the fashion article). But it was Sakamoto's recording of the song that became the definitive Japanese-language version: it entered the *Music Life* domestic hit chart at number 3 in January 1961 (in fact, four of the eight songs listed that month are by Sakamoto) and remained in the charts until May.

In his performance on the record, Sakamoto adopts many of Presley's vocal mannerisms, including the slurring and hiccupy flourishes characteristic of American rockabilly. The singing style is quite distinct from that Sakamoto had used on his previous hit singles, which feature softer, crooning-style vocals, but is likely closer to what he had used in his early live performances. The band behind Sakamoto plays a swinging arrangement by Danny Iida, a tight rockabilly weave accented with jazz-influenced drumming and dueling guitar and piano fills; it runs circles around the fairly staid arrangement on Elvis's original. The lyrics are translated into Japanese, except for a refrain that remains in English: "Hop two three four occupation G.I. blues" (somehow, "hup" has become "hop" in translation). Although Elvis's version is clearly sung from the perspective of a GI stationed in Germany—including references to the Rhine River, German food, and pretty fräuleins—these local references are erased from Sakamoto's version.[28] In fact, Sakamoto's translation seems to relocate the speaker to Japan, so that the relevant Occupation is the U.S. Occupation of Japan.

Sakamoto's "G.I. Blues" raises a number of questions. First of all, what did it mean, at the dawn of America's Vietnam War and so soon after the massive anti-American protests that accompanied the 1960 renewal of the U.S.-Japan Security Treaty (AMPO), for a Japanese singer to sing lyrics mostly in Japanese but to adopt in them the enunciative position of an American GI complaining of homesickness, the squalor of barracks life—and suggesting himself as an object of desire to local (Japanese) residents?[29] In a 2003 interview, Sasaki Isao, one of the other Japanese rockabilly singers who recorded "G.I. Blues," discussed how his mother sewed his military uniform costumes for him, as well as why his father did not oppose his dropping out of school to become a singer in the first place. His father was completely taken in by what Sasaki calls the American 3-*s* strategy in occupying Japan: "Screen, song, sports—those were the 3 *s*'s, and supposedly that was the strategy to lure the Japanese people away from politics. I think the sudden boom in pop and movies after the war was due to this strategy, and we can still see traces of this today. That's why the struggles against the 1960 AMPO and the 1970 AMPO Security Treaty renewals both collapsed: in the end, it was because this strategy succeeded."[30] The problem becomes even more complex when we note that up through the mid-1960s, Japanese rock-and-roll musicians—including both Sasaki and the early Sakamoto—found their most stable source of income in performances at clubs on U.S. military bases—where, no doubt, "G.I. Blues" went over very well with audiences.[31]

We should also consider the question of whether Sakamoto's version of the song—or any of his earlier translated covers of American pop music (including songs by Paul Anka, Bobby Darrin, and others)—could have been a hit in the United States. I suspect the answer is no.[32] A Japanese singing American pop "straight" was certainly acceptable in Japan, but in the United States, it could be viewed only as an exotic joke, one that would elicit appeals to the supposed "authenticity" of Elvis's original. In a 1958 story on Japanese rockabilly, *Time* caricatured the English pronunciations of Japanese singers as "a transoceanic mutilation, as in *Rub Me Tender* and *Rittoru Dahring* (*Little Darling*)."[33] In the United States, Sakamoto the Japanese rockabilly singer of "G.I. Blues" could only produce laughter—laughter in the Bergsonian sense of a technique for the violent disciplining of anything that might jam up the smooth functioning of the social machinery.[34] But if that was so, why was there no resistance to the idea of Elvis singing in German or, for that matter, to his singing a song that claimed to be an African American blues number?

Elvis, singing from the supposedly universal position of an American white man, could cite the particularity of German folk music without raising eyebrows. Likewise, Sakamoto as a particular Japanese could invoke the universal of American rockabilly within the context of Japan. But Sakamoto singing Japanese rockabilly in America would result in cognitive dissonance, a discomforting confusion of hierarchies between universal and particular, one that might even suggest that the universal was simply another particular. Just as was the case for African American performers, crossover success into pop was possible, but only in forms that left intact the crucial boundaries that were being temporarily transgressed.

As Marcus notes, rockabilly in the United States was above all a white genre. But Gilroy reminds us that "gender is the modality in which race is lived."[35] American rockabilly was not only racially exclusive, but also almost exclusively male. Despite the presence of many well-known female voices in both country and blues, virtually all the successful rockabilly singers were men.[36] Within the Japanese market, Sakamoto was able to perform the masculine role of an American soldier. But to achieve success in the West, as we will see, he had to take on a more feminized, nonthreatening "cute" role, more like a JAL stewardess than an American GI. Sakamoto's translations of rockabilly showed that borders could be crossed, but only in certain directions, at certain times, and by persons carrying the proper cultural passports.

✳   ✳   ✳

On the second song I deal with here, Sakamoto was backed by the Toshiba Recording Orchestra (the stable of studio musicians under contract to Sakamoto's Japanese record label). The single version of "Ue wo muite arukō" was released in Japan in late 1961, after Sakamoto performed the song to great acclaim on the NHK television variety show *Meet Me in My Dreams* (*Yume de aimashō*) (figure 6). The song's title might be translated as "I Will Keep My Head Up as I Walk." The music was composed by Nakamura Hachidai, and the lyrics by Ei Rokusuke, a duo who composed many hit songs for Sakamoto and others. Sakamoto uses an unusual vocal style in his performance, something akin to rockabilly's hiccupping style but drastically slowed down, so that a single vowel sound—the "o" in the title phrase's "arukō," for

FIGURE 6 The jacket for Sakamoto Kyū's single "Ue wo muite arukō" (1961). (Courtesy EMI Music Japan)

example—is broken up into several distinct syllables: "arukō-wo-wo-wo." "Ue wo muite arukō" immediately became an enormous domestic hit. The single sold more than 300,000 copies in Japan but did not win the coveted Nippon Record Taishō award because, in the mind of at least one member of the prize jury, the song sounded too American—this despite the standard *yonanuki* pentatonic scale used in the main melody.[37] This was perhaps because, unlike so many minor-key Japanese hits, "Ue wo muite arukō" is written in a major key—though one attractive hook in the song is the way it shifts briefly into a minor key during the bridge section.[38]

This is the same song that under the title "Sukiyaki" became a number 1 hit in the summer of 1963 when it was released by Capitol Records in the United States, the first Japanese-produced record to sell a million copies worldwide. The origin of the "Sukiyaki" title remains obscure; according to a 1981 interview with Sakamoto, a British deejay who liked the song but knew only three words of Japanese—*Fujiyama*, *geisha*, and *sukiyaki*—was responsible for the song's title in the English-speaking world.[39] The song had already become a hit in a number of European countries in 1962, either as "Sukiyaki" or under a number of other titles—in Belgium, for example, it was known as "Unforgettable Geisha Baby."[40] It was originally introduced in England through a Dixieland jazz instrumental version by the Kenny Ball Orchestra, recorded after Pye Records president Louis Benjamin heard Sakamoto's hit while on a trip to Japan. The popularity of the cover version prompted Pye to issue Sakamoto's original recording in the United Kingdom, also under the title "Sukiyaki." In early 1963, deejays at West Coast stations in the United States began playing Sakamoto's record to great response, and another cover version by Billy Vaughn and His Orchestra began to enjoy chart success. These developments led Capitol Records to release the original Sakamoto version in the United States. The single entered the *Cash Box* hit charts on May 4, 1963, and reached number 1 seven weeks later; it remained at number 1 for four consecutive weeks. Numerous cover versions were also released, some with English lyrics. By July 1963, the song had been released in twenty-three different versions in thirteen different countries, including one by Masako, a Japanese-American singer from Hawaii (she would travel to Japan to appear together with Sakamoto on a television special celebrating the song's international success).[41]

The song's success abroad and the Gold Record award it earned the following year (again, the first ever for a Japanese performer) were widely reported in the Japanese media. One critic was quoted as saying that the song's breakthrough in the West shows that "our eighteen years of struggle in the postwar period have not been in vain."[42] Domestically, Sakamoto took on enormous symbolic value as an icon of Japan's ascending star in the global firmament of nations. As we have already seen, when Sakamoto arrived at Los Angeles International Airport in August 1963 to perform the song live on *The Steve Allen Show*, he was met by thousands of screaming teenagers, foreshadowing what would happen the following February when the Beatles arrived in New York City. Incidentally, while in Los Angeles, Sakamoto asked to meet his idol but was told that Elvis was too busy filming his latest movie.[43]

Ei Rokusuke's lyrics in the original Japanese version of "Ue wo muite arukō" present a man who is determined not to allow sadness and loneliness to overcome him; he vows to fight back tears, keep his chin up, and walk forward. The melancholic lyrics stand in odd contrast to the cheerful major-key melody, which—particularly in the passages whistled by the singer and those accented by an upbeat xylophone—seems to take an active role in buoying his spirits. But most American listeners could not know this, because when Sakamoto's single was released in the United States, the lyrics were left in the original Japanese, with no translation. Yet as I have already noted, the song was given a new title.

"Sukiyaki," then, is not a translation of the original title—yet in another sense it might be the ultimate translation. Sakamoto himself was quoted at the time as saying, "At least 'Sukiyaki' is a Japanese word," and of course that was the whole point.[44] "Sukiyaki" was chosen because the word emitted a strong sense of Japaneseness or foreignness—an effect that literal translation would have spoiled. Somewhat incredibly (or predictably?), the single that Sakamoto released in the United States to follow "Sukiyaki" was a cover version of the old warhorse "China Nights" (Shina no yoru), the orientalist fantasy about romance between a Japanese man and a Chinese woman that had first scored as a hit in Japan for Watanabe Hamako in 1939 during the heyday of the Japanese empire.[45] An article from a 1963 Japanese magazine retracing Sakamoto's trip to Los Angeles quotes him on board the Pan American jet carrying him to America: "Next we'll see if I can get 'Shina no yoru' to catch on. With 'Ue wo muite arukō' becoming a hit, we know that Japanese teenagers and American teenagers are the same. Japanese pop songs are no longer an underdeveloped country. With my generation, at last Japan has become an international power."[46] In the same article, he is quoted again, this time on the plane ride home, to the effect that the best part of the trip was when an executive for Capitol Records told him that if he could produce two more hits, he would get his own star on the sidewalk in front of Grauman's Chinese Theatre. Given the orientalist nature of the follow-up single, the location was perfect. But "China Nights" peaked in the low fifties on the hit charts, and Sakamoto never got a star for us to see as we walk down Hollywood Boulevard.

Japanese music journalists in 1963 were well aware of the exoticization involved in retitling Sakamoto's song as "Sukiyaki."[47] The song's lyricist, Ei Rokusuke, found this translation a jarring experience. He happened to be traveling in the United States just as the song was starting to break. In a travel diary published at the time, he describes the envy he felt for the song's composer, Nakamura Hachidai. Nakamura's music can be appreciated by anyone, no matter what language they speak.

> When he sits down at a piano, he doesn't need any words. But my work uses the Japanese language.
>
> When I write poetry, when I write prose, only people who can read Japanese—no, really, only a part of those who can read that language—understand my work.
>
> In New York, I heard "Ue wo muite arukō." The melody was exactly the same, but the title written on the record label was "Sukiyaki." In the lyrics were words like "geisha baby" and "Fujiyama."

Ei goes on to analyze the situation: "Even if someone were to translate my Japanese, it still wouldn't be my words, because it would be a translation." His article concludes emphatically, " 'Ue wo muite arukō' is *not* 'Sukiyaki'!"[48]

It's unclear which version of "Sukiyaki" Ei heard in New York. We should note that even as Ei is criticizing the politics of translation, he is at the same time invoking a certain ideological representation of translation: the belief that music is universal, a homogeneous medium of communication shared by all humans. As musicologist Robert Walser has noted, "Musical constructions . . . are powerful in part because they are made to seem so natural and unconstructed. We experience music's rhetorical pull apart from language, seemingly apart from all social referents, in what is usually thought a pure, personal, subjective way. Yet that impression of naturalness depends on our responding unself-consciously to complex discursive systems that have developed as historical and socially specific practices."[49] The seeming naturalness of music, just like that of national language, is a social fiction, one that functions to mask the heterogeneity and unequal power relationships in which we are always caught up. Even when we seem to be innocently tapping our toe in time to a pop song, we are "musicking": producing meanings within specific social and historical situations, accepting certain visions of the world and our relation to it. As a result, for example, "Sukiyaki" now sounds "Japanese" to our ears, even though there is nothing particularly "Japanese" about the music: it debuted in the West as a Dixieland number, after all.[50] Hence, producers of subsequent cover versions of the song using translated English lyrics had to foreground its supposed Japaneseness by introducing new, highly exaggerated musical cues, such as the koto playing featured in two recordings of the song that charted decades later: A Taste of Honey's soulful version (a top-ten hit in 1981) and vocal group 4 P.M.'s 1995 version.[51]

Accordingly, Ei misses the way that our musicking can also be a form of translation. Even with this blind spot, though, it is clear that Ei discovered on his visit to New York in 1963 that translation is a site of politics and ideology, one in which his own identity was being constructed for him by a dominant culture. Ironically, the dish sukiyaki chosen as the English title for the song because of its exotic resonances was a modern creation, a product of the Meiji period and the reintroduction of beef eating into Japan after a thousand-year prohibition due to the influence of Buddhism. In Meiji Japan, the dish sukiyaki signified the ingestion of Western modernity, not the preservation of tradition. Obviously, these overtones had been lost, in both Japan and the West, by 1963, and it was for the signification of Japaneseness that the word was chosen and the song lyrics were left untranslated. It should also be noted that one reason the word *sukiyaki* had entered the vocabulary of many Americans was the large number of returned American soldiers who had encountered the dish during their tours of duty in Japan and Okinawa—the same soldiers who had filled the base clubs where Sakamoto and other Japanese musicians got their start.

Why were the lyrics to "Sukiyaki" left untranslated for the American release? Perhaps we can speculate that, whereas Sakamoto singing in English could produce only a sense of alienation, Sakamoto singing in Japanese could be consumed and enjoyed—just like the markings of Japaneseness found on JAL airplanes. Gilroy notes that the "discourse of authenticity has been a notable presence in the mass marketing of successive black folk-cultural forms to white audiences";[52] with "Sukiyaki," Sakamoto discovered that Japan, too, could function as a commodity. What was to be communicated was not the semantic content of the song's lyrics but the semiotic content of the music and the ethnicity of the performer and his language.[53]

To borrow Sakai's words, Sakamoto singing in Japanese to an English-speaking audience provided a reassuring "*experience of understanding the experience of not comprehending.*"[54] English-speaking listeners could represent their incomprehension tidily through the schema of cofiguration: they did not understand Sakamoto because he was singing in a foreign language. Sakamoto could even be the object of great praise.[55] Asian difference was not to be erased or feared but enjoyed, thereby producing the bonds of intimacy and integration that the Cold War geopolitical order needed. Rather than a troubling experience of discommunication, Sakamoto's Western listeners were permitted to enjoy what was quite literally a harmonious misunderstanding. It was a different sort of misunderstanding from, for example, the panic set off by the cryptic English lyrics of the Kingsmen's hit single "Louie Louie" (1960) or by any number of Little Richard singles from the 1950s, when parents feared that the slurred lyrics might contain obscene passages.

Moreover, given the Cold War context of 1963, I would argue that only by singing in Japanese could Sakamoto demonstrate that he—and the nation of Japan, which had so recently exploded in violent protest against the United States—was in fact singing in our language all along. "Sukiyaki" in the West presented the image of a Japan that was ready to take its place within the U.S.-dominated security order for East Asia. It was an exotic peripheral member of this community, speaking a kind of marginal dialect—and yet nonetheless a fully integrated member, just like the Asian American characters in Rodgers and Hammerstein's musical *Flower Drum Song*, which had achieved enormous popularity just a few years earlier. In the schema of cofiguration that became ideological common sense during the Cold War, Japan was "one of us." Unlike Red China or North Korea, it belonged to the community on this side of the Iron Curtain, an adopted member of the family of free nations.[56] Performing this role was, it seems, the precondition for Sakamoto to enjoy the status of a globally famous pop singer. It is also true, however, that by singing in Japanese, Sakamoto—unlike, for example, the Beatles—condemned himself in the West to the status of a one-hit wonder, more specifically an ethnic novelty act, akin to Chinese acrobats, even as his global success helped pave the way for the Beatles.

*　　*　　*

Given the racializing and gendered tendencies of orientalism in its Cold War guise, whatever potential Sakamoto Kyū had for transgressing social boundaries lay not so much in a translation like "Sukiyaki" as it did with one like "G.I. Blues." Sakamoto's "G.I. Blues" was a major hit in Japan (albeit in the relatively marginal cultural world of popular music), where it probably reinforced hegemonic notions about America and Japan, as well as about gender and race. But had it been released in the United States, the same song might well have become what Tejaswini Niranjana calls a disruptive translation, a form of colonial mimicry that troubled listeners' ability to believe in the authenticity of Elvis's (and America's) rockabilly.[57]

In other words, Sakamoto's ability to adopt the posture of an honorary white man had one effect in Japan, but it also had the potential to produce a different effect for American listeners. To realize this act of reverse "camouflage"—pretending to be a soldier—Sakamoto had to play lip service to America's hegemony and its claims to a dominant masculine position in relation to a feminized, demilitarized Japan.[58] He had to, that is, accept the notion embedded in "G.I. Blues" that Elvis occupies the dominant center of the world, in terms of both popular music and geopolitics. At the same time, by successfully taking up the role of a white male in his recording of the Elvis song, Sakamoto could assert Japanese masculinity in the face of American orientalism that insisted on feminizing Japan. But the song remained unheard beyond Japan, its potential as disruptive translation unrealized.

There is, then, something tragic about the story of Sakamoto, who in America is remembered as a one-hit wonder because his numerous hit records in Japan don't count. With "Sukiyaki," the schema of cofiguration was reconfirmed, and Sakamoto finally chose to represent Japan rather than rockabilly music.[59] In subsequent years, he would be trotted out again and again whenever Japan needed an "official youth spokesman" for international expos and the like. And, like Elvis in the early 1960s, Sakamoto drifted away from the marginal genre of rockabilly and into mainstream pop ballads. Eventually, he became better known as a television personality than as a singer—although Sakamoto tried more than once to revive his music career. In 1975, timed to coincide with the first visit to America by Emperor Hirohito, Capitol Records invited Sakamoto to return to Los Angeles to record new material, mainly English-language versions of songs that had been hits for other artists in Japan. A single, "Elimo" backed with "Why," was released in the United

States in October 1975. Although it received some media coverage in Japan, it sank without denting the American charts. Then again, just days before his death, Sakamoto approached Ei and Nakamura, the songwriting team that had produced "Ue wo muite arukō," to ask their help in restarting his singing career. But unlike Elvis, Sakamoto was never going to have his great come-back—at least not during his lifetime.

Still, along with tragedy, there is also something astonishing about Saka-moto's story, the pimply-faced Japanese teenager who went from singing "Hound Dog" to U.S. soldiers in Tachikawa to worldwide fame in just five years. His career involved a series of productive mistranslations and misun-derstandings, but as Lipsitz has argued, artists from marginalized cultures "have often profited from less than perfect knowledge about the exclusionary rules devised from within other cultures. Their 'ignorance' of the intentions of others to exclude them has often served as an impetus to creativity; not knowing they were supposed to fail enabled them to succeed."[60] No one told Sakamoto that he couldn't become a rockabilly star, that he didn't have the right passport, and so, for a brief moment, he did. His success hints that alongside the schema of configuration, there are other ways to practice transla-tion: not as a simple reproduction of existing boundaries between languages but as a playful practice that produces new identities and languages. In the hands of the subaltern, as Lydia Liu reminds us, translation can become a weapon for creating new possibilities for agency and for disrupting the hier-archies that divide "original" from "copy."[61]

*　　*　　*

Thousands of mourners gathered for Sakamoto's funeral on September 9, 1985. Like the plane crash, it was a major media event. In the weeks before and after, Japanese musicians of all generations and genres paid tribute to him. One musician was quoted as saying that he was surprised to find himself more deeply affected by Sakamoto's death than he was by John Lennon's.[62]

When Sakamoto died, the Japanese economy was near its bubble peak as the nation enjoyed unprecedented prosperity. Japan was the world's wealthi-est, healthiest, and best-educated nation; its products and services set global standards for excellence. Flights into and out of Japan were booked to capacity as Japanese traveled abroad in astonishing numbers to enjoy their new prosperity. The contrast with the United States, stuck in its post-Vietnam economic doldrums, was lost on no one. While JAL flourished, American airlines like Braniff (1982), Pan American (1991), and TWA (1992) went bankrupt. Japanese didn't screw things up, the way Americans did. The drug-related death of Elvis Presley in 1977 and the murder of John Lennon in New York City in 1980 helped contribute to the image of an America whose undisciplined culture threatened its position as hegemon in East Asia. Japan seemed poised to take its place as the next superpower.

In retrospect, it now seems that the JAL crash in 1985 signaled the beginning of the end for that version of Japan. Although Japan's economy would continue to boom for another five years, anyone who was there at the time of the crash will remember the obsessive news coverage of the incident (television networks suspended regular programming for days to devote airtime to the disaster) and the way it left an indelible scar on Japanese public self-confidence. Enormous efforts were made to determine which side of the border blame rested on—was JAL or the (American) Boeing Company at fault? The eventual finding, that sloppy maintenance work at Boeing caused the crash, provided little comfort.[63] In the late 1980s, the Japanese government slid into another series of ugly bribery scandals, and then in the early 1990s the economic bubble burst and hard times began. Privatized in 1987 under the neoliberal policies of the Nakasone Yasuhiro cabinet, JAL struggled to survive in a new environment of cutthroat competition.

Given the timing and nature of his death, it is perhaps unsurprising that even today, Sakamoto continues to hold a unique place in Japanese popular memory. Despite repeated efforts, no Japanese artist has broken through in Western pop charts the way he did. On December 31, 2000, during *Kōhaku uta gassen*, the annual musical extravaganza broadcast on the NHK network, the producers marked the end of the twentieth century by having all the performers gather on stage together to sing "Ue wo muite arukō," with Sakamoto's widow and daughters present in the audience. And with Japan still sunk in seemingly endless recession, 2001 would see a Sakamoto Kyū nostalgia boom, centered on a rediscovery of his single "There's Always Tomorrow" (Ashita ga aru sa, 1963), a lively big-band number. If Sakamoto is remembered as a one-hit wonder in the West, in Japan he more and more became the unshakable ghost haunting a once high-flying empire.

*   *   *

What can we learn from all the translations that Sakamoto performed—and that were performed on him? And what can we learn from Sakamoto's ill-fated career as an airline passenger? That overly simplex models of the "postmodern" situation as transnational miss the ways that capitalism redraws boundaries of nation (and race, gender, class, and so on) even as it promises to erase them. When Sakamoto's personal effects were recovered from the JAL crash site, it was learned that he had carried on board with him a portable tape player. The song on the tape was USA for Africa's "We Are the World." According to his widow, Sakamoto loved the song and sang it frequently in the months before his death.[64] On the one hand, we see here what (at least from the perspective of a rock fan) seems to be the bad taste and sentimentality that led Sakamoto to follow not the early Elvis but the bland pop of Pat Boone and Paul Anka (or, for that matter, the Hollywood Elvis). On the other hand, perhaps we see yet another sign of the tragedy of Sakamoto. Having been pigeonholed as an oriental novelty act, he was unable to secure his star in front of Grauman's Chinese Theatre. Had things turned out differently, had "China Nights" or "Elimo" become a hit, Sakamoto might well have been one of the superstars who jetted into Los Angeles for the "We Are the World" session. As it was, the song simply repeated a familiar pattern. It was performed almost exclusively by North American and English musicians who nonetheless confidently proclaimed (in English, of course) that they, indeed, were the world. No translation needed. No Asian performers appeared on the recording.

Sakamoto the air traveler crossed national, ethnic, and racial boundaries, but some lines he could not cross. A few years before his death, Sakamoto would look back on his whirlwind airplane trip to Los Angeles in 1963: "On the way back from Los Angeles, we stopped in Hawaii. There was this really pretty beach there. But when I tried to go there with my friends, they told us no coloreds allowed. I went, 'Huh? Oh, I get it—I'm colored.' I was just stunned. I felt like I had yet again brushed against the hugeness, the complexity of America."[65] This was Hawaii, Elvis's home away from home, a regular stopover for JAL flights since 1959, and the only American state whose population in 1960 included a *majority* of persons of Asian ancestry and where Japanese constituted the single largest ethnic group. Advocates of Hawaii's statehood in the late 1950s had stressed that the state's ability to symbolize American racial tolerance made it the ultimate "melting pot" and hence a powerful symbol to rebut Communist accusations about American racial violence.[66] A crucial node in the transnational airline networks, Hawaii was also supposed to be the symbol of ultimate global integration.

In translating rockabilly, Sakamoto crossed the color line only to find that the color line stood intact—even in Hawaii. To become an international star, he was required to perform as an "authentic" Japanese, and that meant staying to one side of the color line. His claims to translate rockabilly, likewise, have to be denied implicitly by those who would tie the genre's authenticity to American culture.

But if we listen carefully to Sakamoto Kyū's translations, and if we pay close attention to the trajectories of his flight paths, we can perhaps trace not the clash of civilizations, not the clash between civilizations, but the clash within, the noise that disrupts the myth of a homogeneous national culture. Perhaps we can hear a sonic boom that cannot be explained away either as a foreign language or as a marginal dialect of some national tongue. Perhaps we can obtain hints about how to translate outside the schema of cofiguration, about how to fly airplanes that don't simply return us to the same identities they promised to transgress.

4

WORKING WITHIN THE SYSTEM

GROUP SOUNDS AND THE COMMERCIAL
AND REVOLUTIONARY POTENTIAL OF NOISE

By listening to noise, we can better understand where the folly of men
and their calculations is leading us, and what hopes it is still possible to
have.

JACQUES ATTALI, NOISE: THE POLITICAL ECONOMY OF MUSIC

In Japan [fuzz boxes] became popular a year or so ago, but in America
lots of bands have been using them for about three years. The Ventures
had them, right? It's really become the center of attention with the boom
in psychedelic music. I started using one three years ago. I bought it for
twenty bucks when I went to America; it was probably the first one to
reach Japan.

EDDIE BAN (LEAD GUITARIST, GOLDEN CUPS)

In August 1968, the Tigers, one of the most successful of the
mid-1960s "Group Sounds" bands, vowed that their forthcoming third album would mark a new departure for the
quintet.[1] The popular weekly *Shūkan heibon* quoted bassist "Sally"
(Kishibe Osami) as declaring, "We want to shed the skin of what the
Tigers have been up to now. This LP is the first step in that image
change." Lead singer "Julie" (Sawada Kenji) reaffirmed the point: "I
think Group Sounds has reached a turning point. And the Tigers
need to undergo an image change too."

What sort of transformation did they have in mind? The article goes on to describe the forthcoming *Human Renascence* LP as a concept album, marking a shift in focus away from hit singles to more extended, complex works. Moreover, all the songs on the new album would explore "humanism," each taking up a different aspect of that theme: birth, death, rebirth, and so forth. In other words, the lyrics would make an artistic statement—in sharp contrast to the lighthearted celebrations of teen life that characterized earlier Tigers' hits such as "Seaside Bound" (1967) and "Love Only for You" (Kimi dake ni ai wo, 1968). This new depth would be conveyed musically as well: the songs on *Human Renascence* would feature sophisticated arrangements, mixing in elements of jazz and classical, including a full forty-eight-piece orchestra. Moreover, the statement the album made would be personal. For the first time, members of the band would compose two of the songs included on it (the remaining ten were by professional songwriters). The article concludes with another quote from Kishibe: "From now on, I want to get a little ahead of our fans so that we can pull them along with us."

Why would a spectacularly successful band suddenly change course? Then again, this was 1968, a time of great turbulence in Japan as elsewhere. Teen culture, centered since the 1950s on the pleasures of consumption, monogamous love, and the family, was giving way to youth culture: politically rebellious, sexually liberated, and openly dismissive of the strictures of domestic life.[2] The mainstream media had often depicted Group Sounds negatively, associating it with juvenile delinquency (a near riot by Tigers' fans in 1967 got them banned from NHK),[3] but now something even more troubling had arisen, rebels with a cause: revolution. The new youth culture was dominated by a political radicalism that rejected the traditional Left—the Japan Communist Party and the Japan Socialist Party—which it viewed as part of the establishment. As one historian has argued, Japan in 1968 saw "an expansion of the field of the political itself as it came to encompass a much wider range of potential issues, actors, and possibilities," attracting the active participation of supposedly nonpolitical students and citizens.[4] Most Japanese universities were the targets of student strikes or takeovers, as were many high schools. That the student-age demographic was one of the fastest-growing sectors of the national population magnified the impact of this campus unrest.[5] At the same time, massive street demonstrations protested the Vietnam War and

Japan's complicity in it (U.S. bases there and in Okinawa remained major staging areas for the conflict). Between 1967 and 1970, some 18 million Japanese participated in antiwar protests, including Tezuka Osamu's cartoon superhero Astroboy, who sacrificed his life (temporarily) to protect North Vietnamese villagers from American bombing raids.[6]

Opposition was also building up to the scheduled 1970 renewal of the U.S.-Japan Security Treaty (AMPO), the pact whose renewal in 1960 had provoked popular revolt in the streets of Tokyo. In response to those earlier AMPO protests, the Japanese government had pledged to double national per-capita income within a decade, a policy that included a new emphasis on promoting consumption alongside production.[7] By 1968, the income-doubling goal had already been achieved (it tripled by 1973), and in the same year Japan surpassed West Germany as the world's second-largest economy, a success that was paralleled by the increasing electoral dominance of the conservative Liberal Democratic Party.[8] Older Japanese seemed largely satisfied with the results, but New Left activists attacked rampant consumerism and the blind worship of growth as forms of oppression. Real human emotion, they argued, was being replaced by social management and artificially generated "needs." Student radicals explicitly linked the state's economic policies to U.S. imperialism: one of the events that brought the New Left to public awareness was the October 8, 1967, attempt by hundreds of activists armed with wooden staves to block Prime Minister Satō Eisaku from reaching Tokyo's Haneda Airport to depart for a visit to Saigon in support of the American war effort in Vietnam.[9]

To put this back into the context of the Tigers, the 1960s wave of mass consumerism and economic growth had been the band's ticket to success. Perhaps the most prominent symbol of the new consumerism was the color television set, which the 1964 Tokyo Olympics had transformed from luxury good into middle-class necessity. By 1968, household television ownership in Japan for the first time exceeded 100 percent—which is to say, the age in which ownership of two or more sets was normal had begun.[10] The Tigers were fixtures of commercial television, regularly appearing on the numerous pop music shows that filled broadcast schedules by the mid-1960s. Their collaboration with the commercial mass media went beyond that: the band recorded numerous advertising jingles for Meiji Chocolate. When they weren't taping commercials or television appearances, the Tigers kept busy filming exploitation movies aimed at the teen market. For a conventional Group Sounds band like the Tigers, market success was sufficient proof of talent—talent at entertaining a specific segment of the market: the teenage girl.[11] Until 1968, the Tigers seemingly understood and accepted their place in the culture industry. Their debut album, *The Tigers on Stage* (1967), a live concert recording, included their transposed version of the Monkees' theme song: "Hey, hey, we're the Tigers . . ."

But by August 1968, this was no longer enough. Rock and roll was becoming rock, and the social functions and uses of popular music were changing. In tandem with the turbulent geopolitical situation, a new musical ideology and aesthetic were quickly becoming central components of the rising youth culture, in Japan as elsewhere in the industrialized world. Sociologist Minamida Katsuya has argued that the *ba* (usually translated as "place" or "location," but Minamida himself cites Pierre Bourdieu's notion of a "field") of rock was crisscrossed by three sometimes contradictory tendencies: it was supposed to be simultaneously a form of art, a kind of outsider culture, and a mode of entertainment.[12]

Under this novel regime, rock was increasingly romanticized and judged against a new criterion. "Authenticity" was an ambiguous concept that meant different things at different moments, cobbling together meanings that were often mutually incompatible.[13] For starters, authenticity was defined in opposition to commercialism, and the charge of "selling out" now became a common epithet. As sociologist Simon Frith has noted, this stance is self-contradictory: rock is a mass-culture form that claims to be at essence critical of mass culture.[14] Nonetheless, it became crucial for rock musicians to appear indifferent to the concerns of the market. They frequently released records on underground record labels, and they declined to make commercial endorsements or to participate in such promotional gimmicks as appearing on television hit parade programs. A distinction of taste began to emerge, as defined by Bourdieu in his study of nineteenth-century French literature: the very lack of popularity, a failure to chart, was now celebrated as evidence of artistic integrity.[15] As we will see, however, the rock ideology's rebellion against the pop music market ultimately achieved the production of another market, the rock market of the 1970s.[16]

Second, rock was supposed to be authentic because it was rooted in the real life of nonelite folk—Minamida's "outsiders." It was the music of an egalitarian community, one that resisted the hierarchical norms of bourgeois society. Here, rock music borrowed from the worldview of protest folk, as important to student demonstrators in Japan as it was in the United States (I explore this more fully in chapter 5). Rock performances were valued because they provided intense experiences of collective, communal emotion. Rock achieved authenticity by being political as well: by rebelling against the establishment and bourgeois morality, including societal expectations for sexuality, success, and community. It became common sense among its partisans that rock music, when done right, was somehow intrinsically subversive and libratory. It was also assertively masculine: the squeaky-clean teen idol soliciting screams from girls gave way to the strutting-cock rock guitarist, his phallic instrument providing a model of power to a largely male fandom.[17]

Finally, rock achieved authenticity by being artistic. A good rock song was supposed to be creative and original in both music and lyrics, and it was supposed to express the unique personality of the musicians who created it. This contradicted rock's claims to represent a nonelite communality: artistic value depended on staking a claim to the genius of the creator, thereby distinguishing him or her from ordinary fans (hence, the Tigers' desire to get "a little ahead" of their audience).[18] A September 1968 magazine article surveying the current pop music scene in Japan declared that "originality" was now all important and that formulaic bands were on the way out. "The Tigers are really manufactured stars," it declared. "New bands will start pushing their way up from below."[19] This increasing insistence on originality also rendered illegitimate the hitherto standard practice in Group Sounds of recording material written for bands by professional songwriters. Musicians were now supposed to compose their own songs, works that somehow expressed their unique outlook on life. Moreover, those artistically ambitious compositions could no longer be confined to the standard format of the commodified three-minute pop song.

The new aesthetic placed unprecedented demands on listeners, too. It was no longer sufficient simply to enjoy pop tunes for their entertainment value; a true fan had to acquire critical skills and knowledge to appreciate musical works that were valued for their complexity. Serious magazines devoted to rock criticism appeared: *New Music Magazine* began publication in Tokyo in 1969, two years after the first issue of *Rolling Stone* appeared in the United States.[20] Its articles frequently discussed politics and music in tandem, insisting that rock music had an important social role to play.

In sum, by August 1968, something was happening in Japanese popular music. A revolution was coming, and the Tigers and everyone else keyed into youth culture could hear it. You could spot signs in all the cultural forms associated with the young: film, theater, *manga* comic books, fashion. In popular music, moreover, you could hear the coming revolution as a specific kind of noise: the intentionally distorted sound of an electric guitar. In both Japan and the West, rock musicians began exploiting feedback and other effects that deliberately muddied the sound that resulted when output from the pickups on an electric guitar was fed through systems of amplification and recording. This new fuzziness had not only aesthetic but also ideological implications: it was a rebellious yelp. What had been "noise" was becoming "music," a change with revolutionary implications.[21]

Jacques Attali's seminal *Noise: The Political Economy of Music* (1977) provides a useful tool for understanding the implications of the new guitar sound. Attali rethinks the social role of music, beginning with noise. Noise is a kind of aggressive force or violence—loud noises can indeed injure. But noise is also a potential source of power, and it is the taming of its enormous energy that allows a social order to emerge. We call the codes that tame noise music, and they are at the core of the most basic rituals through which human society first appeared. Music, then, is the appropriation and channelization of the chaotic energy of noise into orderly codes, codes that help establish the differences that define a society and its hierarchies. This suggests that music is inherently political, or, in Attali's words, a "reflection of power." The organization of noise into codes of music is "a tool for the creation or consolidation of a community, of a totality."[22]

Noise is thus a lawless violence that must be civilized for a social order to emerge. Because "noise is the source of power, power has always listened to it with fascination."[23] And because music consists of channeled noise, it too is fascinating—the current of noise it struggles to contain is always ambiguous and potentially subversive. Music "is simultaneously a threat and a necessary source of legitimacy; trying to channel it is a risk that every system of power must run."[24] This is because the code that distinguishes music as a form also unintentionally creates its opposite—it opens the possibility for noise as that which lies outside music, beyond the control of authority. The creation of a rule, after all, always also creates the possibility for a violation of that rule. The code that is music captures and channels noise in order to produce a social order, but that very act of codifying in turn opens the possibility for new noise, any sound that erupts outside the domain governed by the dominant code.

Attali throws down an even bolder claim: "Music is prophecy," he writes, and its "styles and economic organization are ahead of the rest of society because it explores, much faster than material reality can, the entire range of possibilities in a given code. It makes audible the new world that will gradually become visible."[25] He asserts that every great social transformation in history was first audible in music, that, for example, the great bourgeois democratic revolutions of Europe's nineteenth century were first audible as noise irrupting in eighteenth-century compositions by Bach and Mozart. Attali stands on its head the Marxist notion that transformations in cultural superstructure (including ideology) lag behind ruptures in the economic base or substructure. In Attali's ears, a coming revolution shows up initially as a new form of noise, disrupting the established codes by which a given society orders itself.

In 1968, Group Sounds bands like the Tigers were confronted with the noise of distorted electric guitars. As Attali suggests, coping with this noise was not simply a technical musical problem (although it was also that). In grappling with it, Group Sounds bands were struggling with the emergence of rock ideology and rebellious youth culture: guitar feedback was a discordant bugle call proclaiming imminent revolution. Attali writes that an established "network can be destroyed by noises that attack and transform it, *if the codes in place are unable to normalize and repress them.*" If the established formulas fail to neutralize noise, that noise will mutate those codes and push society forward into a new network: "For despite the death it contains, noise carries order within itself; it carries new information." Noise creates meaning by interrupting the operations of the existing code, thereby opening up a space for imagination, for the creation of a new order: "The absence of meaning is in this case the presence of all meanings, absolute ambiguity, a construction outside meaning. The presence of noise . . . makes possible the creation of a new order on another level of organization, of a new code in another network."[26]

Here, in a nutshell, was the problem the Tigers faced in August 1968. Could they integrate guitar feedback into the existing Group Sounds formula, or did that distorted noise in and of itself explode the formula—did it necessitate the "creation of a new order on another level of organization"? The Tigers' *Human Renascence* LP, released in November 1968, offered a provisional model for solving the dilemma, a method that at least temporarily worked. The album did in fact lend a more sophisticated image to the Tigers, and it even spawned two hit singles: "A White Dove" (Haikyo no hato; number 3 on the Oricon hit chart) and "The Blue Bird" (Aoi tori; number 4 on Oricon). The Tigers' new artistic ambitions did not, at least immediately, bar them from commercial success.

Nonetheless, the writing was on the wall. The Tigers would soon disband, unable to locate a place for themselves in the emerging new network that was 1970s rock.[27] In November 1970, noting the cool reception that the group had received in recent concerts, a magazine ran a "where are they now?" story tracking down five members of the legendary inner circle of Tigers fans, now that the boom had ended and the band were "fallen idols."[28] One month later, the same magazine breathlessly announced the band's breakup.[29]

Human Renascence suggests reasons for this outcome. The album lacks any song longer than 3 minutes, 50 seconds. Fills and solos are more likely to be played on harps, violins, or flutes than on guitars. An early review of *Human Renascence* lauds the band for shifting its focus from singles to more ambitious concept albums but also laments the fact that the backing orchestra drowns out the sound of the band members' guitar playing, "erasing with it their individualities."[30] Only two songs feature distorted guitar noise: "Flower Festival" (Rira no matsuri) and "The Broken Earth" (Wareta chikyū).[31] The songs on the LP basically follow the existing Group Sounds pattern and with only a couple of exceptions give the impression of controlled regularity, formulaic repetition rather than wild abandon.

Four songs from the album were featured in the Tigers' third feature film, *Wonderful Invitation* (Hanayaka naru shōtai; dir. Yamamoto Kunihiko), released in December 1968. A glossy musical, the film contains a fascinating sequence that directly employs guitar noise. Playing high-school dropouts who run away to Tokyo in hopes of making it as a band, the Tigers can't catch a break. To impress two girls they have met, they borrow musical equipment and rig up an electrical connection at a barn and launch into a rendition of "Flower Festival." Just before the guitar solo, however, as the guitar chords pick up in intensity, the jury-rigged electrical system overloads. The amplifiers crackle with static, then begin to smoke, and finally explode. Rather than leading to a moment of orgasmic frenzy, à la the climactic rituals of destruction that ended contemporary performances by the Who or Jimi Hendrix, in the film the Tigers and their companions flee in terror, their concert devolving into a comic shamble.

The performance is, however, recorded by one of the girls. Later in the film it is precisely the taped noise of the amplifiers distorting the guitar sounds that allows a talent agency to identify the musicians as the Tigers. This leads to their being signed to a contract. They are now on the verge of achieving commercial success, but at this point a melodramatic plot (the linchpin narrative form of mass culture, as I explore in chapter 6) erupts to provide moral cover. One of the girl fans is hit by a car as she tries to help the Tigers. She cannot pay for the surgery that her injuries require, and on the eve of their debut, the band members sell their musical gear to pay her medical bills. This threatens to derail their promised success, but of course replacement instruments appear, the debut concert takes place as scheduled, and the movie closes with a montage of film clips, still photos, and newspaper headlines (much of it documentary materials from actual Tigers shows) attesting to their ultimate success.

As should be obvious by now, both the film and the *Human Renascence* album mark attempts to appropriate elements of the new rock ideology and its iconic noise, guitar distortion, into the otherwise unchanged formula for Group Sounds. They are used, precisely, to mount an "image change" for a brand that seemed in danger of losing its market viability. As we will see later, this strategy of appropriation and neutralization was tried by a number of other musicians as well, but it ultimately led to a commercial and artistic dead end. You couldn't get to the 1970s riding this vehicle.

In 1967, Group Sounds was king of Japanese pop; by 1971, it was deader than a doornail, an embarrassment. In January 1970, guitarist Narumo Shigeru (formerly of Group Sounds band the Fingers) would denounce the genre as a "monstrosity" and vow that "what those guys in that freak of nature called Group Sounds are doing is *kayōkyoku*, that's what their audience comes to see. It has absolutely nothing to do with rock!"[32] Yet like Narumo (soon to be leader of the influential band Flied Egg), many musicians who had been central to Group Sounds were able to reinvent themselves and become successful "new rock" or "new music" artists in the 1970s. The Tigers as a band couldn't make it, but their lead singer Sawada Kenji could (albeit more as a pop star than as a rock musician). Bassist Kishibe Osami would likewise remain in the public eye—not as a musician, however, but as Kishibe Ittoku, an award-winning film actor.[33] Guitarists Morimoto Tarō and Kahashi Katsumi stayed in the music industry, although with little rock credibility: the former became a producer and the leader of "oldies" bands; the latter, a composer of theme songs for children's television programs. In contrast, drummer Hitomi Minoru announced his retirement from show business when the band broke up, declaring that he was fed up with the entertainment industry.[34]

We see similar diverging patterns in the afterlife of other Group Sounds musicians: some were reborn as 1970s rock stars, while others faded away. Mizutani Kimio of the Out Casts became a key figure in underground acid rock, and Kosaka Chū of Floral remade himself into a star of mid-1970s folk rock. But Jackie Yoshikawa and the Blue Comets ended the 1960s as a middle-of-the-road dinner-show attraction, recording inoffensive *kayōkyoku* pop ballads aimed at the adult market. Why were some artists able to make the leap from Group Sounds to rock, and others not? Which strategies worked, and which failed? Those are questions I pursue in this chapter. But first, what exactly was Group Sounds?

GROUP SOUNDS: HERE TODAY, GONE TOMORROW

The phrase "Group Sounds" (often abbreviated GS) came into popular use around March 1967.[35] Within a few months, it had become an essential keyword in Japan's teen vocabulary, with popular magazines offering special issues that promised to educate readers in all aspects of the latest craze.[36]

The phrase was new, but the phenomenon it named had already been in existence for a couple of years before the moniker emerged. The origins of Group Sounds can be traced back to the rockabilly boom discussed in chapter 3. A number of the musicians (for example, Kamayatsu Hiroshi, Mickey Curtis, and Uchida Yūya) and institutions (for example, the Watanabe Productions agency and its Nichigeki Western Carnival) central to GS debuted in the late 1950s as part of that earlier fad. An early version of GS heroes the Blue Comets, for example, backed rockabilly singer Gene Vincent during his 1959 tour of Japan.[37]

A more direct ancestor for GS was the *ereki būmu* (electric guitar boom) of the mid-1960s.[38] Successful Japanese appearances by such Western guitar groups as the Ventures (1962, as opening act for Bobby Vee on a tour of U.S. military bases, then twice in 1965 as headliners of bills aimed at Japanese audiences), as well as hit instrumentals by groups like the Tornados, Champs, and Shadows, spurred local teenagers to form their own trios and quartets to play surf, rockabilly, and other genres of early rock and roll. Increasingly, pop music was becoming a do-it-yourself project. The mass production of inexpensive electric guitars by Japanese firms like Arai, Teisco, Yamaha, Kawai, and Guyatone around this time was another important factor.[39] Soon, every high-school and university campus had its amateur *ereki* band competing for popularity with its folk music club,[40] and commercial television networks launched successful "battle of the bands" shows featuring the new sound. Given that most of the tunes played by *ereki* bands were instrumental numbers, the tricky problem of English lyrics was at least temporarily avoided.

Existing rockabilly and country-western bands also converted to the new style—in part because it was popular among audiences at their high-paying gigs in clubs serving U.S. military personnel. Terauchi Takeshi emerged quickly as the Japanese king of surf guitar, releasing a flood of popular instrumental recordings backed by his group, the Blue Jeans. Movie actor Kayama Yūzō was another popular star of the boom, slinging his guitar on silver screen and concert stage, alongside his band, the Launchers. Although *ereki* was resolutely apolitical, the sheer loudness of its amplified noise, as well as a few scandalous incidents of misbehavior, made it a target for criticism by PTA groups, school officials, and police.

Ereki began morphing into Group Sounds around 1964. The Tokyo Beatles were formed in March 1964 by a group of musicians who had been gigging at clubs on U.S. bases and who learned from their GI contacts about the Fab Four's stateside popularity.[41] Soon, *ereki* bands like the Blue Comets and the Spiders started introducing a new style, one in which vocal numbers outweighed instrumentals. Clearly influenced by the Merseybeat sound, these bands nonetheless still kept one foot in 1950s styles of rock and roll and pop. Most featured saxophones, for example, as well as polished choral harmonies. Early GS was resolutely hybrid, as the new style slowly emerged out of many competing pop genres. The Tokyo Beatles' recordings of Japanese-language covers of early Beatles hits, for example, feature big-band orchestration played primarily by jazz veterans. The Blue Comets' smash "Blue Eyes" (Aoi hitomi, 1966), which sold 500,000 copies and is sometimes claimed as the first true GS hit, is built around interweaving fills between a 1960s-sounding electronic keyboard and a 1950s-sounding sax. Tellingly, the lyrics are in Japanese (an English-language recording of the song, released a few months previously, had failed to chart for the band).[42] Visually, this first generation of GS musicians sported short haircuts and conservative matching suits, again carrying on the legacy of 1950s pop.

In this early phase, Group Sounds was just another brand of pop, open to all comers. One of the biggest hits in the new genre was recorded by none other than Misora Hibari: "Deep Red Sun" (Makka na taiyō, 1967), on which she was backed by Jackie Yoshikawa and the Blue Comets. In television performances of the tune, Hibari appeared in a miniskirt and sang the groovy lyrics and syncopated melody with restrained fire, and the song became one of her signature numbers. It also featured a pentatonic scale missing the second and sixth steps and ending on a major second interval, a scale that would become increasingly common in Group Sounds and later forms of Japanese popular music.[43]

The Blue Comets were clearly the forerunners at this early, hybrid stage. The band won the Japan Record Award for "Blue Chateau" in 1967, the same year they backed Hibari on "Deep Red Sun." The following year, they would travel to America to appear on *The Ed Sullivan Show*. But the GS style was also rapidly evolving. Already in September 1967, observers were cautioning that the Blue Comets sounded dated. Their music was dismissed by some as mere "*enka ereki*," as lacking a certain necessary "wildness" that left the band's future prospects in doubt.[44]

Group Sounds really came into its own after the live performances by the Beatles in Tokyo in the summer of 1966.[45] Jackie Yoshikawa and the Blue Comets opportunistically recorded the song "Welcome Beatles" to herald the event, but their days were numbered. With their harder sound, the Spiders (who rejected an invitation to perform as an opening act for the Beatles) were much better poised to survive. Moreover, a second generation of GS bands now emerged and quickly garnered massive popularity. Groups such as the Tigers, Carnabeats, and Tempters (usually with five or more members) played both original numbers and cover versions of Western hit songs. The saxophones disappeared, hair grew longer, and costumes became increasingly flamboyant (figure 7). Noninstrumentalist lead vocalists, standard in the first wave of GS, became rare, since guitarists and bassists were now expected to sing while they played. As with the rockabilly and *ereki* booms, the most

FIGURE 7 The jacket for *The Tempters First Album* (1968). (© Shinkō Music Entertainment Co., Ltd., Tokyo, Japan. Used by permission)

popular bands were under contract to major talent agencies, including Watanabe Productions and Hori Productions. By late 1967, GS bands had become
an omnipresent force not just on the pop music charts but also in television, radio, film, and mass magazines. Group Sounds was, to borrow Attali's
vocabulary, the dominant network holding together teen culture.

From about 1968, as we have seen, bands began expressing dissatisfaction with the manufactured image that they were required to present. As
the new rock aesthetic/ideology gained sway, a pronounced generation gap
yawned, and in the attempt to fill it a third wave of Group Sounds bands
arose, including the Mops and the Golden Cups. Their music often featured
a harder, psychedelic sound and their public images stressed rebellion and
unconventional behavior, even as they remained fixtures of the mainstream
culture industry.[46]

For example, the Mops, a group from Saitama Prefecture, were signed by
Hori Productions in 1967. Looking for an angle to garner the band attention
in the overcrowded GS field, the agency's president, recalling scenes that
he had witnessed on a recent trip to San Francisco, proposed marketing the
band as Japan's first "psychedelic" group. In November of that year, when
the Mops released their first single, "Can't Wait for Morning" (Asa made
matenai), the agency organized a press reception that it called the Mops'
LSD party. Band members showed up in flower-child clothing and handed
out small bags of dried banana peel (rumored to have a hallucinogenic effect
when smoked).[47] This sales campaign was moderately successful: the debut
single reached number 38 on the Oricon hit chart.[48] The Mops would also
participate in one of the first experiments in combining symphonic music
with rock, a 1968 joint concert with the Japan Philharmonic organized by
Ichiyanagi Toshi, a frequent collaborator with John Cage and Yoko Ono.
During the Mops' portion of the performance, they were conducted by composer Takemitsu Tōru.[49]

Despite these attempts at adaptation, however, the new rock aesthetic
ultimately spelled the end of the line for Group Sounds. GS was simply too
closely identified with what was now perceived as inauthentic, commodified
pop music: in Minamida's terms, its stress on entertainment overwhelmed
any claim it might make to artistic or outsider status. For all their noisy
bluster, the Mops' advocacy of psychedelic nonconformity was after all just

another marketing gimmick—even if, invoking the new rock ideology's con-demnation of commercialism, lead singer Suzuki Hiromitsu would boast that their records didn't really sell all that well.[50] By late 1970, most of the major GS bands had split up, and the music press had turned its attention to what was called the new rock. A few of the third-generation GS bands hung on a bit longer, but even they were finished within a year or two.[51] Group Sounds vanished as suddenly as it had appeared.

GROUP SOUNDS AND GUITAR NOISE

A large proportion of the songs recorded by Group Sounds bands were cover versions of tunes that had originally been hits for Western bands such as the Beatles, Animals, and Rolling Stones. Following a pattern set in 1950s pop, lyrics for these foreign hits were often translated into Japanese, though it was also common to retain English for chorus refrains. In addition to these cover versions, GS bands also frequently recorded original numbers, often composed by songwriting teams under contract to recording labels. These were usually formulaic *kayōkyoku*-style pop ballads, especially early in the boom, although as GS matured rock-oriented numbers featuring up-tempo beats and loud guitars became increasingly common. But even songs that leaned toward a harder rock style tended to feature easy-listening strings and vocal choruses as a kind of safety device, softening the overall effect in the direction of pop. Many GS hits were written in minor-key signatures, usually in common time, and they frequently used pentatonic scales. These features enabled numerous crossovers with other Japanese pop music genres (for example, Misora Hibari's "Deep Red Sun"). A characteristic hook seen in many GS numbers involved ending the coda unexpectedly on an emphati-cally nontonic chord, thereby generating an ambiguous effect that combined a feeling of closure with a sense of unresolved tension (although the constant repetition of this trick weakened its impact).

The formulaic quality of so many Group Sounds hits has caused the move-ment to be something of an embarrassment to critics. It is not uncommon today for canonical listings such as "The Hundred Greatest Japanese Rock Albums of All Time" to completely snub the genre. Given the cut-and-dried feel of so many studio recordings by GS bands, it is sometimes hard to fathom how they could have caused such a sensation at the time. Live recordings provide part of the answer. Albums such as *The Tigers on Stage* (1967) and *Tempters on Stage* (1969) give a much clearer sense of the excitement that the bands evoked during their heyday. Hearing proto-punk versions of such rockers as "(I Can't Get No) Satisfaction" with thousands of hysterical fans screaming in the background, we feel more clearly the electricity the bands generated, especially on the concert stage, where they were freed from the shackles of record-company executives seeking safe, surefire radio hits. But there are also many studio recordings by GS bands that have deservedly attained the status of garage-rock classics—the Mops' debut single, for example, or the Spiders' "Ban Ban Ban" (1967).

The new rock ideology that began emerging around 1968 located authenticity in the intense expression of emotion. Musically, this tendency promoted the increasing centrality of the electric guitar, because it was understood to voice keenly the emotions of the player—in rock, the guitar is perceived to be almost a vocal instrument.[52] And if there was one feature above all that defined the sound of GS, it was the electric guitar, more specifically the almost fetishistic use of distorted electric guitar noise. Rock music is, almost by definition, associated with loudness: "The rock community has reworked the *concept* of noise in a way that converts an epithet of disdain into one of achievement."[53] And distorted guitar sounds were the preferred form of rock noise. As one critic has noted, rock guitar arose in the 1950s out of a "shift that was built around the musical incorporation of tones and timbres that had previously been classified as little more than noise."[54]

In favoring feedback, fuzz, and other forms of guitar distortion, Group Sounds bands were in synchrony with recent developments in rock music abroad. As one observer has noted, "For some, rock guitar is not rock guitar without distortion."[55] Recording engineers who for decades had been refining their techniques to minimize the static noise that adhered to the recording process, moving from mechanical to electronic recording technology in the 1930s, and then to high fidelity in the 1950s, found themselves mystified in the 1960s when musicians deliberately started provoking feedback from their amplifiers. Those guitarists had realized that amplification did not simply make their instruments louder: it changed the timbre and sound that were produced, becoming a source of new musical effects that they could exploit with increasing sophistication.[56]

It is common to cite the opening of the Beatles' song "I Feel Fine" (1964) as the first deliberate use of feedback in a rock record, although this attribution says as much about our need to celebrate iconic genius figures as does about musical history.[57] In fact, many guitarists in the blues, jazz, rock, and country traditions had been toying with the possibilities for noise inadvertently generated through the processes of recording and amplification. As critic Robert Palmer has noted, "virtually every innovation associated with rock guitar playing in the 1960s can be traced back to black musicians of the middle and late 1950s."[58] Muddy Waters's blues band in Chicago, for example, had since the late 1940s been exploring the new sounds that became possible when guitars, harmonicas, and other instruments were electronically amplified, even placing the amplifiers in a tiled bathroom to produce echoes.[59] The song "Rocket 88" (1951), recorded by Ike Turner and the Kings of Rhythm, often credited as the first real rock-and-roll song, featured a distorted guitar sound that arose because one of the band's amplifiers was damaged in transit to the studio.[60] Fuzz tones date back to at least 1956, when Paul Burlison, guitarist for Johnny Burnette's Rock 'n' Roll Trio, dropped his amp and accidentally loosened one of the tubes inside—a sound he exploited on the group's recording of "Train Kept A-Rollin'" (1956).[61]

Significantly, the sources for this new noise—the technologies of recording and amplification—were the very means that made possible the emergence of music as a mass-culture form: these technologies made it feasible for corporations to sells songs in enormous quantities, whether via prerecorded media or large-scale concerts.[62] In other words, the new noise that rock guitarists began widely exploiting in the 1960s was as much a product of the business model of pop music as it was auditory in nature. This was due in part to the centrality of the recording process to rock music, in which amplifiers and other equipment took on as central a role in producing the sound as did the actual instruments.[63] Amplifiers, tape decks, and the recording studio became prime musical instruments.

The one recording that seems to have startled Japanese guitarists into taking notice of the new guitar sound was "(I Can't Get No) Satisfaction" (1965). The Rolling Stones recorded several takes of the tune before they got the guitar sound they wanted, using Keith Richards's new fuzz device.[64] Japanese GS guitarists struggled to capture this electrifying new noise. The Dynamites began purposely miswiring their amps, producing similar results, but at the risk of electrocuting the guitarist; the Blue Jeans tried poking holes in their speakers; the Launchers rigged up their own homemade proto–fuzz boxes.[65] Rock historian Kurosawa Susumu identifies the Blue Comets' "Crying Guitar" (Namida no gitā, 1966) as the first confirmed use of a fuzz box in a Japanese recording. The model the band used had originally been purchased by the Spiders' guitarist Kamayatsu Hiroshi on a trip to the United States, but Kamayatsu could never make the device work. He lent it to the Blue Comets' guitarist Mihara Tsunaki, who managed to figure it out. Soon, Acetone was manufacturing a copycat model of the device for the Japanese market, and before long every GS band was featuring fuzz boxes, along with other effects—wah-wah pedals, string bending, heavy echo and reverb, overloaded amps, flanging, feedback—that would produce cool-sounding guitar noise.[66] It sometimes took recording engineers by surprise: the Mops' guitarist Hoshi Katsu reported that at the recording session for the band's debut single, the producer (who obviously had never heard a fuzz box) came running out of the control room to order him to fix his broken speaker.[67] The Spiders' lead guitarist, Inoue Takayuki, reports a similar incident when he overloaded his amp during a recording session for the band's major-label debut single.[68]

Distorted electric guitar sounds not only sounded cool, but were radical. That is to say, they were "noise" in Attali's sense of the word. They proclaimed rebellion not only against the aesthetic codes that defined beauty in music but also against the social order and morality. Advocates of the new rock ideology celebrated the link between aggressively distorted guitar noise and political radicalism, both inside and outside Japan: to them, guitar feedback sounded authentic, artistic, and revolutionary.

The Jacks, for example, released their debut single, "Vacant World" (Karappo no sekai), in March 1968, followed six months later by their first album.[69] Led by vocalist and guitarist Hayakawa Yoshio, the band never enjoyed commercial success, but its impact on the pop music scene, both at the time and in subsequent years, was incalculable. The Jacks began as a campus folk group in 1965. They began attracting critical notice for their strikingly dark original numbers after they played a series of folk jamborees, theatrical events, and radio and television appearances. Eventually the group signed a record deal.[70] Blurring the boundary between folk and rock, as well as between the commercial music industry (they were signed originally to the DOT Productions talent agency) and the anticapitalist realm of underground art, they received wide coverage in the music press. A July 1968 article previewing their upcoming debut album in *Music Life*, for example, compared the Jacks with the Rolling Stones and Bob Dylan and praised Hayakawa for his poetic lyrics and his "passionate singing."[71] A review of the band's second single, "Marianne," in the same issue vowed that the band was producing "a new Japan-based pops (?) capable of being appreciated by adults" and lamented that the Jacks had yet to win the popularity they deserved: "In terms of its hit potential, the record might not be a success by industry standards, but if we consider it in terms of the essence of song, it seems close to ideal."[72] Later that year, the journal celebrated the band's debut album as "epochal," declaring it an unprecedented expression of the emotions of contemporary youth: "Our latent feelings toward life and love, and the vital force and sexual passions that accompany these: the Jacks do nothing but sing these out without any ornamentation. This sounds so fresh, like nothing we've heard before and attracts so many sympathizers because we are already castrated beings, isolated elements crushed under the enormous power that is society, and because up until now we'd been living each day so neat and prim, hearing only pretty, soft songs."[73]

The Jacks generated a loud, harsh noise. Hayakawa's vocal technique "is better called screaming than singing."[74] Their tunes, though melodic, were often dissonant and carried unusual time signatures, and minor-key compositions had never sounded so morbid. Hayakawa once described his musical philosophy: "The essence of songs is not to make us forget our sadness; it is to make us not forget our sadness." Moreover, "after all, it is not a question of whether a song is conveyed or not conveyed; what's crucial is that the person who sings is conveyed."[75] "Marianne," the opening track of the debut album (a different version from the debut single) presents 5 minutes, 20 seconds of barely organized chaos. After a jazzy drum flourish at the opening, a rhythm guitar kicks in, and for the rest of the song it provides the only sense of order, incessantly strumming a simple two-chord pattern fixed in a relentless ¾ rhythm. Around this crude structure, all hell breaks loose: the drums and acoustic bass toss out fluid, swirling patterns that refuse to stay on the beat. Hayakawa wails lyrics (written for the band by poet Aizawa Yasuko) about death, alienation, and doomed love. Above all, Mizuhashi Haruo's distorted lead guitar dominates the track with a powerful, almost overwhelming noise that seemed to point the way to the future of Japanese rock.

In "Marianne" and other remarkable songs, the Jacks suggested a link between guitar noise and social critique. These hints were amplified into overt manifesto by another band, Hadaka no Rallize (or, as the band is also known in bogus French, Les Rallizes Dénudés).[76] Founded at Dōshisha University in Kyoto in late 1967 by guitarist/songwriter Mizutani Takeshi, the band's appearances at underground festivals quickly became legendary, even as it refused to participate in the capitalist music industry, its recordings circulating only on erratically distributed underground labels or as bootlegs. A typical Hadaka no Rallize song would begin with a minor-chord pattern strummed on the guitar; it would end twenty minutes later in "total sensory assault,"[77] an explosion of howling feedback and other distorted guitar noises, with all existing musical codes lying in a heap of rubble. The band not only sang about revolutionary insurgency, but made good on its promise: original bassist Wakabayashi Moriaki was one of the Japanese Red Army Faction militants who in 1970 hijacked Japan Airlines Flight 351 to North Korea. Guitar noise in this guise became part of a general rethinking circa 1968 of the relationship between politics and violence.[78]

Even the kings of GS pop could not ignore the tantalizing new noise that was erupting outside their castle walls. Virtually all GS bands made attempts to capture the guitar distortion, but only some succeeded. In the remainder of this chapter, I take up three case studies, musicians who launched musical and political strategies to transform the new noise into useful musical code, to remake the artistic and political network of Japanese popular music. Which ones were able to turn the corner into 1970s rock, and why?

CASE STUDY 1: TERAUCHI TAKESHI

In June 1967, at the peak of the Group Sounds boom, a popular magazine ran an article proposing an all-star dream GS band, and there was no controversy among the selection committee over whom to pick for lead guitar: Terauchi Takeshi.[79] The same year, another critic declared, "Terauchi's guitar is the best in Japan. No, in fact, I guarantee he's the best in the world," and lamented that fans at his concerts were too busy screaming to sufficiently appreciate his technique.[80] Narumo Shigeru in his 1970 screed against GS for derailing Japanese rock nonetheless had kind words for Terauchi's early *ereki* band: "That weird monstrosity called GS has blocked the way and rock is no longer understood in Japan. Things were better before. Back when the old Blue Jeans used to run around the Nichigeki stage as if it were too small to hold them, it was really manly, powerful: you could hear rock in Japan back then."[81]

Despite his godlike status, Terauchi is one of the GS figures who did not make the leap to 1970s rock. This seems odd. For example, many of Terauchi's bandmates and protégées during the *ereki* and GS booms went on to become major figures in new rock a decade later. "Joe" Yamanaka of Flower Travellin' Band had been a member of the GS group 491 managed by Terauchi, while singer Uchida Yūya (a central figure in the 1970s "rock in Japanese" debate discussed in chapter 5) was an early vocalist for the Blue Jeans.[82] Terauchi himself continued to record prolifically and to appear live throughout the 1970s and beyond, including a successful tour of the Soviet Union in 1976. But his post-1970 record-jacket photos often depict him and his band wearing tuxedos, clean-shaven, and with neat haircuts. His later musical output consisted largely of instrumental versions of contemporary pop hits aimed at an adult audience. While still widely respected for his guitar prowess, Terauchi after 1970 had increasingly little connection to youth culture and its dominant rock ideology.

Terauchi was born in 1939 in Tochigi Prefecture. He received his first guitar at the age of five, and his initial musical instruction came from his mother, a music teacher who specialized in traditional samisen and *kouta* songs. Wanting a louder sound even as a boy, Terauchi experimented by rigging up various electronic speakers to his guitar (his father owned an electronics store).[83] Recruited by composer Koga Masao, he briefly enrolled at Meiji University, intending to join its famous mandolin club, founded by Koga before the war.[84] In his teens, he began playing gigs at U.S. military bases to earn cash, and in 1959 he joined the country-western band Crazy West, where Mickey Curtis was one of his bandmates. In 1960, Terauchi switched to a country-western outfit, Jimmy Tokita and the Mountain Playboys, and with them he made his recording debut.[85] Kamayatsu Hiroshi of the Spiders remembers seeing Terauchi play in country-western bands at American base clubs in the mid-1950s, when the guitarist's showcase number was a medley including all forty-eight U.S. state songs—GIs would stand and cheer when they heard their home state's tune.[86]

In 1962, Terauchi formed a new band, the Blue Jeans. Signed by Watanabe Productions, they appeared with singer Uchida Yūya at the Nichigeki Western Carnival in January 1963. Undergoing intense choreographic training based on the film *West Side Story*, the band developed an engaging performance style.[87] The early lineup was composed of jazz-scene veterans and featured a saxophone, but that was quickly replaced with a second—and then a third—guitar. The band's original upright bass and acoustic piano likewise gave way to electric models. When the *ereki* boom took off, the Blue Jeans were poised to become Japan's most popular band. Between 1963 and 1966, when Terauchi left the band, the Blue Jeans released no fewer than sixteen LPs and eleven singles, almost all their recorded material built around Terauchi's lightning-quick guitar playing.[88]

Terauchi next moved to join the ongoing Group Sounds boom, setting up his own management agency in the process. Gathering together amateur musicians who had been active on the Yokohama club circuit, he formed the Bunnys, a five-piece group that made its recording debut in late 1966. Their first hit came in 1967 with "Let's Go Shake," a vocal pop number that contains elements reminiscent of the Trashmen's "Surfin' Bird" (1963). A string of hits followed, and the group became the house band on a popular television show, where they appeared alongside such pop icons as the Peanuts and Crazy Cats. In 1968, the ever restless Terauchi once again moved on, forming a new version of the Blue Jeans, his old *ereki* band. The Bunnys soldiered on, with Terauchi occasionally returning for guest appearances, until finally disbanding in 1971.[89] Even after leaving the Bunnys, Terauchi remained remarkably prolific, releasing five singles and six albums in 1970 alone. But, as mentioned, in the new decade he would bear an increasingly tenuous relationship to youth culture and its rock ideology.[90]

A number of the singles released by Terauchi Takeshi and the Bunnys prominently feature guitar distortion. Oddly, the single "Feedback Guitar"

(1969) is not among them: it's a rather tame instrumental featuring Terau-chi playing Ventures-style glissandos, with no obvious instances of feedback. But on other recordings, Terauchi captures the new sound brilliantly. For example, "Summer Boogaloo" (1968), a B side, reworks the riff and distorted guitar sound of the Kinks' hit "You Really Got Me" (1964). Other tracks from the period are even more startling. Terauchi employs the whole range of effects available—fuzz boxes, heavy reverb, overloaded amps, and perhaps actual feedback—to produce a genuinely harsh and cutting guitar sound on such tracks as "Let's Go Shake," "Devil's Baby" (Akuma no bebī, 1967), and "Twilight" (Tasogare, 1969). In addition to his work as a guitarist, Terauchi innovated as a studio engineer: his 1968 production of the Phoenix's debut single, "La La La in Love" (Koi suru ra ra ra) is said to mark the first use of a wah-wah pedal on a Japanese recording.[91]

In other words, in terms of sheer playing ability, Terauchi quickly mas-tered the devices and skills required to produce the new guitar noise. Despite his technical brilliance, he was unable—or perhaps unwilling—to carry out the changes in style and sound that were demanded by the new rock ideol-ogy. The stinging fuzz-box sound that Terauchi lays down on "Twilight," for example, weaves in and out of the main melody, a minor-key pop ballad that features you-broke-my-heart lyrics and orchestration built around mainly easy-listening strings. However radical sounding its distorted guitar fills, the song faithfully reproduces the conventional pattern for GS. Similarly, "Let's Go Boogaloo" lifts the riff and guitar style from Jimi Hendrix's "Spanish Castle Music," only to frame the noise in a 3 minute, 16 second teen dance number, complete with a girls' chorus calling out the dance-step rhythms. The frenetic "Flowers of the Sun" (Taiyō no hana), a number 10 hit on the Oricon charts in 1968, gives a feel of constant acceleration and even features a heavily filtered screaming voice laid over a wildly fuzz-boxed guitar solo—but chaos gives way to prim order with each return of the chorus and its 1950s-style vocal harmonies.

These records show that Terauchi knew how to make all the right noises. But he steadfastly refused to pursue the new musical and political network that 1960s guitar noise seemed to prophesy. Critic Robert Christgau once de-fined rock as "all music derived primarily from the energy and influence of the Beatles—and maybe Bob Dylan, and maybe you should stick pretensions in there someplace."[92] In Terauchi's GS recordings, we can hear traces of the Beatles and even of Dylan. What we don't find are pretensions. Terauchi failed to claim either artistic or outsider status for his music. He rejected the affectations of the new ideology, eschewing its self-contradictory claim to transcend the very mass culture that was rock's condition of possibility. He preferred to keep things honest, recording three-minute pop songs that delivered solid entertainment value. He ignored the barrier the new ideology attempted to place around rock, distinguishing its putative authenticity from the falsity of other pop genres. Like jazz composer Hattori Ryōichi (chapter 1), Terauchi was more interested in crossing boundaries that separated musical genres. Terauchi also eschewed the image of rebellion: in 1974, he launched a musical crusade, playing concerts at more than a thousand Japanese high schools to prove that the electric guitar was a respectable musical instrument, one that should not be linked to notions of juvenile delinquency.[93] The outcome for Terauchi was that while he remained the iconic "god of the electric guitar" in the 1970s, the label transformed largely into the object of an affectionate nostalgia. He placed the new guitar noise within the existing musical code, the GS formula, with often brilliant results, but his very skillfulness in exploiting that formula disqualified him from becoming a 1970s rock star.

The indefatigable Terauchi experimented early on with other techniques that pointed the way to the 1970s. With both the Blue Jeans and the Bunnys, he recorded numerous *ereki* adaptations of chestnuts from the classical repertoire—Beethoven's Fifth Symphony, for example, and Schubert's "Unfinished Symphony" (the A and B sides, respectively, of a 1967 single). Later progressive rock groups and new-music artists would repeat this gesture, attempting to certify the artistic value of rock by linking it to the classical canon. Despite this apparent similarity, Terauchi's electrified versions of the classics are marked above all by a characteristic lack of pretension. The well-known melodies simply provide Terauchi more opportunities to display his guitar pyrotechnics in highly commercial settings. In a 1996 interview, he reminisced about those recordings: "I liked to take on the challenge of songs that made me think, that's it! You needed techniques to master them, so I developed them. That's what I liked to do, and I didn't care about genres."[94] Rather than provide a lofty sheen of artistic value, the familiar tunes become the opportunities for pop novelty and spectacular virtuosity.

Similarly, Terauchi also recorded a number of songs that feature GS adaptations of traditional Japanese folk music. The Bunnys' single "Tsugaru jongara bushi" (1967) showcases a musical duel between Terauchi on electric guitar and Mihashi Michiya on samisen. Another single from the same year, "The Temple Solicitation Book" (Kanjinchō), presents an *ereki*-style adaptation of a *nagauta* that had long been sung in the Kabuki theater. Many *ereki* songs by Terauchi and others employ a pentatonic scale that is shared with older Japanese *minyō* folk songs.[95] The tenuous authenticity of Japanese rock music could easily be augmented by appeals to the authenticity of Japanese cultural tradition, thereby satisfying the demands of the rock ideology for the music to be "real." This was the strategy used, for example, by Terauchi's old bandmate Mickey Curtis, who spent the late 1960s performing in Europe with his new band, the Samurais. Their sound increasingly incorporated orientalist elements, as witnessed in their progressive rock album *Samurai* (1970). The lyrics, all in English, repeatedly stress traditional Japanese themes, and the music also repeatedly alludes to traditional Japanese musical instruments and forms. In interviews he gave after returning to Japan in 1970, Curtis bewailed the imitation that marked Japanese rock and claimed that his band had won over European fans by its originality.[96] Originality in this case meant, oddly enough, sounding like other Japanese musical traditions.

By appealing to the authenticity of national culture, veteran Mickey Curtis was able to make a place for himself in 1970s rock, but as usual, Terauchi's emphasis lay elsewhere. His refusal to pay obeisance to the new values of the rock ideology, even as he had mastered its characteristic noise, meant he would be shut out from the new geopolitical and aesthetic network that rock music established in the 1970s. As Terauchi Takeshi jokes in his 2000 autobiography, he takes pride in having achieved the status of "living fossil."[97]

CASE STUDY 2: KAMAYATSU HIROSHI OF THE SPIDERS

Along with the Tigers and the Tempters, the Spiders were one of the most popular bands of the Group Sounds boom. Led by drummer Tanabe Shōchi, a veteran of the 1950s country-western and rockabilly scene, the earliest version of the group was formed in 1961. Playing gigs in hotel lounges, in nightclubs, and on U.S. military bases, they featured a repertoire that included pop, jazz, *ereki*, and other styles—including Hawaiian, chanson, and other forms of musical exotica. A series of member changes took place until 1964, when the group finally settled into the seven-man roster with which it would achieve success. In this version, the Spiders featured two lead vocalists, Sakai Masaaki and Inoue Jun, as well as "Monsieur" Kamayatsu Hiroshi, who sometimes sang lead and also served as the band's primary songwriter.[98]

The Spiders were one of the first Japanese bands to discover and adapt the new Merseybeat sound. Shortly after the album *Meet the Beatles* (1964) was released in the United States, Kamayatsu discovered a copy in the record bins at the Tokyo American Pharmacy. Powerfully taken by the music, he introduced his bandmates to the album. Almost overnight, the Spiders changed musical direction. They began featuring Beatles covers in their act and became noted for their rapid ability to master new Beatle releases, inserting them into their live sets even before the original versions had time to climb the charts. With the timely change in style, attendance at the band's live gigs rapidly increased.[99]

Around this time, at the request of the band's management agency, Kamayatsu began trying his hand at composing. The first song he came up with, "Furi Furi," served as the Spiders' debut single in 1965, and though it didn't sell well at the time, the song would eventually become a classic of Japanese garage rock. The tune is built around a simple three-chord guitar riff, for which Kamayatsu developed a distinctive technique, holding down the tremolo bar while he banged the body of the guitar against his midsection as he strummed the chords. The most memorable feature of the song is its rhythm. According to Kamayatsu, the inspiration came from the 3-3-7 rhythm of unison clapping that Japanese use to mark the end of a party or similar event. "Furi Furi" adapts this into a strongly pronounced one-two-THREE-(pause) beat that is first established with clapping hands in the intro, and then picked up by the rhythm section as the song proper kicks in. The rhythm worked so well that Kamayatsu used it again on the song that provided the Spiders' first minor hit, the ballad "No No Boy" (1966).[100]

The band's first major hit came with the uncharacteristic "Sad Sunset" (Yūyake ga naite iru, 1966), a minor-key *kayōkyoku*-style ballad composed for the band at its record label's behest by hit maker Hamaguchi Kuranosuke.

Despite its soft feel, the record featured a distorted fuzz guitar. The Spiders' debut LP, *The Spiders Album No. 1* (1966), remains a landmark work in the history of Japanese rock and roll and provides a more representative instance of the band's sound than does "Sad Sunset." Unusual for a GS band, the album features all original compositions, many with English lyrics (including a new English-language version of "Furi Furi"), and many of them written by Kamayatsu. (By contrast, the group's second album, rushed out one month later, consists entirely of cover versions of Western hits, including six Beatles numbers on side 1.) The twelve songs include both ballads and up-tempo numbers; all are built around guitar riffs, and most feature vocal harmonies in the Merseybeat style.

In addition to their early predilection for original compositions, the Spiders were also unusual among GS bands in that, after an original tie-in with Hori Productions, they set up their own management company, Spiductions. The band became a regular on a television variety show, helping it build a national audience. The Spiders also opened for a number of Western groups on their tours of Japan in 1965 and 1966, including Peter and Gordon, the Animals, the Honeycombs, and the Beach Boys. Famously, they turned down an invitation to appear on the opening bill for the Beatles' Tokyo concerts in 1966.[101] The band toured Europe in 1966, including an appearance on the BBC's *Ready Steady Go!* television program. This overseas trip was ostensibly intended to promote "Sad Sunset," which had been released in a number of countries there, though in reality the primary aim of the tour (as with Misora Hibari and Kasagi Shizuko's 1950 American tours, discussed in chapter 2) was to improve the Spiders' image in Japan. In an interview published just before their departure, leader Tanabe asserted that the tour would show they were not just Beatle imitators but had their own identity: "Made-in-Japan Beatles? I hate it when they call us that. We're the Spiders!" He vowed that "we won't give up our own originality" in performances for European audiences.[102] In another predeparture interview, Tanabe expressed his hopes that the tour would raise the band's image (and income) in Japan.[103] The following year, the band would play a concert in Hawaii as well as make media appearances in Los Angeles.[104]

The Spiders continued to enjoy hits through the mid-1960s. As with other GS bands, though, they found their popularity waning after 1968. In May

1970, Tanabe announced that he was leaving the group to devote himself full time to the talent-management business. The band recruited a replacement drummer, but this was short-lived. By year's end, the group had decided to disband, and they played their farewell shows early in 1971 in the Nichigeki Western Carnival. Kamayatsu would later recall, "In the changeover from the 1960s to the 1970s, culture and music and everything was changing, and [our breakup] was just a reaction to that."[105]

By the time of their demise, the Spiders had released twenty singles and a dozen LPs. A number of their recordings feature fuzz boxes and other kinds of distorted guitar noise, including their cover versions of "Balla Balla" and "Give Me Some Lovin'" (both included on *The Spiders Album No. 4* [1967]). Among the leading GS bands, the Spiders were perhaps the most consistently ambitious in terms of musical aesthetic. As leader Tanabe told an interviewer in 1967 in response to a question about the future of GS, "I've never thought about Group Sounds as a whole. But for us, we just need to keep growing. I don't think we always want to just be teen idols."[106] A 1967 article praised the Spiders for their rebellious attitudes and their ability to express individual feelings in their music, in contrast to other GS bands: "They don't leave their emotions dragging behind them. It's a sharp contrast with the Blue Comets. For them, the individuality of the members is the top priority."[107]

Perhaps the band's most impressive recorded legacy is their album *100 Years of Meiji, 7 Years of the Spiders* (*Meiji hyaku-nen, Supaidāsu shichi-nen*, 1968). With a striking cover image depicting the famous twelve-story tower in Asakusa, a symbol of Japan's new modern culture during the Meiji period (1868–1912), the album aims to present a unified artistic whole, even if it is not actually a concept album. Side 1 includes seven songs, with each member of the band contributing an original composition and singing lead vocal on it. An early review praised the way "the different tastes of these songs express clearly the individualities" of the various members.[108]

The album offers evidence of the band's growing musical ambitions in other ways, too. On "Mr. Tax" (clearly inspired by the Beatles' "Taxman"), Kamayatsu plays all the instruments, including an electric sitar, and employs filters to distort his vocals, playing creatively with the possibilities for noise generated by the recording process. Other tracks feature an assortment of musical modes, including R&B–style horns, Dixieland jazz, and Chuck Berry–style rock and roll. The album begins with the sounds of a symphony tuning up (reminiscent of the opening of *Sgt. Pepper's Lonely Hearts Club Band*), and it includes spoken-word or musical passages as linking interludes between tracks. Some of these incidental pieces feature trite piano tunes in which the surface hiss and pops inadvertently produced through the recording process are deliberately foregrounded. On the second side of the album, the song "End of Love" features a guitar sound reminiscent of that of Jimi Hendrix (whose "Stone Free" provides the tune's model), a psychedelic-style shifting of volume back and forth between the right and left stereo channels, and even a touch of genuine guitar feedback at the fadeout. The album closes on straightforward modern jazz with "Blues for Wes," an instrumental composed by keyboardist Ōno Katsuo to celebrate jazz guitarist Wes Montgomery. *100 Years of Meiji, 7 Years of the Spiders* achieves a level of complexity that makes it a landmark album of 1960s Japanese pop.[109] It suggests how quickly the band was internalizing the newly emerging rock ideology and its aesthetic principles.

Nonetheless, the Spiders had to disband in order to move beyond 1960s GS. After the band's dissolution, singers Inoue Jun and Sakai Masaaki would remain in the public eye, but primarily as television personalities. Drummer Tanabe Shōchi remained a music industry executive, keyboardist Ōno Katsuo became a successful songwriter (composing, among other works, some of former Tiger Sawada Kenji's biggest solo hits), while bassist Katō Mitsuru largely abandoned the music business. Lead guitarist Inoue Takayuki and rhythm guitarist Kamayatsu Hiroshi were the most successful at re-creating themselves in the world of 1970s rock. Inoue scored a major hit in 1972 with the guitar-based instrumental theme for the popular television police drama *Howl at the Sun!* (*Taiyō ni hoero!*), starring Ishihara Yūjirō (see chapter 6) and former Tempters singer Hagiwara "Shōken" Ken'ichi.

Kamayatsu's reinvention of himself in the 1970s was even more successful. "Monsieur" Kamayatsu would remain one of Japanese rock's most respected elder statesmen for several more decades. In the 1980s and 1990s, he would record with such rising young superstars as Komuro Tetsuya and Oyamada Keigo (better known as Cornelius). Kamayatsu's ability to adapt to changing musical styles from the 1950s to the present day (he is still releasing new CDs as of this writing in 2010) while retaining a characteristic personal style makes him one of the most fascinating figures in Japanese rock history.

Kamayatsu was born in Tokyo in 1939, the son of a Los Angeles–born Japanese American jazz musician who married a local woman after moving to Japan in 1929 to seek a musical career.[110] Raised in a musical family, Kamayatsu took voice lessons at the jazz music school his father established, alongside such future rockabilly stars as Mickey Curtis and Hirao Masaaki, and in his mid-teens he began singing for local country-western bands in gigs at jazz coffeehouses and U.S. military clubs.[111] He turned pro in 1958 with the Wagon Masters, a country-western group led by Kosaka Kazuya.[112] Kamayatsu also began recording rockabilly numbers around this time, though he writes in his autobiography that he never really felt at home with that genre: he always felt himself more a country-western singer.[113] He signed a record contract with the Teichiku label in 1960 and released a series of singles, many of them covers of American rockabilly and pop hits (including "G.I. Blues," as we saw in chapter 3), but with little commercial success.

In 1962, he spent several months in the United States, performing nightclub shows in Hawaii, visiting his father's relatives in Los Angeles, and hanging out at jazz clubs in New York City. Soon after he returned to Japan, he began sitting in as a guest vocalist with the band known at that point as Tanabe Shōchi and the Spiders. Before long, he became a full-fledged member.

Kamayatsu may well have been the first Japanese musician to fully grasp the new music style introduced by the Beatles. Terauchi Takeshi cites Kamayatsu's composition "No No Boy" (1966) as the first Japanese original composition to capture the new sound.[114] In his autobiography, Kamayatsu reflects on the early reception of the Beatles in Japan:

> The Japanese entertainment and music worlds' understanding of the movement launched by English beat groups like the Beatles was shallow [ama-katta]. Words like counterculture had yet to appear, but even so, watching the response of the Japanese entertainment world, I would mutter to myself, "No, that's not it."
>
> Their stance, their way of thinking about music was fundamentally different. That Western way of thinking about music didn't enter Japan until the

1970s. When I think about it now, except for a small number of people, the 1960s Japan music world was, at least on this point, incredibly primitive.[115]

Later, he reflects, "From around 1970, I heard bands like the Grateful Dead, and I started to have at least some understanding of the philosophy that lay behind the hippie movement. You couldn't play the music without that philosophy. From fashion to philosophy to lifestyle, without adopting it all you couldn't make that sound. Around the time I started encountering the culture shock of Jimi Hendrix's avant-garde rock, I realized that the Spiders were finished."[116] In 1969, while still a member of the band, Kamayatsu helped organize a concert at a Tokyo club featuring the Jacks, folksinger Okabayashi Nobuyasu (backed by the members of what would become Happy End), and other underground acts. Around this time, he also recorded his first solo album, *Monsieur* (1970). As this album indicated, Kamayatsu was increasingly attracted to acoustic music: his reaction to guitar noise, as we will see, was increasingly to move away from it.

Things Will Work Out Somehow (*Dō ni ka naru sa*, 1971), his second solo album, was another largely acoustic collection, with new songs that included lyrics reflecting the situation of Japanese youth culture in the wake of the failure of the 1970 AMPO protests. Kamayatsu also began playing gigs at college festivals on campuses that were still hotbeds of radical politics and protest, sharing the bill with such underground folk-rock acts as Mikami Kan, Asakawa Maki, and Brain Police (Zunō Keisatsu):[117] "Whenever I played a campus festival concert, something was bound to happen. Up until then, I'd been living with absolutely no connection to the student movement, and so it had a huge impact on me. To tell you the truth, I was shocked." [118] He also played the Third Nakatsugawa Folk Jamboree, a legendary 1971 event that devolved into chaos when young political activists occupied the stage in protest to the commercialization of the festival.[119]

In 1971, he recorded an album with his father, Tadashi "Tib" Kamayatsu, taking advantage of the elder Kamayatsu's native English on cover versions of songs by Free and the Animals. He also recorded with folk superstar Yoshida Takurō, who composed the title song for Kamayatsu's album *To My Dear Friends* (*Waga yoki tomo yo*, 1975). That song, which features striking guitar work by Takanaka Masayoshi, became one of Kamayatsu's biggest hits, with the single selling some 900,000 copies. It became one of Kamayatsu's sig-nature numbers, as did the B side of the single, "Have You Ever Smoked a Gauloises?" (Gorowāzu wo sutta koto ga aru kai), on which Kamayatsu was backed by the American funk band Tower of Power.

He spent the remainder of the 1970s as an independent artist and pro-ducer, releasing critically acclaimed records that generally enjoyed only mod-erate sales.[120] In subsequent decades, Kamayatsu would retain the status of Japanese rock's elder statesman, continuing to work with rising young art-ists and producers. In sum, Kamayatsu was able to make the transition from 1960s Group Sounds to 1970s rock. His GS background did not prevent him from acquiring legitimacy under the new rock ideology; in fact, Kamayatsu has continually revisited his Spiders compositions in later decades, reworking them in creative fashion as part of his artistic legacy.

What were the strategies that allowed him to make this turn? Kamayatsu was clearly aware of the new guitar noise. In his 2002 autobiography, he writes,

> In those days, the Who used to slam guitars into their amps and kick their drum kit to pieces. Jeff Beck used to smash his guitar. Those kinds of violent performances really felt like "rock." I mean, it was so cool when Jimi Hen-drix sprinkled lighter fluid on his guitar and set it on fire. Back then, in the period from the 1960s to the 1970s, that was what rock was all about.
>
> The Spiders sometimes used to imitate the Who, smashing our guitars on stage. I never used my own favorite guitars for this, only ones supplied by our sponsors. I hereby apologize to all guitar makers.[121]

Yet guitar noise was not the primary strategy that Kamayatsu employed in reinventing himself. In 1970, shortly after returning from a visit to England and France, he commented on the rock concerts he had seen in Europe: "In general, the sound there is too loud. It felt like instead of trying to have us listen, they were trying to knock us out [yowaseru; literally, "intoxicate us"]. In Johnny Winter's performance, one guy was using six Wembley amps. When I saw Blue Cheer last year, the lead guitarist alone had eighteen amps. It was just too much. I didn't like it."

In the same 1970 article, he also rejects the notion of trying to achieve rock authenticity by including exotic orientalist elements, the strategy deployed by Mickey Curtis and the Samurais: "To clumsily include Japanese-sounding elements only makes matters worse. It just doesn't fit the image." Still a member of the Spiders at this point, Kamayatsu says that the band hopes to undergo a radical transformation and undertake "really interesting" projects—but also notes how hard it is to shed an established image: "I recently saw the Dave Clark Five on TV and was really disappointed. They may feel they've changed, but in the end, it's hard to erase the image everyone already has of them inside their heads."[122]

After the Spiders broke up, Kamayatsu did successfully change his image. Instead of becoming noisier, though, he became quieter. His solo albums show him reinventing himself as a 1970s-style singer-songwriter with a softer sound, one closer to his roots as a country-western singer. The cover of *Monsieur*, his debut solo album, features a soft-focus black-and-white photograph of Kamayatsu wearing a heavy coat and sun glasses; below the image appear in English the words "composed, played, sung & produced by Monsieur" (figure 8). The album does include some passages of loud, distorted guitar noise (the opening number "Paper Ashtray," for example), but these are relatively scarce and mixed at relatively low volume. More predominant throughout the LP is a quiet feeling. The widespread use of a subtle echo effect on both vocal and instrumental tracks and the tendency to favor unadorned musical arrangements give a sense that these recordings are the product of a solitary man working late at night in a deserted studio (which, in fact, describes accurately the circumstances under which much of the album was produced). One critic praised the "private feel" of the release, noting that it sounded more like a collection of demos rather than a polished album.[123] With the exception of guest vocalists who join him on several tracks, Kamayatsu treated the album as a one-man project, playing all the instruments and singing all the songs. (*Monsieur* appeared before Paul McCartney's similarly produced solo debut album.)

Three of the tracks included on *Monsieur* were previously released under the Spiders' name but actually recorded as one-man projects by Kamayatsu (including "Mr. Tax," discussed earlier). The remaining numbers include

COMPOSED, PLAYED, SUNG & PRODUCED BY

MONSIEUR

FIGURE 8 The jacket for Kamayatsu Hiroshi's debut solo album, *Monsieur* (1970). (© Shinkō Music Entertainment Co., Ltd., Tokyo, Japan. Used by permission)

new material (all composed by Kamayatsu, although some of the lyrics were written by others), as well as re-recordings of songs he had originally written for the Spiders. In each case, the songs are transformed by the context and recording style into intensely personal statements: the album skillfully gives the sense that we are overhearing a private self-to-self conversation. In this way, despite the relative paucity of guitar noise on the album, Kamayatsu was able to meet the new rock aesthetic's demand that music provide a unique personal and artistic expression rooted in the authentic genius of the performer.

When we compare, for example, the original 1966 Spiders' recording of "No No Boy" to the remake that appears on the 1970 solo album, we find that the latter is a stripped-down version, as if the song were being reduced to its bare bones. The polished multipart harmonies of the earlier version are largely absent (although there are a couple of points in the later interpretation where simple harmony parts are overdubbed); the vocals by Kamayatsu and guest singer Fukuzawa Emi in the remake are restrained and deliberately flattened, while the pedal steel guitar of the original is replaced by comparatively plain fills played on a regular electric guitar. The effect of all these changes is to transform a successful product of mid-1960s GS commodity culture into a 1970s artistic statement that seems to express the individual personality of Kamayatsu. The center of gravity had shifted from a 1960s stress on music as generating a sense of community to a 1970s mode in which songs seemed to circulate through a mode of seemingly personal, one-on-one communication from singer to listener.[124]

The reinterpretation of "Lonely Man" produces a similar effect when compared with the original Spiders' recordings of the song. The orchestral strings are dropped, and we are left with what feels like an unadorned, sincere version of the song. Two other tracks on *Monsieur* include guest vocalists who highlight the personal nature of the statement being made. "My Heart Beats Dum! Dum!" (Boku no hāto wa dan! dan!) features Kamayatsu's father, Tadashi. "Monsieur & Tarō," originally released under the Spiders' name in 1969, features Kamayatsu singing over recordings of his infant son, Kamayatsu Tarō, crying. The comical lyrics depict a father's desperate attempts to keep his baby happy. This pair of father–son duets drives home the point that the album expresses Kamayatsu's own experiences and his unique perspective on life.

Ironically, guitarist Kamayatsu Hiroshi—one of the first Japanese musicians to hear the noise of the coming musical revolution and to feel a pressing need to transcend the limitations of Group Sounds—successfully made the turn to 1970s rock by turning away from guitar noise. He continued to enjoy moderate commercial success in the 1970s and beyond, but as he notes in his autobiography, it was more satisfying to him that he was able to preserve a sense of aesthetic integrity. This allowed him to meet the demands of the new rock ideology—even though his solo music contained barely a hint of political rebellion.

CASE STUDY 3: FROM THE TEMPTERS TO PYG TO VODKA COLLINS WITH ŌGUCHI HIROSHI

If the Tigers were the Beatles of Japan, the Tempters were said to be its Rolling Stones.[125] Like Mick Jagger and company, the band featured an earthier sound with ties to American rhythm and blues, as well as a more rebellious image than that of their clean-cut rivals. The Tempters were conspicuous among Group Sounds bands for their refusal to wear matching uniforms, again taking their cue from the Stones.[126] When they performed "(I Can't Get No) Satisfaction" live, lead singer Hagiwara Ken'ichi used to swing around a wooden stave—reminiscent of the weapons that student radicals used in violent protests.[127] Hagiwara, popularly known by the nickname Shōken, radiated a charisma that Spiders lead guitarist Inoue Takayuki found almost overpowering: "The anger and sadness he harbored toward the absurdity of life and society, the sense he gave of sheer resistance, defiance, antiestablishment: it was piercing, almost painful."[128]

A five-piece group led by guitarist Matsuzaki Yoshiharu, the Tempters originated in 1965 as a high-school band in Ōmiya, a bedroom community on the northern fringes of Tokyo. In 1966, they began gigging at a local dance hall, and later that year they started appearing regularly at discotheques in Tokyo proper. In early 1967, Tanabe Shōchi signed them to the Spiductions management agency: the Spiders, concerned about the suddenly exploded popularity of the Tigers, were seeking a younger group that might compete with their new rivals.[129] Later that year, the Tempters won the Best New Band Award at the Nichigeki Western Carnival, and their debut single, "I Can't Forget You" (Wasureenu kimi), an up-tempo number composed and sung by Matsuzaki, became a hit, supposedly selling some 350,000 copies when it was released in late 1967.[130]

By the following year, the band had achieved its stated goal: it began to contest the Tigers in terms of popularity.[131] The Tempters enjoyed two massive hit singles in early 1968: "Please, God" (Kamisama onegai; number 2 on the Oricon hit chart) and "Emerald Legend" (Emerarudo no densetsu; number 1 on Oricon). Singer Hagiwara in his 2008 autobiography is generally disdainful of the Tempters' music but expresses continuing affection for those two songs.[132] An early review of their debut LP, *The Tempters First Album* (1968), described the band's "explosive popularity" and praised the way leader Matsuzaki's compositions "expressed his humanity in his own language."[133] The Tempters would continue to enjoy hits for another year or two, but like their rivals saw their popularity fade as the decade closed. Already in September 1968, the mothers of the band members were quoted as worrying that the GS boom may be ending.[134] They played their final gig in January 1971 at the Nichigeki Western Carnival on the same bill at which the Spiders played their farewell performances.[135]

In addition to their rougher image and sound, the Tempters sought authenticity using a number of strategies. Their live album, *The Tempters on Stage* (1969), featured raucous concert recordings of a number of hard-rock and blues classics, anticipating the sound that would dominate rock in the coming decade. Another LP released in the same year, *5 – 1 = 0* (1969), captured a similar energy in the studio on many tracks. The most forward-looking Tempters record, however, was an LP that the band released in December 1969. One critic described *The Tempters in Memphis* as an album "drenched in the aroma of the '70s."[136] It featured twelve original numbers by top composers (mostly outside songwriters, including Nakamura Hachidai and Kamayatsu Hiroshi, though group leader Matuzaki contributed some lyrics), but that is not what made the record stand out. Its unique status derives from the fact that it was recorded at the Sounds of Memphis studio in Memphis, Tennessee, making it one of the first instances of a Japanese rock band recording abroad.

Billed as a Tempters album, in fact it is virtually a solo work by lead singer Hagiwara. Participation by the other Tempters is limited to a single guitar solo by Matsuzaki on one track. Instead, Hagiwara's vocals are backed by a remarkable collection of local musicians, including the Memphis Horns, perhaps the top horn section in American popular music at the time.[137] The album even includes two new compositions by an up-and-coming American songwriter, Bob McDill. Not surprisingly, the LP skillfully captures the sound of American soul music circa 1969, albeit with Japanese lyrics. An early review celebrated the album, declaring, "Together with the quality of the songs, Shōken's passionate vocals and his interplay with the backing singers are wonderful."[138] By traveling to the heart of American popular music tradition (the album cover features a photograph of Hagiwara standing beneath a Beale Street street sign) and working with local musicians, the Tempters attempted to claim authenticity under the terms of the new rock ideology. Unfortunately for the band, however, neither the album nor the singles released from it achieved commercial success, perhaps because its soulful bent veered from the rock sound that Tempters fans had come to expect.

Following the breakup of the Tempters, the band members followed various career paths. For our purposes, I trace the subsequent activities of drummer Ōguchi Hiroshi (1950–2009), who was particularly successful in reinventing himself to suit the demands of 1970s rock. Immediately after leaving the Tempters, Ōguchi became a member of PYG, a new supergroup formed at the behest of Watanabe Productions. PYG represented a last-gasp effort to revive the fortunes of Group Sounds. Kamayatsu Hiroshi jokingly nicknamed the new group Spi-Tem-Tigers, because it included two members each from GS superstar bands the Spiders (Inoue Takayuki and Ōno Katsuo), the Tempters (Hagiwara and Ōguchi), and the Tigers (Sawada Kenji and Kishibe Osami).[139]

The name PYG was the brainchild of American Alan Merrill, a part of the GS scene since 1968. Watanabe Productions asked him to come up with a good moniker for its new headliner, and Merrill based it on his then-favorite American band, the Byrds.[140] According to Inoue Takayuki, PYG aimed from the start at "a more rock-sounding, antiestablishment music," but it was paradoxically backed by Watanabe Productions, one of the most powerful mainstream talent agencies.[141] In other words, the project strove to appropriate the new rock aesthetic in terms of music and image but to retain the GS business model.

The band's debut single, "Flower Sun Rain" (Hana taiyō ame; music by Inoue Takayuki, lyrics by Kishibe Osami), required more than a hundred hours of studio time to record. The song's lyrics were inspired by Albert Camus's novel *The Stranger*.[142] The recording opens with a dirgelike flourish that would have fit comfortably on a track by the Jacks: a heavily reverbed guitar strumming an open E power chord four times slowly, like the tolling of a church bell, the degree of distortion increasing with each repetition. This intro gives way to a brief drum fill, whereupon the song's main theme kicks in. Sawada and Hagiwara share the lead vocals, backed with lush harmonies from the rest of the band. Ōno's mournful organ shapes the musical tone of the midtempo song, which also features stinging guitar fills and solos by Inoue. Ōguchi's drum work on the song is restrained and tasteful, marked primarily by extensive use of cymbals.

"Flower Sun Rain" is a fine instance of early 1970s West Coast–style rock, reminiscent of Crosby, Stills, Nash, and Young, with touches of British progressive rock. But it, as well as PYG's subsequent records and live appearances, largely failed to connect with an audience, whether mass or subcultural. For GS fans, PYG's sound was too hard and dark. For hard-core rock fans, on the contrary, the group was too closely tied to the commodified pop of Group Sounds. PYG's regular concerts were poorly attended, and when the band played free rock festivals in hopes of reaching the new rock audience, it frequently found itself the object of catcalls from spectators, who found the band's GS roots and management style an affront.[143] Festival audiences pelted the band with garbage on more than one occasion. PYG quickly faded from the scene, betraying Watanabe Productions' high hopes for the band.

There was nothing wrong musically with PYG. The group's talented members made the new rock sound their own, including its characteristic guitar noise, and their repertoire consisted largely of original numbers composed by the band's members, songs that featured the musical and lyrical complexity demanded by the new aesthetic. The problem with PYG was instead purely ideological and sociological: its reliance on the old GS business model rendered it wholly inauthentic in the eyes of rock fans. Rock critic Kitanaka Masakazu, writing in early 1970, recalled the hopes that GS had aroused among its listeners a few years earlier, a belief that Japan's popular music was heading somewhere new and exciting. But in the end, he wrote, GS largely failed to fulfill those expectations, even in its more recent adaptations (he cited Kishibe Osami's pre-PYG band, Shirō), and, "with very few exceptions, the musicians in GS were never able to leave behind the existing industrial production system for songs."[144] The avowedly commercial basis of PYG disqualified the band from rock legitimacy—even as other bands with similar roots managed to enjoy both legitimacy and commercial success.

It wasn't only fans who felt this way. Members of PYG were likewise uncomfortable with the group's position in the music industry. From the start, Hagiwara felt constrained by the band's management style and by fellow singer Sawada Kenji's acquiescence in Watanabe Productions' marketing strategies for the band, writing in his autobiography that "in PYG, I couldn't express myself—there was no place for me."[145] Drummer Ōguchi may have felt even more keenly dissatisfied with PYG: he left the group only a few months after its debut.

After leaving PYG, Ōguchi played in a number of groups, including the Inoue Takayuki Band and Orange, an experimental combo led by underground musician Shinki.[146] In 1971, together with American Alan Merrill, he founded Vodka Collins, a band that would succeed in garnering critical and popular success under the terms of 1970s rock, winning acclaim in Japan and achieving cult status abroad as one of the pioneers in the new glam-rock style. Merrill, the son of jazz singer Helen Merrill, had played guitar in a number of bands in the New York City area before moving with his mother to Japan in 1968. Still a teenager, he quickly became a GS idol as a member of the Lead, an all-foreigner band. After that group disbanded, he signed with Watanabe Productions as a solo artist, appearing on the Nichigeki Western Carnival bill and elsewhere, and releasing a solo album.[147]

Ōguchi and Merrill first began playing together as part of Kamayatsu Hiroshi's backing band around 1971 (in the 1990s, when Vodka Collins reunited for a series of tours and recordings, Kamayatsu became a full-fledged member of the group). The two began recording some of Merrill's original compositions, later joined by bassist Yokouchi Take. The release of the acclaimed album *Tokyo New York* in 1972 brought the group wide attention (figure 9), which they maintained until they split up in late 1973, largely due to Merrill's dissatisfaction with the band's management. Merrill subsequently traveled to England and enjoyed popular success as a member of the Arrows, for which he composed the song "I Love Rock 'n' Roll," later a hit for Joan Jett. Ōguchi headed for Africa, where he jammed with local percussionists, later returning to Japan to try his hand at acting and at fashion design.[148]

Tokyo New York, rushed out by the record label in semifinished form to meet the demand generated by Vodka Collins's sudden popularity, remains a classic work of early 1970s rock. "Automatic Pilot," the band's biggest hit, opens the album. The song begins with an extended organ introduction played in progressive-rock style before the thumping drums and bass enter, followed shortly by the song's signature guitar riff. Merrill sings the lyrics primarily in Japanese, although the title phrase remains in English in the chorus (the band also recorded an English-language version of the tune). A seductive midtempo rocker, "Automatic Pilot" put Vodka Collins very much in the forefront of the glam-rock style of T. Rex, Gary Glitter, and David Bowie. T. Rex's Marc Bolan became a fan of the band when he toured Japan

FIGURE 9 A publicity shot of Alan Merrill and Ōguchi Hiroshi of Vodka Collins, 1972. (Photo by Koo Saito; from the collection of Alan Merrill. Used by permission)

in 1972, while Bowie would later hire away Vodka Collins's designer for his own costumes.[149] Another standout track on *Tokyo New York* is "Sands of Time," a reflective ballad marked by an infectious melody and lyrics (again sung in Japanese) that express a feeling of world-weariness. The sense that the song represents a creative expression rooted in the musicians' personal experiences is reinforced by the conversational bantering by band members (in often nonsensical English) mixed into the track over the last half of the song. "Scratchin'," the last track on the album, is a muted blues shuffle that is kin to any number of Rolling Stones recordings from the period; it features extensive slide guitar and even that indelible birthmark of 1970s rock, an extended drum solo by Ōguchi.

Like the 1960s purveyors of rock noise, Vodka Collins presented a rebellious, nonconformist image. But the locus and the politics of this subversiveness had shifted: instead of calls for revolution and political struggle in the streets, the band's lyrics and image celebrated a nonconformist lifestyle centering on hedonism, intoxication, and sexual pleasure. "Vacuum Girl," from *Tokyo New York*, for example, is a tribute to promiscuous groupies sung in

English by Ōguchi, and many of the band's other songs voice an aggressive, highly masculine sexual desire. Like their glam-rock peers in the West, Vodka Collins deliberately engaged in gender-bending, with band members wearing makeup, high heels, scarves, and other markers of femininity. Gender-bending showed up in the music as well: in the playful English lyrics to the rocking "Billy Mars," for example, the speaker laments losing his girlfriend to a cross-dressing transvestite.

This image of a noncomformist, hedonistic lifestyle differentiated the band's members from their audience: there was no mistaking that the members of Vodka Collins were rock stars. As a counterpart, although the album features extensive electric-guitar playing, relatively little of it is distorted in obvious ways. Rather than foreground the noise of distorted guitar sounds, Vodka Collins's recordings tend to emphasize virtuosity of musicianship, stressing cleanly recorded lines. The loud guitars are still there, but instead of functioning as noise, they now represent the new musical code or network that was quickly becoming dominant. In 1970s rock, guitar noise produced by fuzz boxes and other devices tended to give way to more complex playing techniques that produced natural distortion from the amplifier.[150] Similarly, in the West in the mid-1970s, it became a common practice for liner notes of rock albums to assure listeners that no synthesizers were used in recording the guitar parts—that the technical virtuosity of the playing was "authentic."[151] This stress on technical skill suggested that members of Vodka Collins, like those in other successful 1970s rock bands, were not simply like their audience. The music still produced a strong sense of emotional solidarity with the audience, but this revolved around a fundamental split between audience and musicians: the latter were special, a quality demonstrated in their musical genius, their deliberately noncomformist appearance, and in the unconventional lifestyles depicted in their lyrics.

For complex reasons, as we have seen, Ōguchi's first post-Tempters band, PYG, was unable to lure the rock audience to invest its affections in the band. In the game the rock ideology plays, the consumerist mass culture that pretends to transcend consumerist mass culture, PYG's detractors could see too clearly the little man (Watanabe Productions) pulling the levers behind the curtain. But Vodka Collins, despite similar roots in Group Sounds, was able to attract a substantial rock audience—even as its music was used in commercials and in television programs. Audiences felt insulted by PYG, but found that they could use Vodka Collins in their own lives. Again, this was not so much a matter of musical aesthetic as it was of ideology and of the meanings that were attached to the music and its relationship to the lifestyles that were emerging in the 1970s: it was a result of the way fans located the two bands on their mental maps of the world.

*   *   *

Hayakawa Yoshio, leader of the Jacks, retired from music around 1972, just as Vodka Collins was emerging. Decades later, Hayakawa would describe his mental state at the time using an odd expression: "All the sounds I was hearing seemed like noise [*zatsuon*] to me."[152] Or, as he wrote in 1972, "just as you'll never find a pretty girl at a coffee shop that advertises its pretty girls, you'll find no folk songs at a folk concert. And of course the same is true at rock concerts, and, naturally, there are no *kayōkyoku* songs on *kayōkyoku* programs. Music only comes from places without music."[153] In a sense, the noise that Hayakawa and the Jacks had generated in 1968 had taken over and become the new music—and yet for Hayakawa, it had lost all musical qualities. The twenty-three-year-old Hayakawa would subsequently open a used bookstore in the western suburbs of Tokyo, avoiding the concert stage for several decades. The rebellious noise of 1968 had become mainstream sound track by 1972, and he wanted no part of it.

Guitar noise in 1968 had seemed to prophesy an overthrow of the existing musical and social orders. But the precise nature of what would emerge next remained an open question: the noise foretold any number of possible futures. The existing codes were overthrown, but in their place arose a new code utterly foreign to what Hayakawa and his peers had envisioned. Glam-rock bands such as Vodka Collins, Sadistic Mika Band, and RC Succession released brilliant albums that still reward repeated listens. But in their music, rock was no longer opposed to a lifestyle centered on consumption: it was a part of it. Rock's always-present complicity with consumerist lifestyle was no longer concealed. Rock's noise was now inescapably a leisure commodity, and the bohemianism that was so much a part of rock's self-aggrandizing ideology now named not a form of political activism but rather a particular lifestyle.

At its most cynical, 1970s rock replaced street demonstrations with partying, collective action with individual indulgence. The very beat of the music had changed, from one that stressed side-to-side swaying of the body in a gesture of solidarity with fellow listeners to one that unleashed an isolated individual pleasure taken from an up-and-down movement of the hips.[154] Glam rock in many ways sealed the deal. In both Japan and the West, it was the style that managed to be "successful in both rock and pop terms."[155] Under glam rock's aesthetic, sex and gender were now images available for creative consumption:

> Sex became just another form of leisure, and the ideology of leisure itself began to change. Free time was used increasingly impulsively, irrationally, unproductively, with reference to immediate gratification rather than to usefulness or respectability or sense of consequence. The expansion of sexual opportunity, in other words, occurred in the context of a new leisure stress on hedonism, and the result was that sex became an experience to be consumed, used up in the moment, like any other leisure good.[156]

Like 1960s Group Sounds, 1970s rock was big business. By the late 1970s, Japan accounted for 10 percent of global record sales.[157] Rock melodies and lyrics were a crucial part of a highly mediated information society, the background music to the world's fastest-growing economy. The kind of political activism aimed at overturning economic injustice and imperial violence that many in 1968 believed guitar noise to signal had been effectively marginalized. Lifestyle and leisure were now the primary domains of youth culture and rock music, and guitar noise was a cultural product packaged for consumption. Cultural studies scholar Lawrence Grossberg, speaking of a similar phenomenon arising a decade later in the United States, describes how the lines of flight unleashed by what he calls the rock formation underwent depoliticization as part of a massive remapping of the space of everyday life. As a result, "the rock formation's lines of flight are disciplined so that they can no longer point to another space," and "their flight now has to be enclosed within the space of everyday life." Subsequently, "what is erased is the very possibility of the political as a domain which both exceeds and transcends the everyday."[158] Jacques Attali saw a similar phenomenon in late 1970s Europe, declaring that music "now seems hardly more than a somewhat clumsy excuse for the self-glorification of musicians and the growth of a new industrial sector."[159]

This did not render impossible the rise of new forms of noise or of new forms of politics. The 1970s saw the rise, for example, of new waves of feminism and environmentalism in Japan, movements that agitated for justice within the domains of everyday life. But the 1960s model of revolutionary political radicalism seemed to come to an end with the police shootout with the remaining Japan Red Army militants in the Asama Incident, a spectacle televised live to the nation on February 28, 1972. The incident and its aftermath finally rendered apparent that the radical New Left "possessed no effective means to analyze or to fight consumer society": even violent political struggle was now a commodity to be exchanged via the medium of television.[160] This mirrors oddly the fate of guitar distortion, originally an accidental and troubling noise produced by overloaded amplifiers, but by the 1970s primarily the effect produced by an electronic commodity, the fuzz box, that you could purchase in any music store.

This was not the future that rock devotees in 1968 thought they were hearing in the intoxicating bursts of guitar noise. The emergence of 1970s rock was in many ways an unexpected coda. It was like one of those final nontonic chords that brought so many Group Sounds songs to a mysterious ending but which turns out to have been built into the song's structure all along as one of its possible, but not inevitable, endings.

5

NEW MUSIC AND THE NEGATION
OF THE NEGATION

HAPPY END, ARAI YUMI, AND YELLOW MAGIC ORCHESTRA

The Left of the Left is the Right.

HAYAKAWA YOSHIO (GUITARIST AND LEAD VOCALIST, JACKS)

The most explicitly political form of popular music in 1960s Japan was folk. As in the English-speaking world, that term encompassed a broad range of meanings. From the early 1960s, there were campus-folk circles, organizing communal sing-alongs at coffee shops and pubs, and harmonizing to acoustic ballads in the mode of the Kingston Trio or Peter, Paul, and Mary.[1] Campus folk was primarily an amateur movement, but it also graduated performers into the ranks of professional music. Mike Maki became the first college-folk star when his recording of "Roses in Bloom" (Bara ga saita; music by hit maker Hamaguchi Kuranosuke) climbed the charts in 1966.[2] A year later, the Folk Crusaders, led by Katō Kazuhiko, enjoyed even greater commercial success with their comic ballad "The Drunk Who Came Back" (Kaette kita yopparai), selling more than 1.8 million copies as a single.[3] Mainstream pop stars such as Yuki Izumi began featuring "Where Have All the Flowers Gone?" and similar numbers in their acts, and the "Ivy look" fashion associated with college folk became trendy even off campus.[4]

Then there was the folk music as recovered by folklorists and ethnomusicologists: the indigenous genres of popular song with premodern roots that came in the twentieth century to be collectively known as *min'yō* (literally, "folk song").[5] Performers such as Takahashi Chikuzan (1910–1998) and Yamaguchi Gorō (1933–1999) revived older, nonelite musical forms, while scholars such as Takeuchi Tsutomu (b. 1937) and Koizumi Fumio (1927–1983) sought cultural identity by locating traces of indigenous Japanese musical forms even in contemporary pop hits.[6] For example, Koizumi expounded on the widespread use in 1960s and 1970s singles by such artists as the Candies and Pink Lady of a pentatonic scale that skips the second and sixth degrees of the Western scale (closely related to the *yonanuki* scale discussed in chapter 2) and linked it to Japanese music of earlier centuries.[7] Radio and television programs, regional music festivals, and performance spaces devoted to these revived (and in some cases newly invented) forms helped build a devoted, if small, *min'yō* audience. Moreover *shakuhachi*, samisen, and *taiko* players appeared frequently at large music festivals, especially those labeled "folk." Updated versions of traditional *min'yō* tunes such as "Sōran bushi" were sometimes performed by college folk acts too, including the Folk Crusaders.[8]

Finally, there was protest folk. First identified in the mid-1960s with the Kansai region around Osaka and Kyoto, by the end of the decade it was a nationwide phenomenon. It rejected the polished, commercially accessible ballads of campus folk, remaining largely acoustic but going for an edgier sound. Lyrics were often explicitly political. Protest-folk musicians played both original compositions and translated versions of songs by such figures as Bob Dylan, Pete Seeger, and Joan Baez. Their music became important components of the movements against the Vietnam War, the construction of Narita Airport, and what students perceived as the increasingly oppressive nature of the Japanese education system. In the spring of 1969, for example, every Saturday night anonymous "folk guerrillas" would perform for crowds gathered near the west entrance of Shinjuku Station in Tokyo—often clashing with riot police in the process.[9] Like the other forms of folk, protest folk was resolutely anticommercial, and yet superstars emerged: Okabayashi Nobuyasu, for example, became known as the god of folk or the Japanese Dylan. Other protest-folk groups popular on what was called the underground (*angura*) scene included the Jacks (discussed in chapter 4), Itsutsu Akai Fūsen, and Rokumonsen. Late-night radio programs, a slew of new, "hip" promotion and management firms, and specialty record labels spread the music to larger audiences—and provoked anxieties about commodification and erasure of political dissent. Large-scale folk music festivals became common events, climaxing in the three Nakatsugawa Folk Jamborees held in the period 1969 to 1971.[10]

Despite this range of styles, there were some suppositions widely shared by the performers and fans of the various types of music called folk. Above all, the music was oppositional: it aimed to negate the existing social, political, and cultural framework of Japan. Since politics frequently revolved around Japan's relationship to the United States, folk music often invoked an antielitist, popular nationalism, one that resisted the policies of a conservative Japanese state that was seen as collaborating in American regional domination. Like the other genres we have explored, its enjoyment implicitly invoked a certain geopolitical mapping of the world. Oppositional folk music called on indigenous culture as a source of resistance against the cultural imperialism of the United States. As such, it relied on a powerful ideology of authenticity, rejecting imitation and commercialism as fake.

Folk initially also defined itself in opposition to popular rock-and-roll music, whether rockabilly, *ereki*, or Group Sounds. In the minds of folkies, rock and roll represented all the forces that folk negated: it was commercial, American, inauthentic, and mindless.[11] Around 1967, it was virtually impossible to be a fan of both Group Sounds and folk. Yet by about 1970, the wall separating acoustic folk from electric rock had broken down: for example, Okabayashi Nobuyasu, the symbol of Kansai protest folk, hired the rock band Happy End as his backing group for his April 1970 concert tour and for his second album, *Leap Before You Look* (*Miru mae ni tobe*, 1970).[12] Rock journalists and fans began referring to "new music" as a distinct genre, one that combined rock with folk. This new hybrid form came to dominate Japanese popular music in the 1970s, critically and often commercially as well. New music also paved the way for developments in later decades. The artistic and historical lineage of much contemporary J-pop can be traced back to 1970s new music.

New music in many ways redrew the map of Japanese popular music. It inherited many of the musical forms, practices, and personnel of 1960s folk, but it largely sidestepped the politics. Repeatedly, new-music performers deconstructed the oppositions through which 1960s folk had defined its ne-gating stance in the geopolitical order. But instead of simply affirming what 1960s folk had negated, instead of flipping its oppositional stance around, new-music performers tended to undermine received political oppositions by negating the negation. This meant not a simple logical double negative (no + no = yes), which would return one to the original starting point, but a more dialectical process in which a new synthesis emerged from a contradiction between thesis and antithesis, a synthesis that redefined the ground on which the original opposition had stood. At its worst, this strategy amounted to a ducking of political responsibility in pursuit of commercial success: the music industry in this period, for example, became increasingly focused on new revenue streams derived from the exploitation of publication, reproduction, and performance "rights."[13] At its best, this characteristic gesture of negating the negation recentered and resituated music in the context of new forms of politics that were emerging in 1970s Japan: environmentalism, consumer movements, and feminism, among others.

As part of this, new music shifted the focus of lyrics and politics. Now, the frustrations of everyday life became prime targets.[14] The seeming piling up of political slogans rejecting bourgeois everydayness that had characterized earlier protest folk began to feel hollow, and in its place new music turned precisely to everyday language and intensely personal modes of communica-tion. According to one history of the genre, the early 1970s were "a time of change, from an age in which social and political problems took the form of clear ideological oppositions fought out on the streets to one in which they were manifested as contradictions or distortions embedded in daily life."[15] Inoue Yōsui's hit "Got No Umbrella" (Kasa ga nai, 1972) seemed to crystallize the new stance: the lyrics begin with the speaker lamenting a recent increase in youth suicide but quickly shift to his real problem: he wants to visit his girlfriend, but it's raining and he has no umbrella. The song caused a con-troversy at the time. Some accused it of betraying the political, while others praised it for skillfully recentering its perspective in the actual daily life of early 1970s youth culture. Whatever one's take, the appeal of Inoue's music to the audience was clear: his album *Kōri no sekai* (*World of Ice*, 1973) became Japan's first million-selling LP, and it occupied the number 1 slot on Japan's album charts for thirty-five weeks.[16]

This change was inscribed in the very bodies of musical performers and fans. As noted in chapter 4, critic Satō Yoshiaki has argued that whereas 1960s concert audiences had swayed rhythmically side to side in an affirmation of community, 1970s spectators tended to bounce up and down in affirmation of the individual self.[17] The rise of new music was also marked by a shift in the dominant musical medium: the LP album replaced the hit single as the definitive unit by which artists were judged.[18] Moreover, the new genre prompted a decisive shift in power within the music industry, away from old-line recording companies and promoters and toward artists and their management offices.[19]

New music produced any number of star performers/composers who would dominate the Japanese pop charts for decades to come: Inoue Yōsui, Yoshida Takurō, Yamashita Tatsurō, Nakajima Miyuki, RC Succession (and its leader, Imawano Kiyoshiro), Off Course, Carol (and its leader, Yazawa Eikichi), Alice, Yano Akiko, and Southern All Stars, among others. Here I focus in particular on three musical acts, linked by genealogy (Hosono Haruomi provides our bass line from beginning to end) but also by a shared praxis of negating the inherited negation. Rock band Happy End destabilized historical narratives centered on a Japan versus America opposition that had fueled much of the political charge of 1960s folk music; singer-songwriter Arai Yumi (known later by her married name, Matsutōya Yumi, or simply by her nickname, Yuming) sidestepped the opposition between art and commerce; while techno-pop pioneers Yellow Magic Orchestra achieved fame by deconstructing the boundary between imitation and authenticity. Each act negated a negation it had inherited from the previous decade and thereby brought Japanese pop forward into a future that had been unforeseeable under the terms of the negations that had driven folk music in the 1960s.

*   *   *

Could Japanese rock be Japanese and still be rock? In other words, where did this new genre of music fit within the framework of Japanese culture? As the discussion of the relation between "tradition" and "rock" in a 1971 Japanese music magazine noted, while rock music in the United States carried on legacies of American folk music, the question was "in England and Japan, which bear different traditions, how does rock relate to tradition?"[20] Japan's own folk music traditions, after all, did not revolve around guitar chords or 4/4 beats, and the very rhythms of the Japanese language seemed at cross-purposes with those of English, the language out of which rock music had emerged.

Happy End is remembered (incorrectly) as the first Japanese rock band to sing its lyrics in Japanese rather than English. Recordings of what are unmistakably rock songs with Japanese lyrics had been made in the 1960s by such groups as the Spiders and the Golden Cups. Nonetheless, as we will explore at greater length in what follows, Happy End did pioneer a new style for linking rock music melodies to the rhythms of spoken Japanese. This gesture can be read as a form of resistance to U.S. cultural hegemony—and yet this resistance was couched in the genre of rock music, a genre generally identified as arising out of American culture. Moreover, late in its career the band struggled to break into the American market, which served as the ultimate arbiter of canonicity in the new genre. In other words, what at first glance may look like resistance to U.S. hegemony also looks suspiciously like complicity in it. The tensions inherent in this irony rose to the surface as these musicians negotiated what historian Igarashi Yoshikuni has described as the "trauma of the present" that Japan faced in the 1970s: subservience to American hegemony, a hegemony that was inscribed in the physical bodies of postwar Japanese.[21] As one Japanese critic wrote in 1971, rock music in Japan amounted to a kind of "colonial culture," in which the very acts of snapping fingers and swaying in time to the music amounted to a colonizing of Japanese bodies.[22]

Happy End responded to this traumatic present not by engaging in a monumental history of national autonomy, or by appealing to an ahistorical fantasy of the timeless national folk, or by appealing to a developmental narrative of modernization—three of the most common historical narratives circulating in the 1970s to explain Japan's place in the postwar geopolitical mapping of the world. Happy End responded instead by performing an ironic remembering of the past through song, one that situated the origins of cultural identity in the unstable and heterogeneous present rather than in the distant past. This was the particular strategy by which they negated the negation they had inherited from earlier forms of folk music.

The four musicians who would form Happy End originally got to know one another in music circles at Tokyo universities in the late 1960s.[23] Two members—bassist Hosono Haruomi and drummer Matsumoto Takashi—had played in the blues-rock band Apryl Fool, which was in turn a descendant of the Group Sounds band Floral. Apryl Fool's eponymous debut album, released in 1969, attracted favorable press attention: one review declared that Apryl Fool had the potential to become a truly Japanese rock band, one that transcended mere imitation of the West.[24] Most of Apryl Fool's songs were original numbers but had English-language lyrics, as was frequently the case for 1960s Japanese rock, especially for bands playing in the blues-rock style.

When Apryl Fool disbanded, Hosono and Matsumoto formed a new band that included guitarists Ōtaki Eiichi and Suzuki Shigeru. At a time when British-style heavy blues and hard rock were all the rage among young Japanese music fans, the new group planned to pursue the softer American West Coast folk-rock sound, especially that of the band Buffalo Springfield, but to sing its lyrics in Japanese. The new quartet began appearing live under the name Valentine Blue in late 1969. Early in 1970, they changed their name to Happy End (Happī Endo, written deliberately in *hiragana* script rather than the *katakana* script usually used for foreign words) and began recording their first album, *Happī Endo*, which was released in August of that year. They would complete two more studio albums before breaking up: *Kazemachi roman*, released in 1971, and then *Happy End*, recorded in Los Angeles and released in early 1973. All the songs on the three albums were original numbers, and all were sung in Japanese.

Although commercial success largely eluded Happy End, they quickly became critical darlings (figure 10). The first album got favorable, if not overwhelmingly positive, reviews and was named *New Music Magazine*'s Japanese rock album of the year. Whatever reservations critics had were swept away with the second album, *Kazemachi roman*, which was instantly acclaimed a masterpiece. Many critics still regard it as the greatest Japanese rock album ever recorded. (For what it's worth, I prefer the earlier album, although I take great pleasure from both.)[25]

Critics praised the band because it seemed to have realized the long-held dream of a Japanese form of rock that was original and authentic and not

FIGURE 10 Happy End, 1971. (© Mike Nogami. Used by permission)

merely an imitation of Western rock. In this sense, Happy End can be understood in the context of the return to Japan that the "ambivalent moderns" of Japan's New Left had been carrying out in many different forms since the early 1960s.[26] This was the same era that gave birth to *minshūshi* (people's history), in which scholars such as Irokawa Daikichi and Hirota Masaki attempted to counter both orientalist and modernization-theory versions of Japan's history by recovering traces of a nonelite past that had been written out of official histories of both the Left and the Right.[27] Musically, as we have seen, this 1960s "return to Japan" also involved a rediscovery of traditional Japanese *min'yō* folk genres as well as the emergence of *enka* as a distinct, specifically Japanese, popular music form.

It was in the midst of this widespread celebration of a specifically Japanese past that Happy End appeared with its hybrid form of Japanese folk-rock. The band's music contained references to Japanese folklore (though the folk culture it cited tended to be more urban than rural; the band's "best of" album was even titled *City* (1973), its farewell concert the same year was named "City: Last Time Around," and one of the alternative names for the emerging genre of new music was "city pop"), and the imagery on its album covers echoed the sorts of folkloric images found in late 1960s *manga* such as *Garo* that were widely read by student activists. The second album, *Kazemachi roman*, was intended in particular as a concept album, elegizing elements of Tokyo that had disappeared in various waves of postwar urban renewal, most notably in the years leading up to the 1964 Tokyo Olympics. More than anything, though, what appealed to a generation that hoped to recover an authentic stratum of native folk culture was the band's insistence on singing in Japanese. Besides the band's skillful use of studio-recording techniques and its mastery of the folk-rock music style (the band members were in constant demand as backing musicians or producers for other artists), what attracted most attention to Happy End was its skillful lyrics, mostly written by drummer Matsumoto Takashi, and the odd way in which the band sung those lyrics, merging the rhythms of spoken Japanese with those of rock music.

As many have noted, the Japanese New Left of the 1960s tended to perceive Japanese folk culture as existing in opposition to the West, especially the United States. In this bifurcated East/West mapping, authentic Japanese culture was situated on the side of the East, alongside the other victims of Western colonialism in Asia, as this generation attempted to address the present-day trauma of American hegemony in East and Southeast Asia, represented most alarmingly by the ongoing Vietnam War and the direct involvement of U.S. military bases in Japan and Okinawa in that conflict. But this perception of Japanese as a victim of Western imperialism also had the effect of erasing memories of Japan's own prewar and wartime empire. Murai Osamu has demonstrated the complicity of the 1920s and 1930s discourse of Japanese folklore studies in legitimating Japan's own expanding empire, and a similar case could be made for the 1960s rediscovery of the folk.[28] In focusing exclusively on the East/West divide, by defining Japan primarily in opposition to the United States, the 1960s "return to Japan" constructed a version of history that erased heterogeneity and hierarchies of power existing within Asia, with the result that too often "Japan's colonial past had been excised from the popular consciousness."[29] This was a period in which the "myth of the homogeneous nation" increasingly held sway in Japan, replacing prewar and wartime versions of national identity that had stressed heterogeneity and foregrounded Japan's interrelationships with other nations in East Asia.[30] That is to say, the radical new forms of historical memory that arose in the 1960s and 1970s could be at the same time an evasion of history, as we saw with the case of Misora Hibari in chapter 2.

Given this historical situation, it is hardly surprising that Happy End's music contains no direct references to the loss of empire, though bassist Hosono Haruomi would address issues of orientalism and Japanese exoticization of both its own and other Asian cultures in a number of solo projects after the breakup of Happy End, as well as in the band Yellow Magic Orchestra, as we will see.[31] This absence situates the band's music within what Lisa Yoneyama has called "the remarkable indifference about Japan's prewar and wartime legacy of colonialism, military aggression, and other imperial practices" that characterizes much (though not all) Japanese historical imagination in the decades following 1945.[32]

While not dismissing the importance or relevance of this interpretation, I would like to argue here somewhat differently. It seems more useful to explore ways in which Happy End's music attempted to remember the past in a different manner, outside the frameworks that led much of Japanese culture, both elite and popular, to erase the memories of empire. The band's music, in other words, did not provide the sort of tidy coming to terms with the past that characterized official narratives of Japanese history, which attempted to restore a "healthy" national identity in the present, one that supposedly arose through linear progressive development out of the premodern past. Nor did the band's music perform a "working through" or "mourning" of the past, such as would characterize a Freudian approach to restore the grieving subject to health after the trauma of wartime defeat.[33] Instead, Happy End tried to break through existing forms of history and memory by negating the inherited negation. This involved stressing the present moment and the possibility it provided to rearrange one's relations with both past and future. What was crucial was the present moment as an opening of possibility for a different kind of practice, a performative practice that was perverse and warped. Happy End's music was genuinely revolutionary—not so much in terms of a Marxist revolution or of a revolution of national liberation (Happy End's members expressed doubts about both) but of a Copernican revolution, one that insisted that the problem of history revolved around the present, not around the past or future.

This required, of course, a rejection of many of the models through which the past was memorialized in 1960s Japan. Yoshikuni Igarashi has shown how much postwar Japanese popular culture worked through the traumatic memories of the war through a variety of melodramatic narratives and imagery, whether it be the sight of wrestler Rikidōzan triumphing against much larger American opponents or romantic narratives that attempted to achieve domestic reconciliation through stories of heterosexual romance and domestic bliss. But starting with its very name, Happy End performed a parodic rejection of mass-culture melodrama as a mode for self-understanding.[34] The band, in fact, recorded almost no conventional love songs—its lyrics were instead characterized by intellectualized expressions of urban angst and alienation.

Yet the band also expressed discomfort with explicitly political forms of music, such as the songs of Okabayashi Nobuyasu, the protest-folk singer for whom Happy End provided backing early in its career. In protest folk in Japan, as in the United States, priority was given to sincerity of voice: a strained, unmusical voice could be valued above a technically skilled one because it seemed to express more honestly the singer's emotional truth.[35] Rather than treat music as a secondary medium, one important only insofar as it conveyed the primary message contained in the lyrics, Happy End insisted on the importance of musicality to any notion of Japanese rock.

What sort of musical remembering, then, did the band practice? Poised on the lip of a trap that seemed to offer only two choices—Japan or America—Happy End sought a way out of the inherited map through the tactical use of ambiguity and irony, as well as through foregrounding the materiality of language itself. Even as they built their lyrics around distinctly Japanese imagery and language, they repeatedly acknowledged that a true and transparent return to Japan was impossible. They sought to "uncover the fragmenting processes of modern westernization itself" without surrendering to the logic of fetishism, to "the wish for an unmediated return to origins, for the identity of difference, and for culture as unity (for which the voice becomes the medium)."[36] The form in which their return to Japan took place involved a deliberate deconstruction of Japan, one that undermined the identities of both America and Japan, East and West.

This is most clearly seen when we examine the "rock-in-Japanese" debate that broke out in 1970 and 1971, largely in response to Happy End's first two albums. As I have noted, prior to Happy End's emergence, the majority of Japanese rock songs were sung in English—even original songs. In contrast, the folk music genre—the other half of the musical sound track to Japan's 1960s student movement—used predominantly Japanese-language songs, so that even cover versions of songs by such American artists as Bob Dylan and Joan Baez tended to be translated into Japanese when performed by Japanese singers.[37] This was in part because, as folk music increasingly became dominated by protest songs in the late 1960s, the primary goal of the music was to transmit the political message of the lyrics to listeners. In folk, it was believed, voice had to act as a transparent medium of communication, and so the lyrics had to be in Japanese, the native language of the listeners. Here we see the reliance of folk music on the notion of a homogeneous Japanese national language, which I analyzed in chapter 3.

By contrast, it was widely believed that rock had to be sung in English to be authentic. Japanese rock bands in the early 1970s were confronted with the same sort of doubts about the "authenticity" of their music as had troubled Japanese jazz musicians since before the war.[38] Rock music was rooted in American and English culture, and so the closer Japanese bands could approach the original models, the more authentic they were thought to be. Flower Travellin' Band, for example, shifted its base of operations to Canada, where its brilliant hard-rock album *Satori* (1971) achieved considerable commercial and artistic success, in part due to the use of English lyrics.[39] Likewise, Sadistic Mika Band (led by former Folk Crusader Katō Kazuhiko) achieved a special status among Japanese rock bands by basing itself in London and working with British producers on its early 1970s recordings (although the band tended to prefer Japanese-language lyrics).

In an article published at the height of the rock-in-Japanese debate, critic Hayashi Hikaru would argue that the music of every local culture was born out of the characteristic rhythms of its spoken language. It would be impossible, he implied, to fit Japanese lyrics to musical forms that had originated with speakers of non-Japanese languages.[40] Likewise, Fukamachi Jun, while expressing sympathy for the experiment Happy End was carrying out, in the end declared, "I just don't believe that the Japanese language can fit rock" and called for Japanese youth to produce their own original form of music that was "neither classical, nor jazz, nor rock, nor pop."[41] On top of such concerns, singing rock in Japanese was perceived as a mark of selling out: those who sang rock in Japanese, such as Group Sounds bands, were producing utterly commodified forms of music, designed not so much for aesthetic integrity as for market success. Finally, Japanese rock bands perceived themselves as participating in a global movement, a participation that seemed to depend on their singing lyrics in a language that was intelligible to audiences beyond the boundaries of Japan.

The assertion by Happy End that rock could be sung successfully in Japanese challenged this common sense and provoked a sharp and sometimes negative response. Skeptics pointed out that the rock-in-Japanese position was self-contradictory. As one noted, "If you're going to say, sing it in Japanese because we're Japanese, then why don't you just go the whole way and come out in favor of *enka* sung in *naniwabushi* style and reject rock? Neither rock in Japanese nor folk in Japanese can lay claim to any traditional lineage."[42] But Happy End sang in Japanese not to lay claim to an authentic tradition: the band explicitly denied that any authentic tradition was available to them. Rather, they chose to sing in a form that no reference to the past could authenticate, precisely so as to create a new authenticity in the present.

In later years, Matsumoto Takashi, Happy End's primary lyricist, would claim to have been a disinterested observer of the rock-in-Japanese debate. The debate broke out mainly in response to the first Happy End album but, Matsumoto wrote, "I wasn't in the least concerned with it. I was happy simply to have our songs understood by those people who understood them; I didn't have the slightest desire to engage in some sort of resistance or protest."[43] It is clear, though, that at the time Happy End was identified as the main proponent for rock in Japanese. A 1970 review of the band's first album declared, "All the songs are their own original compositions, and all are sung in Japanese. According to them, the ones who say Japanese and rock don't go together, that it is foolish, are the ones who are wrong, and that it is meaningless if it's not in Japanese. They don't want rock to end up being a simple import from abroad."[44] In 1970, guitarist Ōtaki Eiichi would declare, "I'm not doing it in Japanese as any kind of protest." If one wanted to participate in a global rock scene, he continued, that was fine, but in every country where rock was being performed, it "had sunk in to become a part of everyday life," and to achieve such an effect in Japan required singing in a language listeners could understand: "Don't misunderstand me, though—my saying 'Japan,' 'Japan' doesn't mean I'm some kind of cultural nationalist [*kokusuishugisha*]."[45]

Writing in 1971, Matsumoto directly addressed the issue of what was "Japanese" about the music that Happy End played. His generation was stuck, he wrote, between a "pseudo-West" (*Seiyō-magai*) and a "sham Japan" (*Nihon-modoki*), in which neither the West nor Japan could provide a stable sense of identity: "The only means left to us is *to seek out our own Japan*. For me, 'Happy End' is a gamble on this, an attempt at a new kind of Japaneseness." Japanese rock lacks any venerable tradition, he continued. "The crucial point is that what we do from now on will become a new tradition." He concludes by directly addressing the reader/listener:

> There is a wind blowing that transcends history. Only to that extent we can call this wind "tradition." And if that's the case, then it isn't so hard to hear a new Japaneseness from *Kazemachi roman*. This takes place when the wind that Happy End has refined is taken up inside your own head. It's quite strange: you and I are both called "Japanese," but our country doesn't seem like our country.
>
> It's time to take a trip.
> To find Japan.[46]

This involved neither a blind yearning for America nor a nostalgic return to Japan. As Matsumoto wrote in another article from the period, "insofar as we are a 'happy end,' the downfall of America and the decline of Japan are both our starting point and our perverse destination." In a consumerist society in which youth rebellion, including rock music, was quickly commodified, the band would seek the gaps and forgotten spaces of contemporary Tokyo, hoping to stop up the social machinery with a "no" (*ie*) that was embedded materially in the name of the band itself: "This is not because we are Japanese or because we are in Japan. Just as Japan has from our perspective become a trompe l'oeil [*kakushie*], the framework of rock itself becomes a Copernican revolution of place—like singing out in a distorted mother tongue [*yuga-merareta bokokugo*]."[47] As Hosokawa Shuhei has argued, Matsumoto's stance differs from that of late 1960s folk singers in Japan, "who argued that they sang in Japanese because they *were* Japanese." Matsumoto did not assume a "'natural' tie between his language and nationality," nor did he believe that singing in English could "resolve the inauthenticity of Japanese as a rock language."[48] For Matsumoto, the Japanese language was above all a source of raw material for use in experimentation.

What sort of lyrics resulted from this experiment? Satō Yoshiaki has traced the process by which from the 1970s a singing style developed in Japan that effectively merged the rhythm of spoken Japanese with the syncopated beats of rock and rhythm and blues. The result was a style based on a standard of four spoken syllables to a beat that made it seem natural to sing Japanese lyrics to Western-originated genres of pop music.[49] But Happy End was after a different sort of effect. "Haru yo koi" (Spring, Come Ye Hence; music by Ōtaki Eiichi, lyrics by Matsumoto Takashi) was the first song on the first Happy End album, and the second song ever written by the band. The lyrics were adapted primarily from dialogue in the experimental *manga Spring* (*Haru*) by Nagashima Shinji, who is thanked in the album credits.[50] The focus of the song lyrics lies not on revolutionary politics or on romance but on ordinary daily life in the city. Specifically, they take up the boredom of one who faces the New Year holiday alone, sitting by himself at his *kotatsu* after having abandoned his rural family home for a new life in the city. Like many Happy End songs, the lyrics are written in *desu/masu* style, a more polite yet also more conversational form of Japanese conjugation. On paper, the lyrics read as a fairly conventional, perhaps existentialist account of urban alien-ation: many commented when the album was released on how successfully the band had used ordinary, conversational Japanese in its lyrics. This is in line with conventional expectations for pop music lyrics, which are not sup-posed to be complex, high poetry but rather foreground the "ordinariness of language," to make "ordinary language intense and vital," thereby establishing an emotional connection with the listener.[51]

The lyrics thus seem unremarkable when you read them, but something strange happens when they are sung. "Haru yo koi" demonstrates how Happy End would resolve the supposed contradiction between the rhythms of spoken Japanese and rock music: the Japanese language they sang would be "warped" and "perverted." As Uchida Yūya, leader of the band Flowers and one of the fiercest opponents of rock in Japanese, would complain about the song in a 1971 roundtable discussion, "if you don't pay close attention when you listen, you can't understand what they're saying. If you're going to take the trouble to sing in your mother tongue, it should come out much clearer."[52]

But for Happy End, the Japanese language functioned not as a repository of tradition or identity but as an alienated and alienating tongue—a source of noise. This singing style fits the narrative presented in the lyric: of a young person who has left home and family behind to gamble everything on a new life. The song rejects the nostalgic discourse of *furusato* (rural hometown) that was so central to postwar Japanese myths of national homogeneity.[53] In tandem with this, the language of the lyrics functions not as a transparent medium that bonds the national community but as a form of opaque materiality to be worked over: accents are misplaced, pronunciations are bent, relatively meaningless syllables are extended to remarkable length (for example, the *ma* in a verb-final conjugation *-mashita*, the *no* in *mono desu*, or the *i* in *nai hazu*). In sum, the band invented an inauthentic, unnatural form of Japanese, what postcolonial theorist Homi K. Bhabha would call an "unhomely" form of the mother tongue.

Similar experimentation with language—the use of wordplay, of non-standard forms of Chinese characters (*kanji*), of *hiragana* script to render words normally written in *katakana*—would characterize Matsumoto's lyrics throughout the band's career. The last song from the second album, "Ai ue wo" (Starved for Love; music by Ōtaki Eiichi, lyrics by Matsumoto Takashi), for example, similarly foregrounds the materiality of language and may perhaps be the band's closing argument in the rock-in-Japanese debate. The song's title, written mostly in *kanji*, seems to communicate a message, one that is repeated in the first line of the lyrics. But as the song progresses, it quickly becomes apparent that nothing is being communicated: the title turns out to be a pun on the opening line of the standard Japanese syllabary, and the remaining lyrics simply recite the remainder of the syllabary (*a i u e o, ka ki ku ke ko . . .*), a string of meaningless sounds—an effect similar to singing the alphabet in English.

When we recall the frequent invocations of the Japanese language as the naturalized ("mother tongue") and transparent bearer of cultural identity, we begin to see the implications of this language play. In Happy End, we hear echoes of Bhabha's description of Frantz Fanon's attempt at a postcolonial form of re-membering, except that of course here the historical problematic is one of postimperialism rather than postcolonialism. Like Fanon, Happy End "speaks most effectively from the uncertain interstices of historical change" in a voice "most clearly heard in the subversive turn of a familiar phrase, in the silence of a sudden rupture." In foregrounding the strange materiality of familiar language, in performing on the unstable margins of American music and Japanese lyrics, the conventional alignments of historical memory—self/other, East/West, America/Japan—are shaken up: the negation is negated. Occupying neither the position of "the colonialist Self or the colonized Other, but the disturbing distance in-between," the band foregrounds the present moment from which it launches into song. "This may be no place to end," Bhabha has noted, "but it may be a place to begin."[54] Or, as Matsumoto Takashi put it in the song "Happy End" from the first album:

happiness isn't a matter of how things end
it's about how things begin.

Happy End marked a moment of optimism, a moment of belief in the present as a beginning, a beginning in which one could bring into existence a new Japanese body through the performance of a new kind of music. This new body would be that of not only children who did not know war[55] but also children who had escaped the capitalist culture industry: the song "Happy End" contains direct swipes at those who define happiness in terms of material consumption. The band's first two albums were distributed by URC Records—the "underground record club," an independent label that eschewed traditional business practices of the popular music industry. At first, its releases were available by subscription only (though by the time Happy End's albums were released, the company had shifted to more conventional distribution channels), and its performers often refused to appear on television or engage in other acts that were perceived as commercializing.[56]

This moment of resistance against the market was brief: as we will see, by the mid-1970s Arai Yumi and other new-music stars (with the backing of former members of Happy End) had negated this negation by redefining the meaning of integrity and co-optation. Moreover, even before Happy End had broken up, the band was attacked for its own participation in the commodification of rock music—most notably at the Third Nakatsugawa Folk Jamboree in 1971, when shortly after a performance by the band with Okabayashi Nobuyasu, a group of audience members occupied the main stage to protest the commercial management of the festival.[57] Likewise, the subsequent careers of the band members after Happy End's breakup in 1973 show them dominating the popular music industry in Japan during the 1970s and 1980s. Matsumoto Takashi went on to write lyrics for dozens of hit songs by such popular artists as Agnes Chan, Tulip, and Matsuda Seiko. Ōtaki Eiichi enjoyed an enormously successful solo career, including the album *A Long Vacation*, which won the Japan Record Award as best-selling album of 1981. And, as we will see, Hosono Haruomi went on to play bass in Yellow Magic Orchestra, the most successful Japanese rock band of the late 1970s and early 1980s. Yet despite the subsequent commercial success of its members, Happy End is ultimately best remembered for being one of the first bands to demonstrate that Japanese rock could espouse values other than those of the market.

Happy End faced the prospect of integration into historical narratives—in fact, into two competing narratives. On the one hand, their music could be narrated as marking the triumph of globalizing American culture and the process of modernization; on the other, it could be narrated as marking a traditional and local resistance to American culture. The band, however, responded to the trauma of the present by performing music that, ambivalently and partially, avoided integration into either narrative—it negated the negation.

In doing so, Happy End occupied the unstable and ironic space of colonial mimicry, performing to undermine the stable identities of being either Japanese or American. The title of Happy End's final single (also the final track on their final studio LP) spelled out the band's position perfectly: "Sayonara Amerika, Sayonara Nippon" (1973). The song, written and sung in Japanese and Japanized English, was recorded in the United States, with an American producer (Van Dyke Parks) and American studio musicians (including members of the band Little Feat). Matsumoto Takashi would recall that the song expressed the disenchantment the band experienced when it realized the dream of recording in America, only to encounter hostility from musicians in Los Angeles: "We had already long ago given up on Japan, and with [that song], we were saying bye-bye to America too—we weren't going to belong to any place."[58] The lyrics, which consist of a repetition of the song's title followed by the phrase "bye-bye," seemed to announce a break with both Japan and the United States. Yet the song goes on repeating this refrain of farewell (with the vocals deliberately distorted through a phase filter) for more than four minutes, with an extended fade-out at the end, as if the point were not so much the break itself but the repeated performance of the act of breaking with the past. As Hosokawa has written, the song demonstrated that "it was neither American music, nor its Japanese simulacra, which provided their model. It was only the difference between the cultures that interested them."[59] The band seemed to understand that "in order to critique the West in relation to Japan, one has necessarily to begin with a critique of Japan. Likewise, the critique of Japan necessarily entails the radical critique of the West."[60]

Literary critic Katō Norihiro and others have recently looked at Japan's postwar historical memory as a misshapen, literally "twisted" (*nejire*) form and sought ways by which the historical trauma of war, defeat, and loss of empire could be confronted and thereby worked through to restore psychic health to the Japanese nation.[61] But it strikes me that Happy End was suspicious of the model of health that underwrites this vision. The band acknowledged the strong desires evoked through memories of loss, and yet it used irony and the materiality of language strategically to avoid the "social disease of nostalgia" in which "the present is denied and the past takes on an authenticity of being, an authenticity which, ironically, it can only achieve through narrative."[62] Happy End cast its lot, rather, with the "twisted" present as a source of possibility and undermined the very processes of historicization—be it via melodrama, nostalgia for empire, or *furusato* discourse—by mobilizing forms of ironic performance in the present. Inheriting the opposition between America and Japan, the band negated the opposition and thereby produced an entirely new space, one that eludes the possibility of easy mapping. As Hosono Haruomi would later reminisce: "The space that Happy

End created was unique, even in global terms. It was warped in a fourth-dimensional kind of way and in conflict with the spaces around it. I'm still caught up in that double-helix structure. I catch on immediately to any music that produces this sort of space."[63]

*　　*　　*

During and after the breakup of Happy End, Hosono Haruomi and Suzuki Shigeru combined with keyboardist Masatōya Masataka and drummer Hayashi Tatsuo to create a crack team of studio musicians who would record and produce other artists. Known popularly as Caramel Mama (the name later changed to Tin Pan Alley), they also released recordings under their own name. But they are best remembered for their work as producers, arrangers, and session players on recording sessions for other performers, including some of the most successful records to emerge in Japanese pop from the 1970s (figure 11). In very real terms, Caramel Mama created much of the sound of new music.

FIGURE 11 The Caramel Mama production team in Hosono Haruomi's home studio, 1973. (© Mike Nogami. Used by permission)

Probably their greatest success came in their work on the first five albums released by Arai Yumi (hereafter referred to by her popular nickname, Yuming), a young singer-songwriter who burst onto the scene in the early 1970s. Yuming combined her own distinct sensibility as composer and performer with the rock-folk hybrid sound and polished studio technique that Happy End had developed, achieving enormous critical and popular success in the process. For all its critical importance, Happy End sold few records during its life span. In contrast, by the mid-1970s Yuming had become a dominant force on the hit singles and album charts in Japan. Moreover, she achieved this commercial success in large part without facing the charges of having sold out. She figured out, that is, how to transform new music into a massively successful commodity without sacrificing artistic ambition or pretension. Accordingly, the inherited negation that Yuming negated was that which opposed artistic integrity to commercial mass culture, and she did so by deconstructing the existing symbols that defined artistic resistance to market co-optation. In doing so, she paved the way for such later best-selling female singer-songwriters as Nakajima Miyuki, Utada Hikaru, and Shiina Ringo.

Yuming (b. 1954) was born and raised in Hachioji, a western suburb of Tokyo. In middle school, she frequently visited PX stores on the nearby U.S. military bases in Tachikawa and Yokota to buy imported rock records by such musicians as Jimi Hendrix and Cream.[64] She had already begun to attract attention in the music industry: Kahashi Katsumi, formerly of Group Sounds giants the Tigers, recorded her composition "Suddenly Love" (Ai wa totsuzen ni) in 1968. As a high-school student, she frequented discotheques, including a club in Roppongi that featured as its house band Floral, the Group Sounds band that would eventually evolve into Happy End. She also developed a particular love of the American band Jefferson Airplane, especially its female lead singer, Grace Slick.[65]

She was still a freshman in art college when she released her first single, "No Reply Needed" (Henji wa iranai, 1972), produced by Kamayatsu Hiroshi. In 1973, she recorded her debut album, and she made her major concert debut the following year (figure 12). Within a few years, Yuming would establish herself as one of Japanese pop's top performers, both in the studio and in live concerts. Her marriage to Caramel Mama keyboardist Matsutōya Masataka in late 1975 was a media sensation, and a 1976 profile in the popular magazine

FIGURE 12 The jacket for Arai Yumi's second album, *Misslim* (1974). (Courtesy EMI Music Japan)

Heibon Punch celebrated her sudden success, declaring her the "queen of the folk scene with amazing popularity," especially among university students.[66] She has continued to release albums with remarkable regularity ever since. When I first arrived in Japan in late 1984, Yuming was clearly the most universally beloved Japanese pop music star among the college students I met, and she remains a potent force on the Japanese music scene, nearly four decades after her debut.[67]

Her debut album, *Hikōki gumo* (*Airplane Cloud*, 1973), was the work that solidified her reputation as a musical genius.[68] Produced by Murai Kuniko, it features ten original compositions and was recorded in Japan's first twenty-four-track studio. The Caramel Mama team provided the backing music and arrangements, which were celebrated for their sophistication and polish. With *Hikōki gumo*, Yuming was recognized as having pioneered a new role for women in popular music, distinct from the *enka* tragic heroine or the lightweight idol singer.[69] For starters, there was a sophisticated, intellectual bent to her music, and as composer of virtually all the songs she recorded, she basically invented the category of female singer-songwriter in Japan. In doing so, Yuming introduced a fresh sensibility into pop music, both musically and lyrically. She shifted the center of gravity away from the electric guitar, the ultimate symbol of masculinity in rock aesthetics, to the keyboard: her debut single, "No Reply Needed," features an extended guitar solo, but in the newly re-recorded version of the composition that appears on the *Hikōko gumo* album, the guitar solo has disappeared, replaced with a keyboard playing to a Latin rhythm on percussion.[70] Her compositions feature instantly appealing melodies constructed around inventive chord changes and invoke a cosmopolitan array of styles, including folk, country, progressive rock, classical, and Latin genres.[71] She sang in a remarkably clear voice, using little vibrato, and her lyrics express a delicate sensibility, that of a young citified woman gazing at passing clouds and reflecting on love and loss, and were not afraid to suggest an existentialist confrontation with darker possibilities.

"Hikōki gumo," the opening number and title track of the album (as well as the source of a brief refrain at the close of the album), is characteristic of Yuming's early sound. It opens with a brief midtempo piano and organ figure establishing the basic chord structure of the song, whereupon Yuming's vocals and the rhythm section come in. The first verse is sung in a gentle voice, but the intensity of the vocals and the backing picks up with the chorus—only to return to hushed tones in the second verse. Subdued strings emerge midway through the song. Written in a major key, the song nonetheless is studded with melancholic minor chords, and it ends on a wistful, extended coda. Classical composer Dan Ikuma praised the tune, calling it a "little treasure": "Listening carefully, I came to feel that its melody—which at first had seemed a little brusque, neither here nor there—was in fact not at all simple or brusque. Am I the only one who feels it is nothing at all and yet at the same time that it encompasses everything?"[72]

The lyrics celebrate an unnamed young friend who, it is hinted, has committed suicide. The words imagine the friend alone, looking up at the cloud-like contrail of an airplane in the sky and seeing in it a path to follow, presumably to an impending death. Despite the dark topic, there is something reassuring about the song, a sense of calm fearlessness that pervades the lyrics, vocal performance, and melody. This is in part because the chord pattern sounds familiar—it mirrors that from Procol Harum's progressive-rock hit "A Whiter Shade of Pale" (1967), a number that had a profound influence on Japanese rock and rollers (it was long a highlight, for example, of live performances by the Golden Cups, who also recorded a cover version of the number). Moreover, both Yuming's and Procol Harum's songs allude to much older music: J. S. Bach's "Air on a G String" and "Sleepers, Wake!" The classical echoes in "Hikōki gumo" lend it an air of seriousness and artistic depth that appealed strongly to listeners in 1972 Japan.[73]

"Hikōki gumo" shared with many new-music hits a powerful sense of nostalgia for a vanished past. This melancholic longing for a simpler time of youthful innocence, poverty, and a seemingly purer lifestyle characterized many new-music records—for example, the group Kaguyahime's hits "Kanda River" (Kandagawa, 1973) and "Paper Lanterns" (Akachōchin, 1974). Ironically, new-music performers were producing successful song commodities that expressed an intense longing for a time when everyday life wasn't dominated by commodity culture.[74] The oil shock of 1973 and resulting economic recession in Japan produced a small blip in a decade that was otherwise dominated by accelerated economic growth, intensified consumerism, and the first sproutings of a sense that Japanese culture was now postmodern. At least in terms of popular music, this remarkable "success" ironically produced a nostalgic longing for simpler, pre–economic growth days.

In 1975, the group Ban Ban scored a number 1 hit with "*The Strawberry Statement* Once More" (*Ichigo hakusho wo mō ichido*), a composition by Yuming that exemplifies this nostalgic tendency. The speaker in the lyric has symbolically abandoned his youth by cutting his long hair and taking on a normal "grown-up" job but now looks wistfully back on the experience of viewing with his girlfriend *The Strawberry Statement* (1970), a Hollywood film depicting campus turmoil in 1968 America that had an enormous impact on Japanese youths. The song symbolizes the way 1960s youth culture became an object of dreamy nostalgia, not to mention a source for new media commodities. The recording's overwhelming success on the charts marked a turning point: new music had replaced folk as the primary musical voice of contemporary youth.[75]

Yuming's own first number 1 hit on the singles charts, "I Want to Return to That Day" (Ano hi ni kaeritai, 1975), likewise exemplifies this tendency.

The song features an attractive bossa nova feel. It opens with breezy vocal scatting by Yamamoto Junko of the group HiFi Set. Yuming enters with the first verse, sung in her characteristic clear, steady voice. The jazzy accompaniment includes acoustic guitar, bass, keyboards, and drums (played by the Caramel Mama team), with accents provided by flutes, a muted slide guitar, and discreet percussion fills. The lyrics voice nostalgia for lost youth and lost love: the singer wants only to return to being the person she was in the past, so that she can meet "you" once again. A long, slow fade at the end, in which Yamamoto's soft scatting returns, provides a musical parallel to the lingering regrets voiced in the lyrics. At least one journalist commented on the irony of a singer barely twenty years old mooning for the good old days.[76] But clearly the song's expression of longing for a simpler past held a powerful appeal to young adults in mid-1970s Japan, who used their rapidly expanding purchasing power to buy Yuming's records in unprecedented numbers. As a result of the song's massive popularity, in late 1975 Yuming was named the most popular female musician in a poll of fourteen thousand university students.[77]

Anticipating the success of the single "I Want to Return to That Day," Yuming's third album, *Cobalt Hour* (1975), was her first to top Japan's album charts. The success extended retroactively to her earlier albums at this point, too. In fact, at one point, in 1976, her first three albums held the numbers 2, 6, and 14 slots simultaneously in the Japanese album charts.[78] By around this time, Yuming had unmistakably become a superstar, a status generated by her market success. As critic Simon Frith reminds us, "The music business doesn't only turn music into commodities, as records, it also turns musicians into commodities, as stars."[79] Yuming would explicitly boast that she herself had become a kind of musical designer label: her first "best of" album, released in 1976, was titled *Yuming Brand*. Her style was frequently described as being "the middle-class sound."[80] A critic in 1976 tellingly described Yuming's music as belonging to the same domain of "image" and "dreams" as popular fashion magazines like *AnAn* and declared that her emergence was "epoch making" not just for the music world but also for the fashion world.[81] When Tanaka Yasuo published his sensational novel *Somehow, Crystal* (*Nantonaku kurisutaru*, 1981), depicting the new consumerist youth lifestyle that had emerged in 1970s Tokyo—a novel famous for the 442 footnotes accompanying its narrative, many of them wryly explaining the semiotics of brand names and other icons of contemporary consumer culture, alongside his explications of the Meiji-ya supermarket chain, Brooks Brothers and Prada, and terms like "brand loyalty"—he included entries for both Yuming and her husband: footnotes 234 and 235, respectively.[82]

Despite her enormous market success and her explicit emergence as a kind of consumer brand, Yuming somehow avoided charges of having sold out, of producing inauthentic mass commodities instead of artistic statements. She sidestepped the negation that 1960s folk had set up between commercial success and artistic integrity, redefining the boundary between the two in the process. The very standards for defining "commercial" and "noncommercial" were shifting with the emergence of the new industry model that accompanied the rise of new music. A new group of "hip" companies devoted to artist management, concert promotion, and music publishing appeared on the scene.[83] This newly risen alternative universe took pride in distinguishing itself from the older entertainment industry (*geinōkai*) and in achieving market success (marked primarily by album sales and concert attendance) without resorting to what it saw as cheap show-business tactics, such as appearing on television or cultivating the tabloid press. As this suggested, popular music was starting to occupy a new position in the cultural field. One critic in 1976 surveyed the new trend, arguing that pop singers had usurped the vanguard role that young novelists like Ishihara Shintarō had occupied twenty years earlier. New-music singers brought on something novel, "giving off the scent not of 'entertainment' but of something like 'culture.'"[84] It is important to remember that the very phrase used to name this novel form of culture, "new music," was itself essentially a marketing tactic, one designed to distinguish records belonging to it from their less-market-friendly roots in noncommercial folk.[85]

Yuming in many ways pioneered this new, oddly noncommercial form of commercial media. Her smash hit "I Want to Return to That Day" was the theme song for the TBS television drama *Family Secrets* (*Katei no himitsu*, 1975) and was also used as the backing music for Mitsubishi stereo-receiver commercials. But under the newly emerging regime, the potentially damaging effect of such close collaboration with the market was negated because Yuming helped establish a new set of markers of authenticity and integrity that became broadly accepted with the rise of new music.[86] The change in name of the collective of musicians that backed her on her first albums was also symbolic. "Caramel Mama" was slang from the 1960s student movement for parents who tried to lure their children into abandoning the barricades and returning to the comforts of home; their new name, adopted around 1974, was Tin Pan Alley—an ironic borrowing of the name of the New York City music-publishing district, home to the most densely commodified form of popular music.

In sum, Yuming figured out how to achieve enormous commercial success without appearing to have compromised her integrity as an artist. Critic Kitanaka Masakazu in 1974 expressed concerns about the "pop" nature of Yuming's early work but concluded that she escaped the faults of the conventional music industry's projects because of a "freshness, a nuance different from earlier singer-songwriters" characterizing her music.[87] Two years later, classical composer Dan Ikuma, writing in praise of the song "Station in the Rain" (Ame no suteishon) from her album *Cobalt Hour*, provided another striking example of how Yuming was perceived. In trying to explain why he was so taken with the young singer-songwriter, Dan wrote: "I think the reason is that I was feeling disgusted with the commercialism of the syrupy songs produced by . . . Japan's commercial lyricists and melody writers, who, with very few notable exceptions, seem to have reached a dead end, and I was looking for songs that weren't born out of the stale planning departments of corrupt record companies." Music should quench our thirsty souls, Dan wrote, but when we are already sated with "coy songs overly saturated with commercialism," it takes a special talent to reach us. He expressed concerns for the future of Yuming's music. Insofar as it cannot exist entirely outside its relation to "the commercialism that dominates in a free market economy," it might be transformed as it "rides along the conveyor belt of commercialism." But he concluded by praising Yuming's talent and intelligence, which allow her to "slip through the net of commercialism" and speak to the rising generation of young listeners who "search within the domain of commercialism for songs that don't feel colored by commercialism."[88]

When I first arrived in Japan in 1984 and discovered Yuming's great popularity among my new friends there, I was repeatedly told two things about her: that she was popular despite not being beautiful and that she refused to appear on television. Neither claim was exactly true: Yuming took great care with her appearance, and she appeared on certain television programs. But each claim took on symbolic weight in redrawing the boundaries for what would be accepted as artistic integrity. Television appearances had become increasingly important to pop stars in the 1960s in the older *kayōkyoku* industry model, which centered on the hit single. This, in turn, produced a tendency to locate new talents based on their appearance and personality as opposed to their musical talents—on, that is, idol singers. Drawing a line between these practices and her own, Yuming was able to open a new space in which massively successful recordings (at first albums but later including singles too) could still lay a claim to artistic integrity.[89] Yuming explicitly refused to appear on conventional pop-music variety shows, yet she would allow her songs to be used as theme songs for television dramas and commercials. She would also appear on concert programs that allowed for her to go beyond the one-song-per-artist practice of most hit-parade shows. By negating the negation that had opposed art to commerce, Yuming shifted the boundaries of the game: one could now seek "within the domain of commercialism" itself popular songs that bore an artistic value that couldn't be eroded by their remarkable exchange value as commodities. If her music was in any sense political, it was a politics that arose not à la 1960s folk, through a rejection of the everyday life of consumption, but from within that world.

＊　　＊　　＊

In addition to his work with Caramel Mama and Tin Pan Alley, Hosono Haruomi released a series of solo albums in the 1970s. These explored in parodic fashion the sounds of musical exotica: Caribbean beats laid down alongside faux oriental melodies, New Orleans piano rags, Okinawan choruses, and allusions to Africa.[90] In 1978, he formed a new group, Yellow Magic Orchestra (YMO), with two other musicians: drummer Takahashi Yukihiro (b. 1952), formerly of Sadistic Mika Band, and keyboardist Sakamoto Ryūichi (b. 1952), who had studied classical composition in college, with special emphasis on the avant-garde.[91] The new unit continued the ironic play with orientalist exotica that had characterized Hosono's solo work but shifted its emphasis to synthesizers and other electronic devices. The plan was to take Hollywood-style musical exotica and place them over a disco-style electronic sound and, it was hoped, use this new style to take America by storm.[92] Sakamoto is said to have coined the word *techno-pop* to describe YMO's music.[93]

Yellow Magic Orchestra released its eponymous first album in late 1978. It initially had little impact in Japan, but the record caught the fancy of executives from the American A&M label, and they arranged to have a remixed version of the album released in the United States in 1979. The first American single, a warped cover version of Martin Denny's exotica number "Firecracker" (1959), became a disco hit. American and European tours followed later that year, and by the time YMO returned to Japan in late 1979 and released its second album, *Solid State Survivor*, the band had attained stardom in the Japanese music scene.[94] On the second album, YMO's disco style started to give way to a harsher sound influenced by new wave and punk, a sign of the band's integration with ongoing musical fashions outside Japan.[95]

Solid State Survivor was the best-selling album in Japan in 1980 and won the Japan Record Award for Best Album. Two of its tracks, "Rydeen" and "Behind the Mask," became signature numbers for the band.[96] Befitting its high-tech image, the band further permeated popular imagination when its song "Technopolis" was used in a television commercial for cassette tapes, the musical playback medium that was achieving mass-market penetration with Sony's just released portable Walkman player. This and other YMO numbers were also frequently used as in-store music by electronics retailers during this period, further underscoring links between the band's image and cutting-edge technology.[97]

The trio released several more critically and commercially successful albums before breaking up in 1984. In the years since, its members have frequently worked together under various monikers, including several YMO reunions. They have also remained active as studio musicians and producers, working with numerous other performers—for example, Misora Hibari (Sakamoto Ryūichi composed and produced her single "Laugh, Moonlight" [Waratte yo mūnraito, 1983]) and Yano Akiko, a singer-songwriter who backed YMO in many early concerts before launching a highly successful solo career (and becoming for a time the wife of Sakamoto). The musicians in YMO also frequently collaborated with their counterparts from Europe and the Americas. Sakamoto is the best known of the band members outside

Japan, due in part to his costarring role with David Bowie in the film *Merry Christmas, Mr. Lawrence* (1983; dir. Ōshima Nagisa), for which he composed the sound track, as well as to the Academy Award he shared with David Byrne and Cong Su for the sound track to *The Last Emperor* (1987; dir. Bernardo Bertolucci; Sakamoto also acted in the film). The band members also function as public intellectuals, participating in political and social movements and explaining their theoretical positions in essays and interviews. Literary theorist Karatani Kōjin approvingly cited Sakamoto and Hosono as thinkers in a 1982 essay.[98]

Like their predecessors in new music, YMO carried forward the negation of the negations that had previously defined the relationship between politics and popular music in Japan. Whereas Happy End invented a sham Japaneseness to escape the Japan versus America binary, YMO went a step further: they appropriated Western stereotypical fantasies of orientalness and performed them back as an empty, parodic identity. And while Yuming had deconstructed the opposition between commercial success and artistic integrity, establishing new artistic possibilities for musical commodities, YMO ratcheted up both sides of the equation: they released some of the most challenging, difficult pop music ever to top the charts anywhere. Their debut album includes several songs based on the background music for the new video games that from the late 1970s were transforming youth culture, assembling the bleeps and blips of game consoles into modernist pastiches and montages. For example, "Circus," the opening number on the album, includes a playful quotation from Chopin's "Funeral March," the musical cue signifying that a player has "died" in a video game.[99]

But perhaps the most radical negation that YMO performed was to undermine the very opposition between inauthenticity and authenticity. Their music, performance styles, and recording techniques repeatedly negate the negation by suggesting that under the conditions of contemporary capitalism and media culture, the fake might be more real than the real itself. Chopin's "Funeral March," which opens YMO's first album, announced, in other words, the death of a certain model of rock music authenticity.[100] The group deliberately and repeatedly undermined the links between popular music authenticity and the performer's interiority, the performer's body as the expression of that interiority, and the implicit masculine gendering of that body that had been central to folk and rock. YMO's music shifted the center of gravity of music from the phallic guitar to the wired networks of synthesizers, their stage costumes stressed anonymous uniformity, and they restricted the expressive body movements of the musicians on stage to a jerky minimum, all in an attempt to decouple the sounds being produced from preexisting notions of music as authentic expression of the interiority of the singer.

As one critic has noted, "techno-pop transmutes the performance-centered traditions of rock by refusing any direct connection between performers' bodies and the production of sound, even to the point that voice itself is revealed on the techno-pop recording as a technological artifact."[101] YMO replaced the musical virtuosity that had become a hallmark of 1970s rock aesthetics by foregrounding machines in place of live musicians. Although YMO's members were all accomplished players, both in the studio and in live performance they yielded center stage to synthesizers, sequencers, and digitized samples. In concert, the band members stood behind electronic keyboards wearing large headphones, implicitly defining the three band members as terminals in an interconnected network (figure 13).[102] Whatever aura their music produced came from its self-evident status as a simulacrum of music. In other words, the band's inauthenticity was its authenticity. Likewise, the deadpan, robotic expressions of the musicians were deliberate quotations of Western stereotypes about inscrutable Orientals, a kind of mirror held up to audiences in both Japan and the West.

Lest their audiences miss the deliberate negation of the negations that had since the 1960s defined rock's politics and aesthetics of authenticity, YMO on its album *Solid State Survivor* went straight for the jugular. Taking its cue in part from the American band Devo's herky-jerky reworking of the Rolling Stones' "(I Can't Get No) Satisfaction" the previous year, YMO went to the heart of the rock canon and recorded a remarkable deconstructive take on the Beatles' classic "Daytripper" (which the Fab Four had featured in their 1966 Tokyo concerts and which had been a featured number in the repertoire of Group Sounds giants the Spiders). In YMO's hands, the song is transformed from an expression of teenage romantic angst into a surrender to the power of the machine. Their version features harsh mechanical drones, electronic squawks and squeals, and an overtly robotic, inorganic beat. At key moments,

FIGURE 13 The Yellow Magic Orchestra in concert in the United States, 1979. (Courtesy Getty Images)

the melody grinds to an alarming halt, as if the machine had lost its power source. Takahashi Yukihiro's always metallic-sounding vocals are run through a harmonizer on the recording to increase their mechanical feel.[103] The familiarity of the song's melody and lyrics coupled with the alienating style of the YMO recording produces a disturbing yet compelling listening experience— a simultaneous celebration and destruction of pop.

The allusions to the Beatles continued on subsequent releases. The most famous album cover of all time, the Beatles' *Sgt. Pepper's Lonely Hearts Club Band* (1967), features a photo of the members of the band standing next to wax museum figures modeled after the early Beatles and in front of a montage of photographs and paintings of famous figures. The cover art of YMO's third album, ×∞ *Multiplies* (*Zōshoku*, 1980), by contrast, features a photograph of the three band members surrounded by plastic mannequins of themselves in a mirror-on-mirror arrangement, stressing the infinitely reproducible nature of the musician as image.

The album itself opens with a fake radio jingle, with famed American deejay Wolfman Jack (or a skilled mimic) introducing the first song. That song,

"Nice Age," was a hit number vaguely reminiscent of Roxy Music and sung by Takahashi—and featuring guest vocals by Fukui Mika, Takahashi's former bandmate in Sadistic Mika Band. The dark lyrics of the song reflect the band members' reaction to an incident that occurred while they were recording the album: the arrest of Paul McCartney at Narita Airport for possession of marijuana.[104] "Nice Age" is followed by the first of several comedy routines by the group Snakeman Show included on the album, this one conducted in English: a Japanese businessman's apparent veneer of comfort at carrying out business in English falls apart. After this, YMO itself gets into the comic game, with a heavily accented, parodic voice introducing the band in English as "the number 1 dance band in Tokyo!" over a techno-pop adaptation of Archie Bell and the Drells' hit "Tighten Up" (1968). The song is given new lyrics, however, built around the repetition (again in English) of the phrase "Japanese gentlemen, stand up please!" Next comes yet another Snakeman Show routine in which the afflicted Japanese businessman becomes the target of increasingly offensive comments by his apparently American business counterpart, his inability to speak English or to confront his interlocutor (who compares Japanese to pigs and monkeys) providing the uncomfortable basis of the humor. The sketch suggests that despite (or perhaps because of) the appearance in the United States of a seemingly Japanophilic trend represented best by Ezra Vogel's best-seller *Japan as Number One* (1979), whose title is alluded to in the comedy routines, hierarchies continued to define the imaginary map by which Americans and Japanese understood their own geopolitical positions—hierarchies that YMO was at pains to undermine by revealing their basis in a hall of mirrors, in which each side looked into the mirror of the other in an attempt to locate its identity through a maze of stereotypes.

As the ×∞ *Multiplies* album continues, it alternates between attractive techno-pop songs and comedy routines highlighting the ways cultural stereotypes are used to produce identity. The final comedy routine consists of a roundtable discussion between several parties (now all speaking in Japanese), each of whom throws down increasingly inflated claims to understanding the authentic meaning of rock music: one claims to own fifty thousand albums, while the next speaker tops this by claiming to own eighty thousand; another claims to host visiting bands from abroad regularly, while yet another claims to wear authentic rock fashion, and so on. The humor derives from the fact that, despite the participants' increasingly desperate attempts to demonstrate their own unique knowledge of rock authenticity, each reaches exactly the same mundane conclusion about the genre: that some of it is good and some of it bad. The album closes with another ironic orientalist number, "The End of Asia," ending with a stereotypical Japanese xenophobic voice that declares, in Japanese, that after all there's no place like Japan.

When $\times \infty$ *Multiplies* was released in the United States, not surprisingly the comedy routines were all dropped from the album. The use of parody to attack cultural stereotypes hinted at the band's politics, which were not grounded in an attempt to protect a pure authenticity from corruption but aimed to produce an affective charge and meaning from the inauthenticity that seemed to rule in early 1980s Japan. Political themes were increasingly foregrounded in the band's final years, when stage and costume design and songs increasingly touched on the history of Japanese fascism and imperialism. In its farewell concert, the band appeared in uniforms that deliberately invoked Nazism, and the film *Propaganda* (1984; dir. Satō Makoto), which combines a fictional narrative with live concert footage, likewise situated the band in the violent history of twentieth-century Japan. In particular, the band increasingly thematized the problems of celebrity culture and the gap that opened between popular musicians and their audiences. In the climactic scene of *Propaganda*, the band's most faithful fan carries out a terrorist attack on a YMO performance. The potential for fascism was lurking, YMO seemed to suggest, in everyday popular culture and fandom.[105] Alongside this symbolic activism, YMO members have long been active in antiwar, antinuclear, and environmental movements, and Sakamoto was a founding member in 2000 of the New Associationist Movement, a brief-lived anticapitalist organization led by Karatani Kōjin.[106] Negating the negation of inauthenticity did not for YMO mean abandoning politics but rather a creative rethinking of the relationship between popular music and politics.

*   *   *

In concluding this chapter on the ways that 1970s new music negated the negation that defined the politics of 1960s folk music, it seems fitting to give the last word to Hosono Haruomi. He was, after all, the bass player for Happy End, for Tin Pan Alley as it backed Yuming on her early albums, and for YMO as the decade closed. In a 1990s interview, Hosono described the role the "exotic" played in his musical life, noting for example that the early postwar boogie-woogie singer Kasagi Shizuko had sounded exotic to his child's ears in the 1950s. Later music that seemed to come from America—rockabilly, country-western, rock and roll—seemed less foreign. Instead,

> things I perceived as exotic were, for example, films from Hollywood in the 1950s where the picture of Japan was occasionally represented in an extremely warped way, and the twisted, surreal mode that they exuded. . . . Japanese people can never be true orientalists. This is because we are trapped within what Westerners term "the Far East." I would say that my own orientalism is a mind's eye view which I arrived at through taking a roundabout, Hollywood-esque perspective. I practiced what Brecht mentioned, "See as through the eyes of a stranger."

He subsequently describes his reaction to the exoticism in Western popular music of such figures as Martin Denny and Arthur Lyman: their music "had a ridiculous liveliness to it that completely turned over the way I viewed Japan."[107]

Hosono's remarks encapsulate the ways the musicking of new music creatively undermined the oppositions that had mapped the geopolitics of 1960s folk. The Japan versus America opposition gave way to a hall of mirrors as Hosono adopted "the eyes of a stranger" to see a fantasy Japan from the fantasy position of an American. This, in turn, called into question the opposition between commodity and art: the most commercial of cultures, the Hollywood film, became the source material for complex musical compositions. Ultimately, the distinction between authenticity and inauthenticity was shed: only by starting from the patently inauthentic—the glossy Technicolor spectacles of the Orient cranked out by Hollywood—could Hosono find a way to do something meaningful and real. New music was certainly guilty at times of hollowing out the political activism that had been definitive of 1960s folk, a politics that ultimately was grounded in the negation of what its advocates saw as inauthentic everyday life. But new music also insisted that any artistic or political activism would have to begin from within that very everyday life and the unreal reality that it seemed to signify in 1970s Japan. New music's failing was also the source of its greatest achievement.

6

THE JAPAN THAT CAN "SAY YES"

BUBBLEGUM MUSIC IN A POSTBUBBLE ECONOMY

There is a painful past between Japan and Asia. It would be very easy to simply apologize to everyone for this past. But it seems utterly insincere for me, who wasn't even born then, to apologize for that past. I would rather be part of a generation that, together with the people of Asia, mourns that past history.

ASKA, SPEAKING TO A CONCERT AUDIENCE IN SINGAPORE

INSTRUMENTAL INTRO (HAWAIIAN SLACK GUITAR): THE ISHIHARA BROTHERS' SEASON IN THE SUN

It was during the mid-1950s period of spectacular economic growth (stimulated by the United States' use of Japan as a staging base for the Korean War) that Ishihara Shintarō first stormed into the public eye—right around the time of the rockabilly boom discussed in chapter 3. In 1956, Ishihara's story "Season of the Sun" (Taiyō no kisetsu) won the Akutagawa Prize, Japan's most prestigious literary award. The story caused a public sensation with its cool depiction of hedonistic upper-class teenagers who reject the morality of their parents and instead seek only the pleasures of cruising, violence, and casual sex.[1] *Taiyōzoku* (sun tribe) became a catchphrase to describe a new breed of postwar teenagers, and the mass media quickly appointed Ishihara (himself the product of an elite upbringing, similar to that of the characters depicted in his stories) as its spokesman. Ishihara relished the role, dashing off a series of melodramatic stories that continued the themes of "Season."[2] The narrative tone in these stories is consistently detached; there is both a distancing from the nihilistic protagonists and a refusal to condemn them. Above all, they are portrayed as victims of the postwar society that made them what they are.

These stories were frequently made into hit movies, often featuring Ishihara Yūjirō—Shintarō's brother.[3] This real-life brotherly link is mirrored in Shintarō's stories. Even as the stories revolve around troubled heterosexual romances, it is clear that the relationship Shintarō is most interested in depicting is the fraternal bond between men, the homosocial community (the sports team, the mahjong circle, the yachting club) in which women are the mediums of exchange by which relationships between men are established. In "Season of the Sun," the protagonist repeatedly sells his interest in his girlfriend to his brother for five thousand yen. She tries to buy herself back, only to be sold again, a vicious circle that ends only with her death. Accordingly, while adults may have feared this new generation with its apparent rejection of "traditional" morality, the *taiyōzoku* were in at least one sense faithful sons: they were the postwar heirs to the patriarchal code of the family-state that had dominated prewar Japan.

"Season of the Sun" was made into a successful film in 1956, featuring, of course, Ishihara Yūjirō. Yūjirō was well on the way to earning his nickname as "the Japanese James Dean." He would soon be known as "the Japanese Elvis Presley," too, because in addition to his status as a movie idol Yūjirō achieved success as a singer. Again his brother played a key role: Shintarō wrote the lyrics for one of his brother's earliest hits, "Crazed Fruit" (Kurutta kajitsu, 1956), the theme song from the film of the same name, which was based on another of Shintarō's stories. The song's expressionistic lyrics seem to tell of a fleeting romance on a summer's day. Nothing is explicit as a series of exotic images float past: the ocean breeze, dreams that disappear beyond the waves, and the hot sun that ripens red flowers, red fruit (and, implicitly, red lips). The speaker's partner is never described. The speaker seems to be a Japanese man, but this too is hazy: cultural identities are in flux here.

The song's instrumental arrangement, however, with its slack guitar and ukulele, provides a more stable cultural reference: Hawaii. In fact, "Crazed Fruit" formed part of the Hawaiian boom in postwar Japanese pop, set off by

Oka Haruo's hit song "The Road to Dreamy Hawaii" (Akogare Hawai kōro, 1948), which was incidentally one of the songs that Misora Hibari featured in her early concerts.[4] The Hawaii signified in such songs is not Hawaii the wartime military target, nor is it Hawaii the prewar destination for Japanese emigrant laborers: this is Hawaii as exotic tourist destination, the island paradise where a few years later Sakamoto Kyū would vacation on his way home from California.

In short, the song "Crazed Fruit" reproduces orientalist visions derived from American pop culture, which as we have seen remained a major force in Japan even after the U.S. Occupation ended in 1952. Tin Pan Alley's romantic fantasies (think "Blue Hawaii," and then think of it again in relation to Korea and Vietnam) are being rearticulated here, ideologically repositioning Japan as an economic powerhouse and as an Asian bulwark against Communism: as America's little brother in the Pacific. Guilty memories of wartime and colonial violence disappear like a bad dream, replaced by the intriguing possibilities of exotic romance between a remasculinized Japan and feminized Hawaii. Swept from view too—*at least, temporarily*—is American pop culture's troubling tendency to imagine Japan itself as a submissive oriental female.[5] Lacking also is the irony that would characterize Yellow Magic Orchestra's appropriation of similar musical exotica a couple of decades later.

As noted in chapter 2, the Hawaiian boom was one of a series of proto–world music crazes to sweep over Japan in the late 1950s, including the Latin boom and the chanson boom. These songs offered new modes not only for mapping Japan's place in the international order but also for establishing connections with the imaginary roots of Japan itself. Local songwriters quickly appropriated exotic-sounding musical elements into their own works, creatively transforming them into a general code used to invoke nostalgia, be it for a lost love or a lost hometown. What signified desire for Hawaii or Brazil could also signify a yearning after an exotic, premodern Japan that was thought to survive intact somewhere beyond the urbanized, industrialized giant that was in the process of forming.[6] Of course, the urban, industrial networks of mass media and corporate music distribution were necessary preconditions for the dissemination of these songs. At any rate, by the late 1960s, the very musical elements that in the 1950s had signified cosmopolitanism—orchestral string sections, Latin dance rhythms, big-band brass arrangements, Spanish and Hawaiian guitar—had been reinflected into that most purely Japanese of pop music genres, *enka*. If you want to find "Crazed Fruit" in a CD store in Japan today, you need to look in the *enka* (or *kayōkyoku*) section.[7]

A surging economy, a melodramatic narrative that takes the public by storm, a hit record, Japanese musicians strumming chords of Asian-Pacific romance, and the translation of American orientalism into Japanese sentiment: all the themes from which I patch together the final song for this book are now in place. Let us turn to the end of the 1980s, when Ishihara again created a splash at another moment of rapid economic growth. This also provides the opportunity to explore music that became popular around the time people first began to use the expression "J-pop" in the early 1990s, as well as the new post–Cold War mapping of the global geopolitical order through which people imagined their relation to that music.

FIRST VERSE: ISHIHARA SHINTARŌ'S TINY BUBBLES

Fast-forward to 1989. Once again, the Japanese economy is surging to unprecedented heights, driven by a speculative bubble that brought with it conspicuous consumption on a world historical scale. Bubble-period consumerism ranges from the massive (Mitsubishi's purchase of Rockefeller Center) to the personal (a boom in ramen noodles sprinkled with genuine gold flakes). Media culture reacts as well: the new consumerism can be seen in the cheerful hit songs of the Southern All Stars celebrating summer vacation and life at the beach and in the television "trendy dramas" that featured stylish young urbanites engaged in rampant consumption. A concomitant reaction also arises, a public gnashing of teeth over the consumer culture that was thought to be corroding spiritual values (especially those of young Japanese women), and forms a key tenet of the muscular conservatism espoused by such figures as Nakasone Yasuhiro, Japan's prime minister from 1982 to 1987.

It was in this tumultuous environment that Ishihara Shintarō, together with Sony head Morita Akio, published the best seller *The Japan That Can Say No ("No" to ieru Nihon,* 1989; hereafter cited as *"No"*), which created a media sensation in Japan and elsewhere. The book sold more than a million copies, and its success drove Ishihara to produce three sequels, each with a different coauthor.[8] None of the sequels was as successful as the first *"No"* book, though, which ranked number 18 in the 1989 annual list of Japan's best sellers, and number 2 in 1990. Both its emphatic confidence in Japan's enhanced position in the world and its spectacular success as a publishing commodity situate *"No"* as a representative product of bubble-period popular culture.

The publishing genre of the book, "business/economics/current affairs" according to its American publisher, reflects Ishihara's changed status since the 1950s: in 1989, he was more famous as a right-wing politician than as a novelist. But in fact lines blur: the political analysis Ishihara provides in *"No"* and its sequels reproduces many of the ideologies that characterized his earlier fiction and song lyrics. While his publishing genre may have changed, Ishihara continued to call on a familiar literary mode to structure his political arguments: *"No"* is even more of a melodrama than "Season of the Sun."

How do I define *melodrama* here? The philological roots of the word— a theatrical performance (*drama*) accompanied by music (*melo*)—are part of the story: Ishihara and his cowriters repeatedly allude to popular music. Moreover, as in the typical melodrama, Ishihara's arguments are anecdotal, a haphazard stringing together of emotionally charged incidents. Ishihara repeatedly cuts structural economic and political difficulties away from their historical contexts and reduces them to stories about personal confrontations between Ishihara and his opponents. Instead of insisting that the personal is the political, Ishihara repeatedly translates the political into the personal.

Ishihara's texts also partake of another definitive quality of the melodramatic genre: "the seductive pleasures of melodramatic wholeness."[9] Unlike tragedy, in which characters find themselves torn in half between conflicting demands, in melodrama conflict is purely external. A homogeneous, self-identical good confronts an equally homogeneous, self-identical evil; the troubles of the hero are not internally generated but imposed from without. In this sense, as Peter Brooks has argued, melodrama is a fundamentally modern form, rooted in the anxieties provoked by the collapse of the authority of earlier sacred myths. According to Brooks, "melodrama becomes the principal mode for uncovering, demonstrating, and making operative the essential moral universe in a post-sacred era."[10] Ishihara and his coauthors, faced with the rapid change and social dislocation brought about under the conditions of capitalism, seek a metaphysical guarantee, an unchanging national morality underlying the appearance of fluctuation. It is a view of history that expresses melodrama's paradigmatic desire for security and wholeness in a world in which all boundaries have given way to capitalism and its processes of deterritorialization and reterritorialization. Taken in this light, melodrama is less a formal genre than a mode for trying to make sense of the modern capitalist world.[11]

Another important factor is gender. Melodramas, particularly film and television melodramas, are frequently aimed at a female audience. In addition, their stories tend to center on the realms that modern capitalist societies code as feminine: the private, domestic space of romance and the bourgeois family. Accordingly, melodramas frequently revolve around questions of marriage, motherhood, and maternal self-sacrifice, often mixing "complicit" images that tend to reinforce dominant ideologies of the family with "resisting" images that tend to undermine or at least question those same ideologies.[12] Ishihara's texts are no doubt primarily aimed at male readers, yet as we will see they partake of this particular version of gendered relations so characteristic of melodrama.

Ishihara employs a melodramatic mode to demonstrate that Japanese culture is immune by its essence to the ravages of capitalism. This is due to Japan's cultural inheritance, the product of two thousand unbroken years of history and rooted, ultimately, in the geography of the Japanese archipelago. Conversely, the ravages of capitalist development—unemployment, class conflict, racism, environmental destruction, military adventurism—are inherently foreign to Japan. They are, specifically, American, and when they seem to appear within the homogeneous space of Japan, it is because external corruption has leaked into Japan, depriving it temporarily of the pleasures of wholeness.[13] The moment of violation is clearly defined in the texts: 1945, the beginning of the American Occupation. Ishihara describes a childhood wartime memory, a naval officer's club near his home where young married couples often stayed before the husband went off to battle: "For us children, it became a kind of cherished holy ground, and we even imagined ourselves presently becoming the sort of person who stayed there." This holy ground of domestic intimacy is violated after the war: "The [clubhouse] underwent a sudden change and became a whorehouse used exclusively by black soldiers.

It was on my way to school, and even in broad daylight the girls came out into the street, wearing flimsy waist cloths, their breasts fully exposed, flirting with the black soldiers. To my childish heart, this was a cruel transformation."[14] And so the *"No"* series calls for Japan to recover the moral purity it lost with the American Occupation, a morality that transcends the corruption caused by Western capitalism. Clearly, Ishihara carries on the imaginary geopolitical mapping of the world centered on a Japan versus America bipolar opposition that has provided the implicit ground for much of the postwar popular music examined in the previous chapters.

Moreover, as this emotional anecdote suggests, Ishihara's arguments are structured with sexual and gender categories at the forefront. National and racial identities are simultaneously gender identities. And in fact it is an inherent, essentially feminine quality that seems—at least at first glance—to provide Japan with its moral essence and its immunity to social trauma:

> Japanese companies are distinctive for their warm interpersonal relations. There is an emotional attachment to company, workplace, colleagues, and even the machinery. To cite an extreme case, workers affix photos of popular singers like Momoe Yamaguchi and Junko Sakurada to industrial robots and nickname the machines "Momoe" or "Junko." Silly as this may seem, it enhances productivity. Thinking of a cold piece of metal in human terms generates a kind of empathy, a personal connection.[15]

There is an essential maternal, mothering quality to Japanese culture, Ishihara argues, a careful attention to details and to people that protects Japanese society from the excesses and failures that mark the United States.

Accordingly, Ishihara figures the relationship between Japan and the United States as one of heterosexual marriage, a marriage that is on the rocks because of the husband's shiftless and irresponsible behavior: "An American politician whom I knew well said to me, 'The Japan-U.S. relationship must be preserved. As you say, it's important to both countries and to the rest of the world. We're married to each other.' 'Well, if we are properly married, okay,' I responded. 'A wife can talk back to her husband. But a kept woman, afraid the man will kick her out, always has to do what he says. Don't ever think Japan is America's mistress.' He was shocked at my metaphor, but we both laughed."[16] The right to say no, then—at least initially—is the right of a woman to refuse a marriage proposal or sexual advance from a man. Ishihara's stated goal is to make America shape up so that marital harmony and a stable world order can be restored: Dad and Mom must join hands over the Pacific so that the kids (the developing nations) can grow up strong and healthy.[17] The melodrama of the suffering wife reaches closure when the husband finally acknowledges her worth. As historian Yoshikuni Igarashi has shown, this kind of sexual melodrama used to figure postwar relations between Japan and the United States reoccurs frequently in the rhetoric of postwar Japanese historical memory.[18]

But a closer examination of Ishihara's argument reveals greater ambiguity. Ishihara suggests another possible resolution to his melodrama: the wife can throw the husband out; she can even become the man in the family. Take, for example, another musical reference Ishihara uses:

At the risk of repeating myself, the first step . . . is to get rid of our servile attitude toward the United States. We should no longer be at Washington's beck and call. The ending of *The King and I* suggests a great beginning for Japan. As his father is dying, the young son who will become king proclaims a new era for Siam: No longer will the subjects bow like toads. They will stand erect, "shoulders back and chin high," and look the king in the eye as a proud people were meant to do.[19]

Here Japan is ambiguously either the son, usurping the father's position and freeing the people, or the newly "erect" people standing up to look the king in the eye. Either way, Japan is assigned a masculine role. Note furthermore that Ishihara is citing a musical built around a romance between an Asian male and a Western female, a reversal—though not a deconstruction—of the usual orientalist sexual fantasy found in its paradigmatic form in Puccini's opera *Madame Butterfly*.[20]

Similar assertions of the need for Japan to adopt a more assertive, masculine position appear throughout the *"No"* series. Postwar Japan "has become a nation-state that is like the eunuchs of ancient China: it is a man with a penis but no balls." Accordingly, in the post–Cold War world, Ishihara argues that Japan's "passive, feminine posture, always following America's lead," has reached a dead end and accordingly asks, "Haven't we now reached an age when we should change directions and fulfill a masculine role as a nation-state?"[21]

In the end, Ishihara claims that the coming postmodern world order, the age of Japan's triumph, will transcend the binary divisions of the Cold War: either it will be a poleless world order or a tripolar one.[22] Does Ishihara's ambiguous gendering of Japan's role in a postmodern, posthistorical Utopia[23] represent the beginning of a postgender order in which the binary structure of patriarchy dissolves? In fact, that hardly seems to be the case. Ishihara, after all, is an author of melodramas: he is concerned primarily with polar oppositions, the unbridgeable antithesis between yes and no. As a result, Ishihara's predictions fail spectacularly to account for the new world order that did emerge following the end of the Cold War.

Japan's shifting gender in Ishihara's argument is partially a result of a double relationship, of bigamy. He portrays Japan's dual role as a wife to America and as a husband to Asia: Japan is simultaneously Mrs. America and Mr. Asia. Going beyond this, though, Ishihara's gender ambiguities also operate as an ideological mechanism for reproducing Japan's modern patriarchal order. Even as he criticizes modern Western societies, Ishihara is not interested in overthrowing the structures of power/knowledge that are characteristic of Western modernity. Instead, his critiques of Western racism and orientalism reproduce those very structures, but with (feminine) Japan on top—that is, in the masculine position. Ishihara's version of "particular" Japanese culture is complicit with the very Western modernity and its "universalism" that he claims to resist. Hence the irony that he must resort to the English word *no* to phrase his rejection of the West.

Accordingly, one of Ishihara's strategies is to appropriate critical theories developed to challenge Eurocentrism, racism, and class conflict in the West and to transform them into legitimations of the existing social order in Japan.[24] Simultaneously, Ishihara is also rearranging an old tune here, one with deep roots in Japan. In the eighteenth century, the nativist scholar Motoori Norinaga posited Chinese culture as an aggressive and invasive masculinity, thereby inventing a Japanese tradition that was essentially feminine, a tradition that was threatened by the intrusion of the foreign Chinese. Subsequently, many (but by no means all) Japanese intellectuals have resorted to this ideology, an attempt to resolve at the level of fantasy (and thereby to reproduce) the power relationships that fracture Japanese society, including class and gender conflict. Masculine domination is translated into the myth of feminine harmony.[25] By seeming to blur the boundaries between male and female roles, Ishihara and his brethren help reproduce the ideologies that underwrite a hierarchical patriarchal order, thereby implicitly reinstalling rigid gender divisions. In Ishihara's melodrama, it is precisely by laying claim to this essential femininity that Japan will at last become one of the boys, a player in the homosocial poker game that is the new world order.

This was a sophisticated ideological strategy that tried to preempt the possibility of a gender critique from within Japan. As Ueno Chizuko and other feminist scholars have argued, the strategy of claiming an essential femininity to Japanese culture not only reproduces the ideologies of Western orientalism but also places Japanese women under a double burden, a double silencing.[26] If Japanese men are supposed to be "feminine" in contrast to "masculine" Westerners, then calls for them to surrender their masculine privilege must be irrelevant. In terms of Ishihara's melodrama, to critique patriarchy from within Japan is already to identify oneself as a non-Japanese, because Japanese culture is essentially feminine and harmonious. In fact, Ishihara's coauthors specifically cite feminism and gay activism as symptoms of the social disease that is afflicting the United States, and accordingly as movements essentially foreign to Japan.[27]

Ishihara's fantasy traps Japanese feminists "in a vicious circle that oscillates between Orientalism and reverse Orientalism."[28] He accepts the ideologies of orientalism, with its presumption of a masculine West and a feminine East, and thereby is able to invent a fantasy of Japan as having transcended the traumas of modernity and capitalism. Simultaneously, he produces a powerful ideological statement that aims to reproduce a patriarchal social structure within Japan, one grounded in the bourgeois ideal of romantic marriage (which, of course, did not exist in "traditional" Japan). The options left open to Japanese women are reduced to a simple yes or no in answer to proposals generated by men. Other questions—about the presumption of normative heterosexuality, for example, or about the need for women to marry at all—are closed off from view: they become fundamentally anti-Japanese, non-Japanese. Ishihara takes a position that has been produced through the workings of modern capitalism, orientalism, and patriarchy; even though his position is complicit with these forces, he pretends to resist them—only to install them all the more securely. It is the generic conventions of melodrama that allow him to hold this self-contradictory structure together.

INSTRUMENTAL BRIDGE: POP!
THE SOUND OF A BUBBLE BURSTING

In January 1990, one year after the publication of *"No,"* the bubble burst. On the first day of trading in 1990, stock prices began falling. By April, the Nikkei average had lost a quarter of its closing 1989 value; by mid-1992, it had lost more than half. Simultaneously, land prices, whose speculative rise had fueled the bubble, collapsed. This staggered the banking establishment, whose loans were largely collaterized on now-vanished real-estate wealth. To make matters worse, the value of the yen soared, making Japanese exports more expensive and leading to a hollowing out of manufacturing as companies shifted production overseas. The Japanese economy entered into a severe recession that would last for more than a decade.

Simultaneously, the Cold War—the justification for the entire postwar order in Japan, including unbroken rule since 1955 by the conservative Liberal Democratic Party, the continual promotion of rapid economic growth within Japan, and the positioning of an extensive network of American military bases in Japan and Okinawa—ground to a rather abrupt halt. The Berlin Wall cracked open in late 1989 (former Spiders lead guitarist Kamayatsu Hiroshi famously mounted it in early 1990 to perform an impromptu solo version of his hit "Ban Ban Ban" [1966]), the Velvet Revolution swept across eastern Europe, and in late 1990 the two Germanys were reunited. An entirely new mapping of the world order was suddenly emerging, one that rendered meaningless Ishihara's vision of a world centered on Japan. It would bring with it new forms of popular music in Japan—forms that were used in unprecedented ways, circulating via novel digital media across what for decades had been unthinkable pathways of distribution.

SECOND VERSE: SAY YES TO *THE 101ST PROPOSAL*

It is now the summer of 1991. The giddiness of bubble-period popular culture gives way to a more somber, reflective tone, one that privileges values other than material consumption. The hedonistic "trendy dramas" so popular in the late 1980s suddenly seem anachronistic and are replaced by a new type of series, one with characters no less attractive yet who deal with economic and social problems and seek spiritual rather than material satisfaction.[29]

One of the most successful of the new series, *The 101st Proposal* (*101 kaime no puropōzu*), was broadcast in the coveted Monday 9:00 P.M. slot on the Fuji TV network, beginning on July 1, 1991. The series, produced by Ōta Toru and scripted by the up-and-coming Nojima Shinji, at first scored moderately successful ratings; in mid-August, the numbers began to pick up. The eleventh episode (broadcast on September 9) broke through the 30 percent barrier, signifying a megahit in Japanese television ratings, and the final episode (September 16) achieved a 36.7 percent mark, then the highest rating in the history of the Fuji network and one of the highest ever for a commercial broadcaster in Japan. In its press releases heralding this triumph, the network's public-relations department declared that the series "broke from the previous mold of the 'trendy drama.' One reason for its success was that it was able to capture not only the young viewers who had formed the core of the audience for trendy dramas, but also middle-aged fans."[30] The nation was being united again, this time around a television drama.

The program's theme song, "Say Yes," by the male duo Chage & Aska (hereafter, C&A), also became a hit, eventually going on to be the year's best-selling single. Given the song's title and the post-bubble, subdued tone of the drama in which it appeared, it may seem that "Say Yes" marks an ideological shift from Ishihara's prebubble insistence that Japan just say no. But this apparent incongruity masks a fundamental similarity that becomes apparent when we explore how the song was used in the television series. *The 101st Proposal* fits the classical definition of melodrama in many ways—not the least of which being philological: *The 101st Proposal* is a *drama* built around a *melody*, "Say Yes." And following classic melodrama fashion (as well as the formula already well established by 1991 for Japanese television dramas), the song was used each week to intensify the emotional impact of climactic moments, usually at the end of each episode: it was precisely this skillful use of theme songs "not just as background music but as a constitutive part of the climactic scene" that distinguishes Japanese television dramas from this period.[31]

The 101st Proposal narrates the tale of Hoshino Tatsurō (Takeda Tetsuya, an actor who first achieved popularity as a singer with the 1970s folk group Kaientai), the hapless forty-two-year-old subsection chief at a construction company who has been refused in ninety-nine marriage proposals, and Yabuki Kaoru (Asano Atsuko), a suave thirty-year-old professional cellist who feels increasing pressure to marry but whose memories of her deceased fiancé, killed in a car accident on the way to their wedding ceremony three years earlier (talk about melodrama!), leave her emotionally unable to commit to another man. The two meet at an *omiai*, an arranged introduction of parties seeking a spouse. Hoshino performs with his usual lack of aplomb, and Kaoru rejects his proposal: she says no. Of course, this is merely the beginning of the melodrama, which follows Hoshino's desperate attempts to prove his worthiness and Kaoru's growing attachment to him. The series ends with a gigantic YES as Kaoru accepts Hoshino's proposal in spectacular fashion: Hoshino—having abandoned all hope of marrying, having thrown away the expensive engagement ring he bought for Kaoru, having lost his job—is reduced to working at night on road construction when he looks up to see Kaoru in a wedding dress running down the nighttime road toward him (the song "Say Yes" plays in the background). She reaches him and vows to marry him despite his loss of everything, a masochistic gesture of self-sacrifice that is consummated when she picks up a muddy lug nut from the pavement and insists that Hoshino place it on her ring finger.

This formulaic story line can be mapped onto its specific historical moment of postbubble Japan in a number of ways. Unlike with the earlier "trendy dramas," now economic considerations abound: the contraction of the Japanese economy means that even fictional television characters have to worry about money. Failure is as likely as success. Hoshino's inability to rise beyond the lowly rank of subsection chief, and his subsequent loss of even that position, reflect this. This melodrama is built not around a glamorous company president but around one of the increasingly numerous losers in the Japanese economy.

Another contemporary theme presented throughout the show is the allegedly decreased virility of men in postbubble, post–Cold War Japan. Echoing Ishihara's complaints about a "eunuch" Japan, Kaoru complains repeatedly about how Hoshino represents the weakened state of Japanese manhood, the lack of masculine self-confidence that she claims is causing an increasing number of women to postpone marriage. And the flip side of, even the causal factor for, this demoralized masculinity is also repeatedly identified, usually by Kaoru: in 1991, men are weak because Japanese women have become too self-centered to properly support their men. Too many women are choosing to become career women, for example, rather than to make the sacrifices necessary to become good mothers.

Hoshino's response to Kaoru's assertion of declining virility indicates the complexity of the plot structure: repeatedly it is Kaoru's intervention that makes a man of Hoshino. This is clearly seen in the third episode, when Hoshino, intoxicated by Kaoru's declaration of her respect for his sense of honor, abandons all hope of finally making section chief by publicly accusing a superior, the sponsor of Hoshino's proposed promotion, of sexual harassment. The editing of the scene demonstrates that it is Kaoru driving the process: in a constant cutting back and forth between Kaoru's instructions to a young piano pupil and Hoshino's confrontation with his boss, Hoshino is portrayed as following to the letter Kaoru's instructions to her pupil. She is the force behind Hoshino's transformation into a self-assured man, one willing to abandon economic success in order to defend moral values, a man who even quits his job out of love for Kaoru.

We seem to see, then, the emergence in *The 101st Proposal* of a new ideal man, one less masculinist and more willing to engage in something like maternal self-sacrifice. Moreover, in the wake of the bubble collapse, this new man seems to have abandoned the goals of capitalist success in favor of defending a deeper, moral order. But it seems to me that we are seeing the same dodge we saw in Ishihara. The apparently "resisting" feminization of Hoshino's position leads directly to a restoration of the patriarchal order: in the end, Kaoru gets the strong man she has longed for all along. And whereas in the first episode Hoshino jokes that a thirty-year-old unmarried woman as beautiful as she could only be a transsexual, by the final episode it is clear that Kaoru is a real woman. Her symbolic humiliation (the lug nut that soils her hand in place of a diamond) signifies her withdrawal from the productive economy of subjects just as the camera transforms her into the spectacular object of Hoshino's (and the viewer's) gaze. She seemingly accepts her destiny as a housewife/consumer who will retreat into the private space of the home, where she will stand by her man.

Moreover, the apparent morality that Hoshino defends represents not so much the rejection of a capitalist economy as it does a surrendering to market forces—just as this melodrama with its message of morality and sentiment over selfish profit became a remarkably profitable commodity, a smash hit. In order to demonstrate this in more concrete terms, I would like to focus on a scene that occurs at the end of the sixth episode (that is, precisely halfway through the series), one that provides the most striking visual image from the entire series. Kaoru and Hoshino are shown walking down a street together at night. Kaoru breaks into tears as she tells Hoshino that though she loves him, she cannot marry him yet: having lost her fiancé on their wedding day, she is terrified to commit to another man for fear that she will lose him too. Suddenly, the opening chords of "Say Yes" sound, instantly producing goose bumps on the flesh of the viewer, who is by now trained, like one of Pavlov's dogs, to associate the music of the theme song with moments of emotional catharsis. This impact is intensified by a shift into slow-motion video. Hoshino breaks away from Kaoru and jumps over a guardrail into the street, directly in the line of an oncoming truck. The truck brakes just in time, and Hoshino—now with tears running down his cheeks too—turns to Kaoru to scream, "I won't die! Because I love you, I won't die! I promise I will make you happy!" Several cuts in close-up (throughout the series, the camera fetishizes the face of the heroine to register emotional peaks) between the two figures follow as the song continues in the background. Kaoru finally announces her acceptance of Hoshino's proposal between sobs. The episode ends as the song "Say Yes" draws to its close, with Hoshino kneeling on the ground, admitting—comically—"Oh, that was frightening, really frightening," endearing him all the more to Kaoru and the viewer.

This masochistic act of self-sacrifice turns the course of the show. By demonstrating utter selflessness, Hoshino has finally broken through to Kaoru's heart (though repeated breakups and reconciliations lie ahead in the remaining episodes). He has apparently demonstrated an allegiance to the spiritual values that a chastened postbubble Japan sought. As Fuji television's public-relations announcements repeatedly trumpeted, this was a series that revolved around the theme of "pure love."

But Hoshino's act signifies no rejection of market values. The very next appearance of "Say Yes" in the following episode is suggestive: there, it is used as background music for a montage portraying Hoshino and Kaoru as happy consumers on a shopping spree. Even in the scene where Hoshino faces death, we see the operation of market principles: in throwing himself in front of the truck, he takes a calculated risk. Rather than invest money in stock and abandon it to the whims of market forces, he invests his person to the whims of chance and comes up a big winner. This notion of love requiring one to speculate recurs frequently throughout the series. In the second episode, Kaoru challenges Hoshino to gamble his entire annual bonus on a horse race: only a man capable of such a decisive act can win her heart, she vows. Hoshino in fact does bet his bonus on a horse and loses it; the pair watches the race on television in another montage sequence backed by "Say Yes." This failed gamble causes Kaoru to reconsider her initial rejection of his proposal: she begins to see Hoshino in a new light, as a real man capable of taking the sorts of risks that market economies require, capable of absorbing losses without abandoning the game. The economic message of the series seems to be that while Hoshino may have suffered losses, his economic fundamentals—demonstrated by his ability to successfully woo Kaoru—are still solid: he will rise again.

If melodrama "expresses the anxiety brought by a frightening new world in which the traditional patterns of moral order no longer provide the necessary social glue" and "demonstrates over and over that the signs of ethical forces can be discovered and acted upon,"[32] the twist that *The 101st Proposal* brings to this is an assertion that the "traditional" moral sentiment of the bourgeois family is not in conflict with the demands of the market economy. In the fourth episode, Hoshino scolds Kaoru's father, the president of a provincial company: any father who misunderstands his daughter as badly as you do will assuredly lead his company into failure. To be a good father and husband, the series implies, is to be a good capitalist, a good manager of women. A 1991 tabloid newspaper reported that one of the reasons that the ratings for *The 101st Proposal* were so high was that in addition to the core audience of young females, male managers were watching the show in great numbers so as to be able to communicate with the young women who worked under them.[33]

This, in my reading, is the message conveyed by the drama and its theme song, "Say Yes." A crisis in capitalism and the family are overcome through a masochistic, feminizing gesture by a man, who thereby paradoxically reasserts his authority as father and husband and simultaneously restores the hegemony of market principles.[34] Maurizia Boscagli in discussing contemporary American television melodramas argues that their depiction of masculine tears represents not a bending of gender boundaries but a strategy for reformulating masculine power in a period of anxiety brought about by the weakening authority of the subject under late capitalism.[35] In these melodramas, the masculine subject appropriates what has been culturally coded as feminine in order to produce a new discourse of universality, one that can be occupied only by men: "While a man who cries is a human being, a woman who cries is a woman. By crying she loses her humanity only to become gendered and 'particular' again."[36] The appropriation of femininity by men reproduces the intimate domestic sphere, the home, as the proper space for women to occupy. We see something very similar in *The 101st Proposal*: it proposes marriage as the solution to economic breakdown.

This sort of critique of the ideological messages of popular culture is necessary, but we also need to go a step further. While a given text might contain a dominant ideological message, it is by no means assured that its consumers will passively accept that message. Consumers can also be producers; they can produce their own meanings from melodrama, meanings that might bracket or even subvert the dominant ideological message.[37] To explore this possibility in more detail, I turn now to the theme song from the show, C&A's "Say Yes," and its actual and potential modes of reception. Here, in addition to looking at the form of the song, we also have to examine how and by whom it was used: how, in other words, it provided the opportunity for what Christopher Small calls musicking.[38]

THIRD VERSE: CHAGE & ASKA ARE THE MR. ASIA

While "Say Yes" provided a major breakthrough for C&A, it was by no means the duo's first record: it was in fact their twenty-seventh single release.[39] Since 1979, C&A had issued a constant stream of recordings and undertaken incessant touring (nearly a hundred shows per year) to build a loyal, largely female audience for their music within Japan. They originated in the thriving 1970s folk music scene around the cities of Fukuoka and Kitakyushu—the same scene that a few years earlier had produced such influential new-music artists as Inoue Yōsui and the band Tulip.[40] In their recordings, C&A combined folk and rock sensibilities, carrying on the lineage of the 1970s new music discussed in chapter 5. Like the most successful new-music artists, they also possessed a canny pop sense, allowing them to achieve a highly commercial sound.[41] Hence, they were well positioned to take advantage of the explosive growth in the Japanese music industry's sales volume that accompanied the switchover from analog records and tapes to the digital compact disc format in the 1980s.

The single "Say Yes" was released three weeks after the telecast of the first episode of *The 101st Proposal*. The album *Tree*, on which the song appears, was released in October, at which point its success was assured: both the television program and its theme song had achieved massive popularity, a fine instance of commercial synergy (both the Fuji TV network and the Pony Canyon record label belong to the same entertainment industry conglomerate).[42] C&A were awarded the Japan Gold Disc Award the following January for the highest sales volume among Japanese artists during 1991: the "Say Yes" single had sold 2.7 million copies, and the *Tree* album nearly 2.2 million. C&A would win the same award the following year, driven by the success of their album *Red Hill* with its anthemic hit single "Yah Yah Yah" (2.5 million copies sold). More than any other pop artist, C&A provided the sound track to the immediate postbubble, post–Cold War years—with the only near competition, at least in sales figures, coming from Matsutōya Yumi.

"Say Yes" (music and lyrics by Aska) is a remarkably catchy tune. From its complicated structure, which weaves together several distinct melodic themes; through the strained emotion of the vocal harmonies, which range from simpering whispers to bold, open-throated appeals; to the skillful arrangement of the recording, which employs all the lush techniques of 1980s synthesizer-based popular dance music, it is hardly surprising that the song became a massive hit. It is also hardly surprising that the lyrics reflect a celebration of heterosexual, romantic marriage. As the chorus insists, all will be right if you (the woman [*kimi*]) simply say yes to me (the man [*boku*]). But the persona of the singer is not entirely self-assured: like Hoshino in the series, he subtly betrays a touch of panic, of hysteria. The man is insisting that the woman say yes precisely because he is not certain that she will. The man tries to define for the woman her own thoughts, a paranoid stance that tries to preempt alternative and (from his perspective) undesirable responses to his proposal.

The weakened stance of the male speaker can be read as another manifestation of the strategy of male feminization we saw in Ishihara and in *The 101st Proposal*. In that sense, when the young women who formed the core of C&A's audience bought the song, they were in a sense buying into their own domination. The lyrics clearly lay out a kind of trap: insisting that words cannot truly convey what is in the heart, the singer declares,

> Even your little lies and displays of selfishness
> Become lover's phrases, as if to test me. . . .
> I will say it countless times, without a doubt, you
> Are in love with me

While he insists that the woman say yes, the speaker creates a tricky language code, a vicious circle: whatever the woman says, even no, it will signify her love for him. In other words, the doubt the man seems to express is in fact feigned: he knows that she will say yes in the end.

Musically, the structure of the song recapitulates this closed circle. Although the instrumentation of the recording foregrounds keyboards and mostly synthesized strings, the very first sound that the listener hears is a powerful sustained E-flat chord on an electric guitar, accompanied by a cymbal crash, a masculine thrust that then gives way to the shimmering keyboard runs and softly chimed triangle couplets that carry us through the rest of the eight-bar introduction and soften the overall feel into something much gentler. The strong, almost overpowering guitar chord at the onset suggests that the answer to the question is determined in advance: the opening hook foretells, that is, the conclusion to the narrative that the song will enact, both in its lyrics and in its music. Only after this authority is established can the tune then back off to suggest a softer musical tone and a less overtly macho speaking position for the lyrics—something akin to the thoughtful, self-sacrificing masculinity of Hoshino in the television series.

After the brief introduction, the complex architecture of the main body of the song shifts between several distinct melodic themes, generating a sense of tension. At key moments in the verses when the speaker stresses his vulnerability, the lyrics are sung in a subdominant (A-flat) harmony that seems far removed from the security of the tonic key, setting up tension that at least temporarily suggests that the outcome is far from certain. But the satisfying return to the tonic E-flat in the chorus effectively resolves the tension, returning us safely to the conclusion that we knew was coming all along.[43] In similar fashion, the lyrics withhold the awaited title phrase until almost the very end: in a song lasting 4 minutes, 43 seconds in the version found on the album *Tree*, the first occurrence of the phrase "say yes" does not come until 3 minutes, 31 seconds. The extended coda consists of five repetitions of that title phrase with various intonations and at various pitches, while the musical backing reprises the shimmering keyboard runs and triangle chimes from the introduction. In the ultimate and most confident-sounding repetition of the phrase, the final sung "yes" settles back into an E-flat chord, now held for a full measure, as if to emphasize that the song has ended precisely where that striking guitar chord at the opening predicted it would.

This complex structure has much in common with the sonata form in classical music, whose narrative form—in which the masculine tonic established at the beginning seems to go astray with the appearance of the secondary feminine key only to overwhelm it and force a triumphant return to the tonic in the finale—is that of a masculine conquest of the feminine Other. As Susan McClary has noted,

> Most popular music avoids this schema, for songs typically are content with the sustaining of harmonic identity. There is usually no implied Other within these musical procedures, no structural obstacle or threat to overcome. However, all that is required to transform these stable procedures into narratives is for a detail to be problematized—to be construed as Other

and as an obstacle to the configuration defined as Self or identity. In such songs, time becomes organized around the expectation of intensified conflict, climax, and eventual resolution. They adopt, in other words, the same desire-dread-purge sequence that characterizes narratives of so much classical music and literature.[44]

"Say Yes" remains in a single key throughout, but it still enacts a narrative of conquest through its lyrics, layering of melodies, and chord progressions. It is in part this structure that made "Say Yes" such an effective and, yes, seductive pop song.

In sum, to enjoy the song—as millions did, myself included—is to consent, at least for four and a half minutes, to a specific ideological vision of the world. Musicologist Robert Walser reminds us that "musical details and structures are intelligible only as traces, provocations, and enactments of power relationships. They articulate meanings in their dialogue with other discourses past and present and in their engagement with the hopes, fears, values and memories of social groups and individuals."[45] "Say Yes" grips its listeners by soliciting their minds and bodies to meld with certain imaginary solutions to fundamental anxieties and hopes.

But like all ideological interpellations, this one is marked by gaps and incoherencies. Like its performers and listeners, the song is living out a contradiction—several contradictions, actually. While I cannot speak for the young women who purchased the single—to do so would situate me in the same enunciative position as the speaker in the song's lyrics—I would like to sketch out possibilities that the song opens up for, in Rey Chow's phrase, "listening otherwise,"[46] possibilities that the song itself creates for a withdrawal from the language game that is being played. The game can be played more than one way, after all, and—to again borrow Walser's words—we need to keep in mind that "ultimately music doesn't have meanings; people do."[47]

Christopher Small's notion of "musicking" may be helpful here. In attempting to shift the focus of musicology from the noun *music* to the verb *to music*, from a notion of music as an object to a notion of music as an action, Small redefines the location of musical meaning. Meaning, he argues, arises from the act of performance, and its active producers include all participants: musician and singers, yes, but also the audience, ticket takers, managers, and anyone else whose participation contributes to the event. The crucial question then becomes, "*What does it mean when this performance (of this work) takes place at this time, in this place, with these participants?*"[48] Furthermore, Small argues, a performance of music has meaning because it establishes in its site a set of relationships, a model for the ideal relationships that participants imagine should exist between sounds, between people, between the musical performance and the world outside. When we enjoy a song, we are enjoying—and in fact learning to enjoy—a certain model of how the world should be; our enjoyment is a sign of our at least temporarily buying into that ideal vision. But each act of musicking is a different performance, enacting different ideal models of the world, even when the piece of music being performed is putatively the same. There can arise "a tension between, on the one hand, the intended meaning of that specific sequence of musical gestures that we call a piece or work of music as we hear it performed and, on the other hand, the meaning of the total act of performing it—musicking—on a specific occasion"[49]

In other words, even an ideologically weighted song like "Say Yes" provides openings for various possible meanings. It all depends on who participates in the act of musicking, and where and when that act takes place. Like Elvis's screaming fans in the 1950s, C&A's audience may "not be so much worshiping [them] . . . as *using* [them]."[50] In "Say Yes," the insistent silencing of the woman's voice that characterizes its lyrical content and musical form can also, when certain actors engage with it, open up an opportunity for withdrawal. As long as the masculine voice monopolizes the dialogue, continually insisting that the female say yes but never pausing for an answer, the very silence of the female interlocutor maintains a negating possibility, a postponement of the melodramatic closure that either a yes or a no would provide. An ideological silencing can be refracted into indifferent silence, into noise, or even into a refusal to speak—as we saw with Kasagi Shizuko in chapter 1. We can figure this kind of silence as a withdrawal from the insistent code of language, from the lyrics, and into the nonsignifying code of rhythm: shut up and dance. It may be possible that in *performing the act of listening* to the song, the listener can postpone answering the ideological hailing that the lyrics and music enunciate.

We should keep in mind that C&A's audience consisted largely of a generation of young Japanese women who in the 1990s increasingly postponed their own marriages, to the alarm of conservatives like Ishihara.[51] Of course, this propensity for Japanese women to delay marriage (their refusal to accept confinement in the private realm) was itself a product of their increasing assimilation into the labor market (their domination in the public realm)—an assimilation that increased their purchasing power, making it possible for C&A to sell their music in such massive quantities. But the consumers of "Say Yes" purchased not only its dominant ideological message but also its blind spots, gaps that they could use to their own purposes to create the "autistic" space of the Walkman listener, momentarily withdrawn into a hiding place marked by a "freedom to be deaf to the loudspeakers of history."[52]

Any discussion of the reception of "Say Yes" has to extend beyond the boundaries of Japan as well. With the end of the Cold War and the bursting of the economic bubble, the bipolar Japan versus America geopolitical map that had framed Japanese popular music since 1945 began yielding to a new mapping that increasingly situated Japan within Asia. Just as Ishihara's *The Japan That Can Say "No"* inevitably led to *The Asia That Can Say "No"* (a literal translation of the title of the fourth *"No"* book), in which Asia is figured as desiring a strong, masculine Japan that can impregnate it with investment capital, so C&A labored to carry their success in Japan into the broader Asian market. Realizing the potential of the pentatonic scale, Chinese characters, and other cultural forms as bridges that might connect Japan to Asia, C&A long had their eyes on the continent. As they declared (in English) in the chorus to the title song of their album *Mr. Asia* (1987), "We are the Mr. Asia." The door to the Asian market finally opened to C&A with the success of "Say Yes," which rode into Asian hit charts following the rebroadcast of *The 101st Proposal* on Hong Kong's satellite channel Star TV (it has subsequently been rebroadcast elsewhere, including Singapore and China).[53]

In a 1996 interview, when asked what career path he would have taken if he hadn't become a musician, Aska replied that he would likely have followed in his father's footsteps and become a member of Japan's Self-Defense Forces.[54] As a Japanese soldier, he would of course be unwelcome in the nations where he now regularly performs concerts: Singapore, Hong Kong, Taiwan, Korea.

When the ban on Japanese-language music performances was lifted in Korea in 2000, C&A were the first Japanese musicians to appear in concert there; a similar ban was lifted in another former Japanese colony, Taiwan, just months before C&A's first concert there several years earlier.[55] C&A have demonstrated a keen sensitivity to the problems of historical memory: during their first two Asian concert tours in 1994 and 1995/1996, they repeatedly addressed Japan's troubled past relations with Asia, expressing hope that their Asian concerts would help bring about a reconciliation.

That is to say, C&A took pains to distinguish their own invasion of Asia from Japan's invasion of Asia some fifty years earlier.[56] C&A's overture to Asia involved not military aggression but sentiment: they invoked the image of romantic love.[57] Their official Asia tour book describes their attitude toward Asia in the following terms:

> Chage & Aska, who first began singing to try to win the hearts of girls they liked—now they sing before the people of Asia with that same feeling they had in their youth.
>
> "Even if it's just a little bit, I want them to think, 'I like Japanese people.' Even if only one person feels this way, it's worth it for us to do our Asian tours."[58]

This sentimental reunion, however, was built on a solidly capitalist foundation. C&A were careful, for example, not to release "Say Yes" in Hong Kong and Taiwan until after their governments had signed on to international copyright conventions, thereby ensuring that the duo's love affair with Asian fans would be a profitable one. Likewise, C&A's second Asian tour was considered financially unfeasible until a number of major Japanese corporations—JTB, JAL, and NEC—stepped up to underwrite expenses. Clearly, the marriage of C&A to Asia was built on market principles, and it has proved a fruitful union. C&A album sales in Singapore, Hong Kong, Taiwan, and Malaysia topped 3 million, while a "best of" album released in China in 1995 sold some 300,000 copies.[59]

C&A were careful to trumpet their Asian success back home in Japan, but always in terms meant to reassure their Japanese fans that they hadn't been jilted. In 1996, they published *Chage & Aska document: Asian tour no shinjitsu*, a photo album of the second Asian tour, containing essays and quotations from Asian fans, promoters, and music critics, celebrating the tour. In the same year, C&A released a concert video documenting their 1995 concerts in Taipei. The book and video transformed the reactions of Asian fans to C&A into a visual commodity to be consumed by their Japanese audience: the spectacle of neocolonial Asian desire for Japan, what Koichi Iwabuchi has called the myth of "Asia-yearning-for-Japan."[60]

But a close look at the video reveals that, while C&A are no doubt selling the "romance of Asian capitalism,"[61] their Taiwanese fans may be buying something else. They are not "passive 'cultural dupes' who, apparently without a critical cultural lens, automatically absorb any messages and ideologies from the dominant center" but rather "actively and creatively consume media texts and cultural products."[62] Concert-goers and record listeners are active participants, after all, in the production of meaning that is this act of musicking, and for them the song may be a commodity like the Sony Walkman, whose global popularity may be a result of its lack of any specific cultural "odor," despite its invocation of allegedly Japanese traits such as miniaturization: "Although such signs of 'Japaneseness' are analytically important, they are not especially relevant to the appeal of the Walkman at a consumption level. The use of the Walkman does not evoke images or ideas of a Japanese lifestyle, even if consumers know it is made in Japan and appreciate 'Japaneseness' in terms of its sophisticated technology."[63] The title and refrain to the commodity—that is, "Say Yes"—are in English, after all, and the song's melodies are constructed primarily around pentatonic scales, like much contemporary pop music across East Asia.

In sum, when we explore the ways East Asian fans use J-pop songs like "Say Yes," we have to keep in mind that "there is no moment, in fact, in which records are 'passively' consumed, simply used up. Music is too volatile, carries too many meanings. It is actively consumed, *used*, in contexts of leisure and pleasure that are not easy to control."[64] In the Taipei concert video, when C&A perform "Say Yes," the cameras pan over the largely female audience. Most sway in time to the music. Virtually everyone shown is moving their lips: they sing along. But this, too (like a refusal to speak), can be interpreted as displacing the demand for a yes or a no: instead, they repeat the proposal back, word for word. Despite the video's attempt to commodify the spectacle of Asian desire for Japan, the Taiwanese fans not only are performing the role of the colonial woman answering the call of the Japanese male, but also simultaneously adopting the position of the Japanese male and repeating the question. It is an act of mimicry that both accepts the message of the song and subtly undermines it: it is no longer clear who is proposing to whom.[65]

At another point in the video of the Taipei concert, C&A attempt to engage their audience in what seems like dialogue. In wretched spoken Mandarin, the duo recite lines they have obviously memorized by rote: they introduce themselves and ask if the audience is having a good time. The audience roars with laughter, just as C&A make wry comments (in Japanese) between themselves about how well this "dialogue" is going. The sequence is funny to both performer and audiences because both sides realize that this is not actually a dialogue but a parody of a dialogue: the performers can only recite their prescripted lines, which are intended to elicit an entirely predictable response. Now it is the performers who imitate their audience, blindly reciting words memorized from a foreign language. Finally, C&A pick up huge signboards and write on them the Chinese characters for "thank you" (which are also used in Japan), holding them up to the audience, which predictably cheers in response.

In a Japanese newspaper article announcing C&A's first Asian tour, Aska declared that whereas their Asian fans had seen their songs performed in cover versions by other Asian artists, "We are the real thing. We're going there to prove that."[66] But is the divide between real and imitation, male and female, yes and no, so clear-cut? Oddly enough, the same page of the newspaper also contains an article praising John Lone's performance as a "remarkable 'woman'" in the film *M. Butterfly*, including a photograph of Lone in drag captioned "Who am I?" Translation and adaptations, as we explored in the case of the rockabilly music of Sakamoto Kyū, can shake up or reinforce boundaries between target and source languages, and sometimes, as we have seen in the case of Happy End and Yellow Magic Orchestra, the rejection of claims to authenticity can lead to creative breakthroughs: the unreal can become oddly real.

C&A sang a melodrama of cross-cultural romance. But as the song dispersed through a newly expanded marketplace, its consumers could transform the commodity into raw material for use in producing unexpected variations.

Their sampling might create new tunes that evade the melodramatic search for cultural and gendered wholeness, for simple yes or no answers. Could this act of musicking be considered a form of resistance? As one critic has noted, "Nothing is as resistant to consumer reinterpretation as the standardized forms, sounds, and verbal devices operating at the conventional core of the popular song," so that "these standardized components probably evoke the entrenched codes of the dominant culture much more powerfully than do the non-standardized components." Nonetheless, even in highly commodified pop music, there is "a constant struggle at the meeting point of production and consumption between the evocation of entrenched codes and the insinuation of alternative meanings."[67]

In a situation where the apparent choice between yes and no offered only the trap of a vicious circle, a refusal to speak or a parodic repeating of the question may not have offered a foolproof strategy of resistance; it may have amounted only to a matter of stalling. But sometimes stalling buys the time needed to think up a better question, to find more interesting ways to use the music. As we consider how Asian fans outside Japan used "Say Yes," we should keep in mind that the decade of the 1990s saw remarkable democratic transformations and other forms of political activism in South Korea, Taiwan, Hong Kong, and elsewhere—just as the decade also ushered in new heights of consumerism (and market failure) across the region. All these developments belong to the period of J-pop and hence lie beyond the scope of this book. But it was the generation of East Asians who grew up listening to C&A (among others) who participated in these changes. At the very least, the case of "Say Yes" suggests that the role popular music played and the ways it functioned in the leisure activities of youths across Asia were complex and contradictory.

* * *

With Chage & Aska, we leave behind the prehistory of J-pop and enter into the moment of J-pop proper. The death of Misora Hibari in early 1989 is symbolic of the closing of that era. The term "J-pop" was apparently first used in 1988, and within a few years it had become widely circulated to name a newly dominant genre of popular music in Japan, one that circulated widely throughout Asia.[68] The song "Say Yes" was one of the first major hits associated with this new genre. J-pop brought with it new imaginary mappings of the world, as well as a new set of geopolitical issues and contradictions. In other words, the story I am telling in this book, a story that began in 1945, comes to a close with the appearance of Chage & Aska and their contemporaries, both inside and outside Japan. With them, a set of new stories begin—stories that are even now remapping the movement of popular music across East Asia and, increasingly, the entire globe.

CODA

The period since 1991 has seen dramatic shifts in both the geopolitical environment in which Japanese performers and listeners "musick" and in the forms and contents of the sounds they make. The Cold War ended, and the imaginary geopolitical mapping of the popular music world organized around two poles, America and Japan, yielded to a more complex world in which Asian neighbors such as South Korea, China, and Taiwan have become predominant trade partners, strategic rivals, and potential markets for and sources of popular music. The bursting of the economic bubble in 1991 also brought to a close the period in which Japanese economic growth could simply be assumed (although the decade between 1988 and 1998 saw a doubling in the size of prerecorded music sales in Japan).[1] The compact disc, which in 1986 surpassed the vinyl record in sales volume to become the predominant format for prerecorded music in Japan, has itself subsequently become an endangered species, replaced by digital files that can be played back on a variety of devices, including cell phones. The Sony Walkman, still a relative novelty in 1990, is now an antique curiosity.

Many of the musicians discussed in the preceding chapters remain active today, producing both old and new sounds. But they have largely surrendered the all-important youth audience to a new generation of performers. Many of those newly risen artists perform what is called J-pop, a term that was coined in 1988 as the name for domestic music segments on the popular Tokyo FM radio station J-WAVE and that achieved wide currency around 1992 to 1994.

Originally the term was a branding strategy that seemed to situate Japanese popular music, regardless of genre, on the world stage. After all, both the *J* and the *pop* were from English, as if the word had been coined abroad instead of by the Japanese marketing executives who were its actual inventors.[2] Gradually, though, the category acquired the traits of a recognizable musical genre as the long-sought merger of Japanese, European, and African American musical styles—made possible by a mutual predilection for melodies constructed on pentatonic scales—was widely achieved by a number of singers, songwriters, and producers who have released a seeming unending string of hits that are unmistakably grounded in rhythm and blues yet also include elements that listeners identify as Japanese: Hamasaki Ayumi, Utada Hikaru, and Misia, to name just three popular purveyors of the new sound.[3]

J-pop seems to presume the existence of counterparts: K-pop, C-pop, and so forth. Many J-pop musicians enjoy success across the East Asian region, following the trail blazed by Chage & Aska. In the years after 1991, the popular music worlds of Japan and its neighbors became increasingly synchronized, with local record companies across East Asia releasing recordings by Japanese artists at the same time as they were issued back home in Tokyo. By the late 1990s, artists such as Dreams Come True, Amuro Namie, and Globe were regularly appearing in hit charts across East Asia.[4] Likewise, artists from East Asia were achieving unprecedented success in the Japanese market, too. From Singaporean musician Dick Lee to Hong Kong singer Faye Wong and South Korean idol BoA, audiences and musicians in Japan since the early 1990s have enjoyed musicking with a variety of pop music genres from across the Asian continent. A book on Asian popular culture published in Japan in 1990 declared that "the popular music of Asia reminds us that Japanese are Asian."[5] Popular music since 1991 is increasingly enjoyed through a map that connects Japan to its neighbors in Asia, and the actual travels of performers, songs, and recordings help transform that imagined map into a real, lived network.

Another pronounced change in J-pop since 1991 involves the structure of the market. The switchover to the CD format and the rise of cheap CD players led initially to a rapid expansion in the market for popular music recordings in Japan, as teenagers and women joined men as key purchasers of albums (in earlier decades, the audience for vinyl records had been primarily adult and male, with other market segments relying on radio, self-recorded cassettes, and other inexpensive media for their pop music fixes).[6] But as members of the family increasingly listened to music on individual playback devices rather than a shared stereo system, and as new digital-recording and distribution technologies reduced the cost of producing and marketing recordings, the mass market splintered. Popular culture in general, including music, has seen an increased specialization among markets by genre. The million-seller hit, such as Chage & Aska's "Say Yes," that could unify the entire pop music audience has since the late 1990s become increasingly scarce in Japan.[7]

Instead, with varying degrees of market size, a wide variety of musical subcultures has emerged, each with its devoted fan base. *Shibuya-kei* became a catchword in the 1990s for bands like Pizzicato Five, Flipper's Guitar, and Number Girl that performed a diverse range of alternative pop and rock styles, often releasing their material on independent record labels and using the Internet and other avenues to attract fans from around the world. *Visual-kei* bands like X-Japan, Glay, and Dir en grey achieved popularity with a hard-metal sound and extravagant costumes, hairstyles, and makeup that echoed the glam-rock styles of the 1970s. Hip-hop emerged as well, quickly giving birth to a multiplicity of subgenres in Japan, both mainstream and underground, just as it had elsewhere.[8] Trance, house, and other ambient electronic dance forms also found their own audiences, with Japan producing internationally recognized figures such as DJ Krush. Smaller audiences, both domestic and foreign, swear allegiance to hard-core punk, experimental noise, and electronica musicians such as the Boredoms and Merzbow.[9] Reggae, dance-hall, and Latin genres have their own well-developed subcultures.[10] Jazz, particularly modern jazz, and various forms of world music retain devoted audiences in today's Japan. Japanese artists performing in these and other relatively uncommercial genres have frequently toured on a small scale in North America and Europe and built cult audiences around the world, though no one has yet to duplicate Sakamoto Kyū's 1963 global-chart success.

Musical forms that claim more traditional roots continued to prosper after 1991 as well. *Enka* remains a force in today's popular music industry and in recent years has revitalized itself with a new generation of young performers, including Jero, who in 2008 became the genre's first African American star performer. Many of the other genres discussed in this book—folk, Group

Sounds, and rockabilly, for example—have also seen revivals since 1991, with new bands creatively revisiting the older genres. Traditional Japanese folk music also continues to evolve. The 1960s "god of folk" Okabayashi Nobuyasu now features a Tsugaru-jamisen and other traditional instruments in his live shows, while the Yoshida Brothers, a pair of samisen-playing siblings, achieved remarkable popularity in the early years of the new century.

One pronounced tendency in recent J-pop is the increased centrality of peripheral Okinawa, Japan's southernmost prefecture and a region with its own cultural and musical traditions. Before and even after its reversion to Japan from U.S. occupation in 1972, Okinawa was already the home of legendary hard-rock bands such as Condition Green and Murasaki, who learned their chops playing in bars for audiences made up mainly of U.S. military personnel.[11] In tandem with J-pop's rediscovery of Asia, Okinawa has since the 1990s increasingly become a site for homegrown exoticism, with such bands as the Nenes and Begin and singer Chitose Hajime (all actually from Okinawa) as well as mainland Japanese musicians such as the Boom and Sakamoto Ryūichi (formerly of Yellow Magic Orchestra) creating attractive hybrids that mix elements from traditional Okinawan folk songs, rock and pop structures, and world-beat aesthetics. Moreover, the prefecture has produced a disproportionately large number of mainstream musicians whose musical styles do not overtly reference local musical traditions, including the female idol group Speed, singer Amuro Namie, and the rock bands Orange Range and High and Mighty Color.[12]

In sum, since 1991 popular music in Japan has moved in multiple directions, undergoing a range of transformations in its audience, geopolitical imaginary, technologies of recording and distribution, musical styles, and in the ways people use it. The multiple linkages of the omnipresent cell phone and Japanese popular music since 1991 is a topic worthy of a book on its own. Although many of the elements and tendencies from earlier decades carry on today, they now operate in a new world and on a new map, that of J-pop proper, a form of musicking whose history is still being written.

I chose to end my story in 1991 in part because of the remarkable complexity of what has emerged since then (though I should here again acknowledge that the music of earlier decades also showed great complexity, which I have necessarily reduced in order to tell the story narrated in this book). As I have tried to suggest briefly here, Japanese popular music since 1991 is harder to collapse into a coherent historical narrative, at least from my current vantage point. If forced to choose a single musician with whom to close my discussion of post-1991 developments, I would pick singer-songwriter Shiina Ringo (sometimes written Sheena Ringo, with other spellings also in circulation). She grew up in Fukuoka—not too far from the home of Chage & Aska— and debuted as an idol singer in 1998 but quickly distinguished herself from the competition with her inimitable, often borderline avant-garde, compositions, which have earned widespread popularity despite their unconventional sound. She quickly won artistic control over her career, not only writing most of her own material but also producing her own recordings. A profile published in 2003 in the Asian edition of *Time* declared that while "her melodies managed to stay just within the boundaries of mainstream pop, she brought a hard-core, grungy pique to many of her songs." It went on to compare her acclaimed third album, *Karuki, zamen, kuri no hana* (*Chlorine, Semen, Chestnut Flower*, 2003), with the Beatles' *Sgt. Pepper's Lonely Hearts Club Band*, noting how it shifts "between ethereal yet densely layered ballads to all-out hard-rock anthems" and describing it as a "bursting yet impressively seamless pastiche of influences including (but not limited to) '40s Big Band and swing, Indian sitar, avant-garde atonal music, trance-house psychedelia, church-organ fugues, electronic multiprocessed voice-overs and traditional Japanese *koto, shamisen* and flute music."[13] In her subsequent solo releases and in her recordings since 2004 with her band, Tokyo Jihen (Tokyo Incidents), she has moved closer to the world of jazz, although retaining her characteristic hybrid and experimental style.

One of the things I find particularly appealing about Shiina Ringo is her sense of musical history. In concert, she has been known to wear costumes alluding to performers from earlier decades. Her recordings, too, sometimes contain musical allusions to earlier genres from the prehistory of J-pop. One song she has recorded more than once, "The Apple Song" (Ringo no uta), first saw light of day in 2003 as a kind of silky tango ballad, vaguely recalling some of Misora Hibari's 1950s cosmopolitan stylings—the lyrics even feature the solicitation *meshimase*, which was the lyrical hook to Hibari's smash hit "Hibari's Flower-Seller Girl" (Hibari no hanauri musume, 1951). Shiina's lyrics are more explicitly erotic than the early Hibari would have countenanced, with the female speaker offering herself up as a kind of sinful fruit, akin to Eve in the Garden of Eden.

The song reappeared in a new grunge-style hard-rock recording on Tokyo Jihen's debut album, *Education* (*Kyōiku*, 2004). In this speeded-up version, another musical allusion became apparent. Both in its title and in its melody, the song references Namiki Michiko's hit "The Apple Song" (1945), the bouncy tune that launched the history of postwar pop music in Japan amid the ruins of bombed-out Tokyo. In Shiina Ringo's remarkable postmodern version of J-pop, the genre's prehistory is translated, liberated, transformed into noise, negated, and then negated again. And you can most certainly dance to it.

NOTES

INTRODUCTION

1. On the culture of homemade cassette tapes in 1970s and 1980s Japan, including the decoration of tape cases, see Carolyn S. Stevens, *Japanese Popular Music: Culture, Authenticity, and Power* (London: Routledge, 2008), 112–13.
2. Harry Harootunian, "Some Thoughts on Comparability and the Space-Time Problem," *Boundary 2* 23, no. 2 (1995): 23–52.
3. One good source on 1930s mass culture in Japan is Miriam Silverberg, *Erotic Grotesque Nonsense: The Mass Culture of Japanese Modern Times* (Berkeley: University of California Press, 2007). On prewar jazz culture in Japan, see E. Taylor Atkins, *Blue Nippon: Authenticating Jazz in Japan* (Durham, N.C.: Duke University Press, 2001).
4. Julian Cope, *Japrocksampler: How the Post-War Japanese Blew Their Minds on Rock 'n' Roll* (London: Bloomsbury, 2007), 10.
5. Jacques Attali, *Noise: The Political Economy of Music*, trans. Brian Massumi (Minneapolis: University of Minnesota Press, 1985), 46.
6. Christopher Small, *Musicking: The Meanings of Performing and Listening* (Middletown, Conn.: Wesleyan University Press, 1998), 13.
7. On the critique of area studies, see H. D. Harootunian and Masao Miyoshi, eds., *Learning Places: The Afterlives of Area Studies* (Durham, N.C.: Duke University Press, 2002).
8. Naoki Sakai, *Translation and Subjectivity: On Japan and Cultural Nationalism* (Minneapolis: University of Minnesota Press, 1997).

1. THE MUSIC WILL SET YOU FREE

1. Tōya Mamoru, *Shinchūgun kurabu kara kayōkyoku e: Sengo Nihon popyurā ongaku no reimeiki* (Tokyo: Misuzu shobō, 2005), 174.

2. I have relied on a number of outstanding studies of early postwar culture in Japan that have appeared in recent years, including John Dower, *Embracing Defeat: Japan in the Wake of World War II* (New York: New Press, 1999); Yoshi-kuni Igarashi, *Bodies of Memory: Narratives of War in Postwar Japanese Culture, 1945–1970* (Princeton, N.J.: Princeton University Press, 2000); Joanne Izbicki, "Scorched Cityscapes and Silver Screens: Negotiating Defeat and Democracy Through Cinema in Occupied Japan" (Ph.D. diss., Cornell University, 1997); Michael Molasky, *The American Occupation of Japan and Okinawa: Literature and Memory* (London: Routledge, 1999); and Douglas N. Slaymaker, *The Body in Postwar Japanese Fiction* (London: Routledge, 2004).

3. "The Apple Song" was featured in the movie *Breeze* (*Soyokaze*, dir. Sasaki Yasushi), released on October 11, 1945—making it the first postwar film to be shown publicly in Japan. See Kyoko Hirano, *Mr. Smith Goes to Tokyo: Japanese Cinema Under the American Occupation, 1945–1952* (Washington, D.C.: Smithsonian Institution, 1992), 155. See also Dower, *Embracing Defeat*, 172–73.

4. On music in *Men Who Tread on the Tiger's Tail*, see Nishimura Yūichirō, *Kurosawa Akira: Oto to eizō*, rev. ed. (Tokyo: Rippū shobō, 1990), 39–44; and Donald Richie, *The Films of Akira Kurosawa*, 3rd ed. (Berkeley: University of California Press, 1996), 31.

5. Akira Kurosawa, *Something Like an Autobiography*, trans. Audie E. Bock (New York: Vintage, 1983), 144. Kurosawa himself came under police pressure during the war, yet in his 1944 film *The Most Beautiful* (*Ichiban utsukushiku*), he produced what was clearly an instance of propaganda, with its stress on individual self-sacrifice for the sake of increased production. The film, constructed in quasi-documentary form, celebrates the heroic efforts of a group of young women working in a high-tech optics plant. In contrast to the pattern of using diegetic music found in Kurosawa's postwar films, which I discuss later in this chapter, here diegetic music (primarily marching songs performed by the girls as they march from their dormitory to the factory) carries positive connotations. For a discussion of the film in the context of wartime propaganda, see Mitsuhiro Yoshimoto, *Kurosawa: Film Studies and Japanese Cinema* (Durham, N.C.: Duke University Press, 2000), 81–88.

6. The song "Fragrance of the Night" (Ch., Ye lai xiang; Jp., Ieraishan), composed by Li Jinguang, had been a hit throughout China around 1940. Hattori became a friend of Li during his stay in Shanghai.

7. Ueda Ken'ichi, *Shanhai bugiugi 1945: Hattori Ryōichi no bōken* (Tokyo: Ongaku no tomo sha, 2003), 153. See also Hattori Ryōichi, *Boku no ongaku jinsei* (Tokyo: Chūō bungei sha, 1982), 205–16.

8. The details of Kasagi Shizuko's wartime life come from an autobiography she published in 1948, just as she was reaching the peak of her popularity as

a singer: *Utau jigazō: Watashi no bugiugi denki* (Tokyo: Hokuto shuppansha, 1948).

9. Hattori, *Boku no ongaku jinsei*, 197.
10. Kasagi Shizuko, "Mijuku na ningen," *Mainichi jōhō*, January 1951, 86–87, quote on 87.
11. Hattori, *Boku no ongaku jinsei*, 217–18.
12. Kasagi, "Mijuku na ningen," 87.
13. Stephen Prince, *The Warrior's Camera: The Cinema of Akira Kurosawa*, rev. ed. (Princeton, N.J.: Princeton University Press, 1999), 197.
14. Dower, *Embracing Defeat*, 27.
15. Kasagi appeared in several dozen films during her career, stretching from the late 1930s through the early 1970s.
16. On the relationship between the two, see Stuart Galbraith IV, *The Emperor and the Wolf: The Lives and Films of Akira Kurosawa and Toshiro Mifune* (New York: Faber and Faber, 2001).
17. Hirano, *Mr. Smith Goes to Tokyo*, 77.
18. Richie, *Films of Akira Kurosawa*, 53.
19. Nishimura calls the sweet theme in E-flat major the "gentle" (*yasashisa*) theme and the darker theme in C major the "violence" (*bōryoku*) theme, and provides transcriptions for both, in *Kurosawa Akira*, 100–110.
20. On diegetic and nondiegetic use of music in film, see Claudi Gorbman, *Unheard Melodies: Narrative Film Music* (Bloomington: Indiana University Press, 1987), 23–30.
21. Nishimura, *Kurosawa Akira*, 73–100. See also Kurosawa, *Something Like an Autobiography*, 107–8, 197.
22. Kurosawa originally wanted to use Kurt Weill's "Mack the Knife" for this song but was unable to acquire the rights to use it in the film. See Nishimura, *Kurosawa Akira*, 93–94.
23. Hattori, *Boku no ongaku jinsei*, 181–82. While 1945 marked the end of wartime censorship of popular music, it also marked the beginning of U.S. Occupation censorship: in 1946, for example, singer-violinist Ishida Ichimatsu was ordered to stop performing a song that satirized the Occupation itself. See Hirano, *Mr. Smith Goes to Tokyo*, 72–73.
24. For example, Richie describes it as an "error of judgment" (*Films of Akira Kurosawa*, 51).
25. The notion of a triangular Oedipal structure to individual subjectivity is suggested visually several times in the film when, through the use of such devices as a three-section vanity mirror or the overlapping of shots in a dream sequence, the viewer is presented with three distinct images of a character's face within a single frame.

26. J. Victor Koschmann, *Revolution and Subjectivity in Postwar Japan* (Chicago: University of Chicago Press, 1996), esp. 170–202.

27. Quoted in Molasky, *American Occupation*, 157.

28. Ōya Sōichi, "Ōya Sōichi no oshaberi dōchū," *Goraku yomiuri*, July 12, 1957, 38–41, quote on 40. Kasagi herself readily agrees with the comment, pointing out that she had engaged in rigorous dance training since the age of four, so that "back then, I could do things that other people couldn't do."

29. Susan McClary, *Feminine Endings: Music, Gender and Sexuality* (Minneapolis: University of Minnesota Press, 1991), 153.

30. On the reception of Ellington's "hot jazz" and "jungle sound" in the Japan of the 1930s, see Hosokawa Shūhei, "The Swinging Voice of Kasagi Shizuko: Japanese Jazz Culture in the 1930s," in *Japanese Studies Around the World 2006: Research on Art and Music in Japan*, ed. Patricia Fister and Hosokawa Shūhei (Kyoto: International Research Center for Japanese Studies, 2007), 159–85.

31. I am indebted to Robert Walser for pointing out the orientalist musical gestures in "Jungle Boogie," and to Loren Kajikawa for helping me understand how these gestures are at work in this piece, as well as in the other songs discussed in the following. On the question of race, the body, and popular music, see Susan McClary and Robert Walser, "Theorizing the Body in African-American Music," *Black Music Research Journal* 14, no. 1 (1994): 75–84. Hattori would repeatedly use jungle references in his works from the late 1940s—for example, in the lyrics (credited to Saeki Takao but heavily revised by Hattori) to his "Ginza kankan musume," an enormous hit for Takamine Hideko in 1949: "Ginza is my jungle, the tigers and the girls, I'm not afraid of either one." Likewise, in 1951 he would write a musical revue titled *Queen of the Jungle* (*Janguru no joō*), starring Kasagi Shizuko.

32. Hattori Ryōichi, "Kawaii onna," in Kasagi, *Utau jigazō*, 152–55. According to Kasagi, Hattori explained to her that although the "natural voice" was not used by Western singers, it was the necessary technique for a Japanese singer who wanted to take on a swing song, because it compensated for the physical strength that a Japanese singer supposedly lacked. She writes that her use of *jigoe* "makes me in that sense a Japanese-style [*Nihonteki*] jazz singer" (61). It was this style that gave Kasagi's voice a feel of "tough volume." See Hosokawa, "Swinging Voice of Kasagi Shizuko." On *jigoe*, which can be translated as either "natural voice" or "chest voice" and which contrasts with, for example, falsetto or bel canto styles, see Christine Yano, *Tears of Longing: Nostalgia and the Nation in Japanese Popular Song* (Cambridge, Mass.: Harvard University Asia Center, 2002), 109–10.

33. Kurosawa discusses his choice of the music for this sequence in *Something Like an Autobiography*, 162–63.

34. E. Taylor Atkins, *Blue Nippon: Authenticating Jazz in Japan* (Durham, N.C.: Duke University Press, 2001), 191; on jazz as a sign of corruption in Kurosawa, see also Prince, *Warrior's Camera*, 85–86. Michael Molasky's fine study of jazz culture in postwar Japan, *Sengo Nihon no jazu bunka: Eiga, bungaku, angora* (Tokyo: Seidōsha, 2005), was published just as I finished work on this chapter; it also includes a discussion of Kurosawa's use of jazz and classical music in *Drunken Angel* and other early postwar films and raises a number of points similar to those I am arguing here. For a detailed analysis of the use of music in *Drunken Angel*, see also Keiko I. McDonald, *Reading a Japanese Film: Cinema in Context* (Honolulu: University of Hawai'i Press, 2006), 33–48.

35. For a discussion of "textual details and figures that allude to the shadow of America" in Kurosawa's *Stray Dog* (*Nora inu*), see Yoshimoto, *Kurosawa*, 164–65.

36. This identification may seem counterintuitive to some, especially in Japan, where Kurosawa's reputation is often defined in contrast to the more experimental film directors who have appeared since the late 1950s. For an extended reading of Kurosawa's early works in the context of the artistic theories of Bertolt Brecht and Sergei Eisenstein, see, for example, Prince, *Warrior's Camera*. Prince downplays the notion that Kurosawa is a specifically "modernist" director yet repeatedly explores Kurosawa's oeuvre as "a cinema of perceptual shocks" (47), one in which the viewer "is continually being reoriented by a succession of noncontinuous spatial fields, complicating the perceptual process" (65), tendencies that call to mind, among other things, cubist paintings and the experimental narrative techniques of such modernist writers as James Joyce and Gertrude Stein. For another Japanese film history that defines Kurosawa as a "modern" director in contrast to the "modernist" filmmakers of the New Wave movement in the 1960s, see David Desser, *Eros Plus Massacre: An Introduction to the Japanese New Wave Cinema* (Bloomington: Indiana University Press, 1988), esp. 15–38.

37. Theodor Adorno and Hanns Eisler, *Composing for the Films* (1947; repr., London: Athlone, 1994). See also James Buhler, "*Star Wars*, Music, and Myth," in *Music and Cinema*, ed. James Buhler, Caryl Flinn, and David Neumeyer (Hanover, N.H.: University Press of New England / Wesleyan University Press, 2000), 33–57.

38. Adorno and Eisler, *Composing for the Films*, 22.

39. Gorbman, *Unheard Melodies*, 55.

40. Theodore Gracyk, *Rhythm and Noise: An Aesthetics of Rock* (Durham, N.C.: Duke University Press, 1996), 157.

41. Theodor Adorno, "Perennial Fashion: Jazz," in *Prisms*, trans. Samuel Weber and Shierry Weber (Cambridge, Mass.: MIT Press, 1981), 121–32, quote on 129.

42. Andreas Huyssen, *After the Great Divide: Modernism, Mass Culture, Postmodernism* (Bloomington: Indiana University Press, 1986), 51.

43. Dogme 95, "Vow of Chastity," quoted in Benjamin Craig, "What Is 'Dogme 95'?," http://www.filmmaking.net/faq/answers/faq37.asp (accessed May 9, 2011).

44. Adorno and Eisler, *Composing for the Films*, 73–4.

45. Kurosawa cut back radically in his use of sound-track music for *I Live in Fear* (also known as *Record of a Living Being* [*Ikimono no kiroku*, 1955]), which uses sound track only over the opening and closing credits (perhaps a form of tribute to Hayasaka Fumio, who died during the making of the film). Likewise, *The Lower Depths* (*Donzoku*, 1957) contains no sound-track music during the film proper and only sparse gongs over the opening credits and a single woodblock strike at the closing credit (after the style of a Kabuki play). Both films contain instances of diegetic music, however.

46. Izbicki, "Scorched Cityscapes," 272–99; Yoshimoto, *Kurosawa*, 147–78.

47. For a detailed discussion of the songs used in the *Stray Dog* montage, see Nishimura, *Kurosawa Akira*, 90–93.

48. For an alternative reading of this sequence in terms of the class differences it reveals between the woman in her bourgeois home and the detective and criminal, see Prince, *Warrior's Camera*, 97–98.

49. As the two men lie exhausted in the grass, we get another instance of diegetic music: children walk past in the distance, singing the children's song "Butterfly" (Chō-chō), a sign of the purity of childhood (and yet another form of apparently uncommodified song). Then, in the final sequence of the film, as Murakami visits Satō's hospital room to report the capture of Yusa, the sound track kicks in again with music clearly derived from Western nineteenth-century classical music orchestration, which continues until the ending credit. See Nishimura, *Kurosawa Akira*, 97–100.

50. I should acknowledge that the classical music used in this sequence is diegetic, rather than nondiegetic, which complicates the basic structure I am arguing for here: that is, masculinity = nondiegetic = classical versus femininity = diegetic = popular. In fact, in three additional films from this period, Kurosawa uses diegetically motivated classical music, always—as here—in the form of a woman playing piano—and in each, the woman ends up banging on the keyboard in anger: *No Regrets for Our Youth*, *Scandal* (in which the woman sings as she plays), and *The Idiot* (*Hakuchi*, 1951). In all these sequences, however, the diegetic is still associated with the feminine, and in all these films the restoration of masculine subjectivity is a crucial thematic, so that this complication does not necessarily invalidate the framework I am proposing.

51. It should also be noted that Kurosawa frequently used specifically Japanese genres of music in his films, especially in his *jidaigeki* (historical films). Even in these films, however, his overall tendency remains to use Western orchestration (albeit often with orientalist flourishes) as the core of the nondiegetic sound track

52. This pattern is not unique to Kurosawa. In Ozu Yasujirō's film *Dragnet Girl* (*Hijōsen no onna*, 1933), for example, the hero is a gangster torn by a desire to go straight. The film's narrative centers on a battle for his soul between two women, the wicked "modern girl" Tokiko, who is associated with jazz music and dance halls (but who turns out to have a heart of gold), and the sweet ingenue Kazuko, who works in a music store and tries desperately to convert the hero to classical music. This battle between jazz and classical music is complicated by the fact that this is a *silent* film: all the musical cues must be conveyed visually. Ozu employs a wide vocabulary of visual cues throughout to convey the missing sound of the music, most prominently the RCA Victor mascot dog.

53. Adorno and Eisler, *Composing for the Films*, 15–16.

54. On Kurosawa's attraction to the title of the symphony, see Nishimura, *Kurosawa Akira*, 58–59; and Yoshimoto, *Kurosawa*, 136. On the gender politics of Schubert's symphony, see McClary, *Feminine Endings*, 69, 143.

55. Kurosawa, *Something Like an Autobiography*, 193.

56. In addition to the films already mentioned, many other Kurosawa sound tracks allude to canonical works, including Bizet's "Waltz of the Toreadors" from *Carmen* (*One Wonderful Sunday*), Ravel's *Bolero* (*Rashōmon*), Mussorgsky's "A Night on Bald Mountain" (*The Idiot*), Dvorak's Symphony no. 9 ("From the New World") (*Seven Samurai*), Beethoven's Ninth Symphony "Chorale" and Haydn's Symphony no. 94 ("The Surprise") (*Red Beard*), and Mahler's First Symphony (*Ran*), among others.

57. Nishimura, *Kurosawa Akira*, 173–74.

58. McClary, *Feminine Endings*, 80–111.

59. On the prewar jazz boom in Osaka, see Atkins, *Blue Nippon*, 57–67. Except where noted otherwise, details on Kasagi's career are based on the account given in the (anonymous) liner notes to the three-CD collection that surveys her career: *Nihon no poppusu no senkutachi: Bugi no joō Kasagi Shizuko* (Nippon Columbia 72CA-2894-96; released in 1998), as well as Kasagi, *Utau jigazō* and "Mijuku na ningen." Details on Hattori's career come primarily from *Boku no ongaku jinsei*.

60. For an English translation of the lyrics, see Alan M. Tansman, "Mournful Tears and *Sake*: The Postwar Myth of Misora Hibari," in *Contemporary Japan*

and Popular Culture, ed. John Whittier Treat (Honolulu: University of Hawai'i Press, 1996), 103–33.

61. On Koga, see Yano, *Tears of Longing*, 36–39.

62. On the tension in the song between the pentatonic and Western minor scales, see Satō Yoshiaki, *J-pop shinkaron: "Yosahoi bushi" kara "Automatic" e* (Tokyo: Heibonsha, 1999), 87–88. I return to the issue of the pentatonic scale in chapter 2.

63. Atkins, *Blue Nippon*, 132–39. On orientalism in Japanese popular music and film during the 1930s and 1940s, see Michael Baskett, *The Attractive Empire: Transnational Film Culture in Imperial Japan* (Honolulu: University of Hawai'i Press, 2008), esp. 53–65; and Edgar W. Pope, "Songs of Empire: Continental Asia in Japanese Wartime Popular Music" (Ph.D. diss., University of Washington, 1993).

64. Hattori tells how Kasagi's appearance, especially her long false eyelashes, caused her to be questioned by the police on suspicion of violating wartime regulations against excessive indulgences in personal appearance, in *Boku no ongaku jinsei*, 197.

65. On *Jazz Carmen* (1947), see Hattori, *Boku no ongaku jinsei*, 220–21. In 1947, Hattori would also write a musical called *Tokyo Carmen*, also starring Kasagi (232). On the gender and racial politics in both the story and musical form of Bizet's *Carmen*, see McClary, *Feminine Endings*, 56–67.

66. Hattori, *Boku no ongaku jinsei*, 231.

67. Ibid., 223–29. See also Take Hideki, *Yomu J-pop: 1945–1999 shiteki zenshi* (Tokyo: Tokuma shoten, 1999), 17–20. On the history and structure of boogie-woogie, see "Boogie-Woogie," *Grove Music Online*, http://www.oxfordmusic online.com/subscriber/article/grove/music/J052100 (accessed May 9, 2011).

68. On the Kurosawa–Yamamoto relationship, see Satō Tadao, *Kurosawa Akira sakuhin kaidai* (Tokyo: Iwanami shoten, 2002), 2–17.

69. On the song's hybrid musical structure, see Satō, *J-pop shinkaron*, 93–97. The song also apparently became quite popular in Hawaii, according to Hattori, *Boku no ongaku jinsei*, 259. For a translation of the lyrics, see Tansman, "Mournful Tears and *Sake*," 110–11.

70. Take, *Yomu J-pop*, 20.

71. Hattori, *Boku no ongaku jinsei*, 199.

72. In 1946, 3.42 million disks were produced; in 1947, 8.85 million; in 1948, 11.96 million; and in 1949, 16.86 million. These were mostly ten-inch 78 rpm records; the switchover to 33⅓ rpm LPs began around 1951 in Japan. Under conditions of postwar inflation, the price of a ten-inch record soared from 3.75 yen in September 1945 to 170 yen in February 1950. See Kurata Yoshihiro, *Nihon rekōdo bunkashi* (Tokyo: Tōkyō shoseki, 1992).

73. McClary and Walser, "Theorizing the Body in African-American Music," 76. On the tendency to seek liberation through the body in early postwar Japanese culture, see Slaymaker, *Body in Postwar Japanese Fiction*; Molasky, *American Occupation of Japan and Okinawa*; Igarashi, *Bodies of Memory*; and Dower, *Embracing Defeat*.

74. Angela Y. Davis, *Blues Legacies and Black Feminism: Gertrude "Ma" Rainey, Bessie Smith, and Billie Holiday* (New York: Vintage, 1998), 4.

75. Satō, *Kurosawa Akira sakuhin kaidai*, 5–7.

76. Huyssen, *After the Great Divide*, 16–17.

77. Masao Maruyama, "From Carnal Literature to Carnal Politics," trans. Barbara Ruch, in *Thought and Behaviour in Modern Japanese Politics*, ed. Ivan Morris (New York: Oxford University Press, 1963), 245–67.

78. McClary, *Feminine Endings*, 79.

79. In fact, I am simplifying here somewhat, since a distinction was made during wartime between unacceptable Western music (Anglo-American forms) and acceptable Western music (primarily music identified with Germany and Italy, Japan's wartime allies). This is a distinction that musicians such as Hattori exploited, claiming German or Italian roots to slip Anglo-American music past the ears of unsuspecting censors.

80. Eric Cazdyn, *The Flash of Capital: Film and Geopolitics in Japan* (Durham, N.C.: Duke University Press, 2002), 242.

81. Michael Denning, *Culture in the Age of Three Worlds* (London: Verso, 2004), 79–80.

82. Hattori, *Boku no ongaku jinsei*, 271–72.

83. Likewise, Awaya Noriko, the Japanese "queen of the blues" who recorded numerous songs by Hattori, was a conservatory-trained vocalist. See Hattori, *Boku no ongaku jinsei*, 79–80.

84. Ibid., 92.

85. Ibid., 91–92. Hattori would in fact compose many extended "symphonic jazz" pieces in his career.

86. Ibid., 267.

87. Ibid., 273.

88. Ibid., 140.

89. Ibid., 149. Hayasaka Fumio, Kurosawa's favorite film composer, also felt a strong compulsion to experiment with orientalist forms of music so that his compositions would not simply represent slavish admiration of Western cultural traditions. See Nishimura, *Kurosawa Akira*, 126–28, 176.

90. Hattori, *Boku no ongaku jinsei*, 276–77. See also Atkins, *Blue Nippon*, 132–39.

91. Hosokawa, "Swinging Voice of Kasagi Shizuko," 169, 170.

92. Yano, *Tears of Longing*, 149. I return to the genre of *enka* in chapter 2.

93. Kasagi, "Mijuku na ningen," 86. Likewise, Hattori is quoted as praising Kasagi for the way she uses her body in performing his songs—he compares her performance style to that of French chanson singers like Josephine Baker, "who convey the meaning of the lyrics not just through the words but through their body movements—in other words, who perform as they sing" (quoted in "Hattori Ryōichi to Kasagi Shizuko," *Goraku Yomiuri*, December 16, 1955, 22–23).

94. The phrase "gestural overstatement" comes from Hosokawa, "Swinging Voice of Kasagi Shizuko," 177.

95. Hayashi Fumiko, "Pari fū no tōki: Kasagi Shizuko no inshō," a testimonial in Kasagi, *Utau jigazō*, 137–40, quote on 138.

96. McClary, *Feminine Endings*, 151.

97. Hattori, *Boku no ongaku jinsei*, 230. Kasagi's popularity among streetwalkers is also noted in Hata Toyokichi, "Kasagi Shizuko to Karumen Miranda," *Mainichi jōhō*, September 1950, 98–100.

98. In addition to multiple renditions of the title song in the film, Kasagi does a nice reprise of "Jungle Boogie" from Kurosawa's *Drunken Angel*, repeating the body gestures she used in the earlier film.

99. Hata, "Kasagi Shizuko to Karumen Miranda," 98.

100. Ironically, Hattori Tomiko began her career in the late 1930s singing exotic orientalist popular songs such as "Manchurian Girl" (Manshū musume, 1938) and playing exotic Chinese female roles in films such as *The Monkey King* (*Songoku*, 1940). See Baskett, *Attractive Empire*, 60–65.

101. Davis, *Blues Legacies and Black Feminism*, 168–69. Kasagi's style also calls to mind African American performers in the nineteenth and early twentieth centuries who adopted performing strategies from blackface minstrelsy, only to alienate the audience from these same strategies (in the sense of Bertolt Brecht's theories of alienation), thereby "critically defamiliarizing their own bodies by way of performance in order to yield alternate racial and gender epistemologies" (Daphne A. Brooks, *Bodies in Dissent: Spectacular Performances of Race and Freedom, 1850–1910* [Durham, N.C.: Duke University Press, 2006], 5).

102. Hattori, *Boku no ongaku jinsei*, 229.

103. Hattori quotes the following lines from Kurosawa's original draft as the source of Kasagi's objection: "In the jungle on the night of a red moon, I felt a love that jolted my legs from under me [*koshi no nukeru yō na koi*]; in the jungle on the night of a blue moon, I felt love shake me down to my bones [*hone no uzuku yō na koi*]" (*Boku no ongaku jinsei*, 229–30). They were expunged from the final version of the song.

104. See, for example, "Rizumu ando burūsu" (Rhythm and Blues), *Asahi shinbun*, August 15, 1955, 12. This article, published on precisely the tenth anniversary of Japan's surrender, contains what must be one of the earliest mentions in the Japanese press of Bill Haley, who is mistakenly identified as being black.

105. "Maiku hanarete," *Hōsō bunka*, June 1955, 40–44, quote on 41.

106. Theodor Adorno, "On Popular Music," in *Essays on Music*, ed. Richard Leppert (Berkeley: University of California Press, 2002), 437–69, quote on 441.

107. Ibid., 437–38.

108. Ibid., 440.

109. Bernard Gendron, "Theodor Adorno Meets the Cadillacs," in *Studies in Entertainment: Critical Approaches to Mass Culture*, ed. Tania Modleski (Bloomington: Indiana University Press, 1986), 18–36. On the importance of timbre to the rock genre, see Gracyk, *Rhythm and Noise*, 59–61.

2. MAPPING MISORA HIBARI

1. Christopher Small, *Musicking: The Meanings of Performing and Listening* (Hanover, N.H.: University Press of New England / Wesleyan University Press, 1998), 210.

2. John W. Dower, *Embracing Defeat: Japan in the Wake of World War II* (New York: New Press, 1999).

3. "Tokyo Boogie," *Time*, June 28, 1948, 34. The bracketed English translations of the lyrics are in the original.

4. Isoda Kōichi, *Shisō toshite Tōkyō* (Tokyo: Kōdansha, 1990), 123–24.

5. Suzuki Noribumi, "Kaisetsu: Dare ka kokyō o omowazaru," afterword in Ōshita Eiji, *Misora Hibari: Jidai o utau* (Tokyo: Shinchōsha, 1992), 607–15, quote on 607.

6. Yamaori Tetsuo, *Misora Hibari to Nihonjin*, rev. ed. (Tokyo: Gendai shokan, 2001). For another book devoted to exploring the Japaneseness of Hibari, see Shindō Ken, *Misora Hibari to Nipponjin* (Tokyo: Banseisha, 1998).

7. Misora Hibari, *Hibari jiden: Watashi to kage* (Tokyo: Sōshisha, 1971), 274–75.

8. Ibid., 232.

9. Hata Toyokichi, "Kasagi Shizuko to Karumen Miranda," *Mainichi jōhō*, September 1950, 98–100.

10. Alan M. Tansman, "Mournful Tears and *Sake*: The Postwar Myth of Misora Hibari," in *Contemporary Japan and Popular Culture*, ed. John Whittier Treat (Honolulu: University of Hawai'i Press, 1996), 103–33, quote on 105. See also Alan Tansman, *The Aesthetics of Japanese Fascism* (Berkeley: University of California Press, 2009), 259–67.

11. Sources for biographical information include Hibari's autobiography: Misori, *Hibari jiden*; Ōshita, *Misora Hibari*; and Honda Yasuharu, *"Sengo": Misora Hibari to sono jidai* (Tokyo: Kōdansha, 1989).

12. Honda, *Sengo*, 74–75.

13. Misora, *Hibari jiden*, 119–20.

14. Ōshita, *Misora Hibari*, 46.

15. Hibari performed the same song in her first film appearance, *The Age of the Amateur Singing Contest Craze* (*Nodo jiman kyō jidai*, dir. Saitō Torajirō, 1949).

16. "Kappa Boogie Woogie" (Kappa bugiugi) was released on July 30, 1949. The B side of a single (the A side was a new recording by the more-established singer Kirishima Noboru), it supposedly sold only seventy thousand copies, something of a disappointment. The song is a standard big-band boogie-woogie number, distinguished primarily by Hibari's nasal voice and an unexpected percussion bridge. A *kappa* is a mythical river imp from Japanese folklore.

17. For a complete discography of the 292 singles that Hibari released during her career, see Mori Akira, ed., *Misora Hibari* (Tokyo: Tokyo FM shuppan, 1997), 191–253.

18. Honda, *Sengo*, 93.

19. Shindō, *Misora Hibari to Nipponjin*, 18–19.

20. Satō Hachirō, "Mitari kiitari tameshitari: Bugiugi kodomo," *Tōkyō taimuzu*, January 23, 1950, 2. Satō was a poet and lyricist; among his compositions was the early postwar hit "Apple Song" (Ringo no uta), discussed in chapter 1.

21. Quoted in Shindō, *Misora Hibari to Nipponjin*, 67–68.

22. "Jidō no fukushi," *Fujin asahi*, October 1949, 4–6. See also Honda, *Sengo*, 94–95.

23. Honda, *Sengo*, 116.

24. On the Kasagi–Hibari dispute, see ibid., 150–57; and Ōshita, *Misora Hibari*, 183–94. For Hibari's version of the events, see Misora, *Hibari jiden*, 65–75. For Hattori Ryōichi's side of the story, see *Boku no ongaku jinsei* (Tokyo: Ongaku no tomo sha, 2003), 250–52.

25. See, for example, Satō Hachirō, "Mitari kiitari tameshitari: Burei naru manajā," *Tōkyō taimuzu*, May 18, 1950, 2. Satō takes Hattori's side in the dispute and blames Hibari's manager for rude and dishonest conduct.

26. Hashimoto Osamu and Okamura Kazue, *Kawada Haruhisa to Misora Hibari* (Tokyo: Chūō kōron sha, 2003), 5–30.

27. In August 2009, I was contacted by a collector of old recording devices who had recently purchased a box of wire recordings that he believed to be of concerts by Japanese performers in California from 1950 to 1951. The collector provided me with digitized copies of the recordings, and I was able to confirm that they were concerts recorded in Sacramento, including those by Misora

Hibari, Kasagi Shizuko, Yamaguchi Yoshiko, and Watanabe Hamako. The origins of the recordings is unknown, although they seem to have been taped off the concert-hall microphone rather than from a microphone in the audience.

28. Yoshikuni Igarashi, *Bodies of Memory: Narratives of War in Postwar Japanese Culture, 1945–1970* (Princeton, N.J.: Princeton University Press, 2000), 13.

29. Christina Klein, *Cold War Orientalism: Asia in the Middlebrow Imagination, 1945–1961* (Berkeley: University of California Press, 2003), esp. 93.

30. Hattori makes similar remarks from the stage in the recording of his Sacramento concert with Kasagi later that year.

31. "Tokyo Kid" (Tōkyō kiddo; lyrics by Fujiura Kō, music by Manjōme Tadashi) was recorded before Hibari left for Hawaii but released in July 1950. The sweet ballad is in Tin Pan Alley style and is famous primarily for its chorus, in which the singer claims to have dreams filling her right pocket—and chewing gum in her left.

32. Hashimoto and Okamura, *Kawada Haruhisa to Misora Hibari*, 38–43.

33. For a discussion of Hibari's early postwar films in terms of their celebration of "the American dream," see Isolde Standish, *A New History of Japanese Cinema: A Century of Narrative Film* (New York: Continuum International, 2006), 196–200.

34. On the ideological reconstruction of the family in Hibari's early films, see Joanne Izbicki, "Singing the Orphan Blues: Misora Hibari and the Rehabilitation of Post-Surrender Japan," *Intersections* 16 (2008), http://intersections.anu.edu.au/.

35. Allan R. Ellenberger, *Margaret O'Brien: A Career Chronicle and Biography* (Jefferson, N.C.: McFarland, 2000), 163–67.

36. Quoted in ibid., 166.

37. On Hibari's image change, see Deborah Shamoon, "Misora Hibari and the Girl Star in Postwar Japanese Cinema," *Signs: Journal of Women in Culture and Society* 35, no. 1 (2009): 131–55.

38. Ōshita, *Misora Hibari*, 230.

39. Honda, *Sengo*, 227.

40. On the irregular rhythm of the traditional *oiwake* genre, I am relying on the work of the great scholar of Japanese traditional music, Koizumi Fumio. In English, see F. Koizumi, "Towards a Systematization of Japanese Folk-Song," *Studia Musicologica Academiae Scientiarum Hungaricae*, T. 7, fasc. 1/4 (1965): 309–13. In Japanese, see Koizumi Fumio, *Nihon no oto: Sekai no naka no Nihon ongaku* (Tokyo: Heibonsha, 1994), 327–53. For an ethnomusicological analysis of "Apple Oiwake," including a translation of the lyrics, see Kay Kaufman Shelemay, *Soundscapes: Exploring Music in a Changing World*, 2nd ed. (New York: Norton, 2006), 441–43. For the fascinating history of the standardization

and popularization of one key song from the genre, "Esashi oiwake," see David W. Hughes, *Traditional Folk Song in Modern Japan: Sources, Sentiment and Society* (Folkestone, Eng.: Global Oriental, 2008), 108–18.

41. Yamaori, *Misora Hibari to Nihonjin*, 83–89.

42. Kata Kōji, "Misora Hibari," in *Ryūkōka no himitsu*, ed. Kata Kōji and Tsukuda Jitsuo (Tokyo: Bunwa shobō, 1979), 369.

43. Shimizu Hideo, "Misora Hibari sutōrī pāto 1," in Mori, *Misora Hibari*, 256–77. The album *Hibari no madoro-san* (Nippon Columbia AL-101) was released May 25, 1958. It was a ten-inch disk (rather than the twelve-inch disk that would soon become the LP standard format) and contained four songs on each side, all recorded in mono.

44. J. Victor Koschmann, *Revolution and Subjectivity in Postwar Japan* (Chicago: University of Chicago Press, 1996), 203–5.

45. Unnamed Japanese critic quoted in Tansman, "Mournful Tears and *Sake*," 122.

46. Arakawa Akira, *Okinawa: Tōgō to hangyaku* (Tokyo: Chikuma shobō, 2000), 158–62; Yakabi Osamu, "Beigun senryōka Okinawa ni okeru shokuminchi jōkyō," in *Sengo Nihon sutadīzu 1: 40–50 nendai*, ed. Iwasaki Minoru et al. (Tokyo: Kinokuniya shoten, 2009), 153–70.

47. Honda, *Sengo*, 270–71.

48. "Misora Hibari o yobu," *Okinawa taimusu*, July 24, 1956, evening ed., 3.

49. "Misora Hibari shō jikkyō chūkei," *Okinawa taimusu*, August 11, 1956, evening ed., 4.

50. "Kūzen no Hibari būmu," *Okinawa taimusu*, August 12, 1956, evening ed., 4.

51. Honda, *Sengo*, 260–98, quote on 295–96.

52. Mori, *Misora Hibari*, 311.

53. Honda, *Sengo*, 402–4.

54. Maeda Yoshitake and Hirahara Kōji, *Nihon no fōku & rokku no jidai 1: 60-nendai fōku no jidai* (Tokyo: Shinkō Music, 1993), 71.

55. Simon Frith, *Sound Effects: Youth, Leisure, and the Politics of Rock 'n' Roll* (New York: Pantheon, 1981), 25.

56. Christine Yano, *Tears of Longing: Nostalgia and the Nation in Japanese Popular Song* (Cambridge, Mass.: Harvard University Asia Center, 2002), 15.

57. Ibid., 28–44. On the shifting boundaries of popular music genres in Japan, see also Kitanaka Masakazu, *Nihon no uta: Sengo kayōkyoku shi*, rev. ed. (Tokyo: Heibonsha, 2003).

58. In fact, "Mournful Sake" did not have a spoken passage when first released. Hibari added the spoken interlude in live performances, and it went over so well with her fans that she re-recorded the song to include the teary-eyed soliloquy. See Ōshita, *Misora Hibari*, 494–97.

59. Frith, *Sound Effects*, 26.

60. On the history of the *yonanuki* scale and its emergence as a new standard in the Japanese popular music industry around 1920, see Satō Yoshiaki, *J-pop shinkaron: "Yosahoi bushi" kara "Automatic" e* (Tokyo: Heibonsha, 1999), 30–65. Satō notes that another commonly used scale in twentieth-century Japanese popular music is a minor scale missing the second and sixth steps (i.e., the relative minor scale to a major *yonanuki* scale). For discussions of the scales used in Japanese folk music genres and their relation to *enka*, see also Hughes, *Traditional Folk Song in Modern Japan*, 35–39, 42–45.

61. Yano, *Tears of Longing*, 90–123.

62. Composer Koga Masao received the same award in 1978, as did Hattori Ryōichi in 1993 and Kurosawa Akira in 1998.

63. Kang Sangjung, "The Discovery of the 'Orient' and Orientalism," trans. Shu Kuge, in *Contemporary Japanese Thought*, ed. Richard Calichman (New York: Columbia University Press, 2005), 84–100, quote on 85.

64. Koichi Iwabuchi, *Recentering Globalization: Popular Culture and Japanese Transnationalism* (Durham, N.C.: Duke University Press, 2002), 61.

65. Yakabi, "Beigun senryōka Okinawa."

66. Harry Harootunian, "America's Japan/Japan's Japan," in *Japan in the World*, ed. Masao Miyoshi and H. D. Harootunian (Durham, N.C.: Duke University Press, 1993), 196–221.

67. Igarashi, *Bodies of Memory*, 35.

68. On the rise of a new postwar stress on Japan's "uniqueness," see ibid., 72–103; Eiji Oguma, *A Genealogy of "Japanese" Self-Images* (Melbourne: Trans Pacific, 2002); and Tessa Morris-Suzuki, *Re-inventing Japan: Time, Space, Nation* (Armonk, N.Y.: Sharpe, 1998). Ironically, the "unique" quality that was taken to define the essence of Japaneseness was often hybridity: the ability of Japanese culture to absorb foreign elements (Asian in the premodern period, Western in the modern period) while retaining its own, unchanged identity. This view rests on an ideological tautology that is remarkably convenient for nationalists: the more Japan changes, they can claim, the more it remains the same.

69. On the role Shanghai and other continental Asian locales played in the development of Japanese jazz, see E. Taylor Atkins, *Blue Nippon: Authenticating Jazz in Japan* (Durham, N.C.: Duke University Press, 2001), esp. 127–63; and Ueda Ken'ichi, *Shanhai bugiugi 1945: Hattori Ryōichi no bōken* (Tokyo: Ongaku no tomo sha, 2003).

70. For the singer's own memoir of his wartime travels, see Fujiyama Ichirō, *Utagoe yo hibike minami no sora ni: Fujiyama Ichirō nanpō jūgunki* (Tokyo: Kōjinsha, 1986).

71. Yiman Wang, "Screening Asia: Passing, Performative Translation, and Reconfiguration," *positions* 15, no. 2 (2007): 319–43.

72. Hattori, *Boku no ongaku jinsei*, 148–51.

73. The most comprehensive source in English on "continental melodies" is Edgar W. Pope, "Songs of Empire: Continental Asia in Japanese Wartime Popular Music" (Ph.D. diss., University of Washington, 1993). See also my "Japan's Orient in Song and Dance," forthcoming; and E. Taylor Atkins, "The Dual Career of 'Arirang': The Korean Resistance Anthem That Became a Japanese Pop Hit," *Journal of Asian Studies* 66, no. 3 (2007): 645–87, and *Primitive Selves: Koreana in the Japanese Colonial Gaze, 1910–1945* (Berkeley: University of California Press, 2010), 147–86.

74. On the Chinese popular music genre "yellow music," see Andrew F. Jones, *Yellow Music: Media Culture and Colonial Modernity in the Chinese Jazz Age* (Durham, N.C.: Duke University Press, 2001).

75. Ueda, *Shanhai bugiugi*, 153. See also Hattori, *Boku no ongaku jinsei*, 205–16.

76. Gavan McCormack, *Client State: Japan in the American Embrace* (London: Verso, 2007).

77. Alex Ross, *The Rest Is Noise: Listening to the Twentieth Century* (New York: Farrar, Straus and Giroux, 2007), 42.

78. Yano, *Tears of Longing*, 9.

79. Shuhei Hosokawa, "Soy Sauce Music: Haruomi Hosono and Japanese Self-Orientalism," in *Widening the Horizon: Exoticism in Post-War Popular Music*, ed. Philip Hayward (London: Libbey, 1999), 114–44, quote on 130.

80. Ōshita, *Misora Hibari*, 64–67.

81. Yamaori, *Misora Hibari to Nihonjin*, 27–34. Even as he acknowledges these links to Korea and the rest of Asia, though, Yamaori wants to maintain a Japanese distinction: its Buddhism and chanting practices, for example, are unlike those found elsewhere on the continent, he argues.

82. Yano, *Tears of Longing*, 9. I am grateful to Jordan Smith for his assistance in reading Korean names and words in this chapter.

83. Robert Walser, *Running with the Devil: Power, Gender, and Madness in Heavy Metal Music* (Hanover, N.H.: University Press of New England / Wesleyan University Press, 1993), 29.

84. Igarashi, *Bodies of Memory*, 104–30.

85. Google search conducted on November 13, 2008.

86. Unnamed performer, quoted in Nomura Susumu, *Korian no sekai tabi* (Tokyo: Kōdansha, 1996), 15.

87. "'Misora Hibari no chichi wa Kankokujin' wa dokomade hontō ka," *Shūkan bunshun*, August 10, 1989, 155–59.

88. Ibid., 157.

89. Mark Anderson notes that he taught English to an elderly woman in Yokohama in the early 1990s. The woman said that she had been raised in the same neighborhood as Hibari and that the status of Hibari's family as Korean was

widely known among the neighbors (e-mail message to the author, June 2, 2006). This seems a strong piece of evidence, and yet we have to question not so much the truthfulness of the woman but the complex process of memory formation. If, for example, you were raised the childhood friend of someone who went on to become a celebrity and about whom you subsequently heard a shocking rumor, it seems to me there would be strong incentive to project, consciously or unconsciously, knowledge of that rumor back onto one's own childhood memories.

90. "Misora Hibari no chichi wa Kankokujin."
91. Kata, "Misora Hibari," 371–72.
92. David Samper, "Cannibalizing Kids: Rumor and Resistance in Latin America," *Journal of Folklore Research* 39, no. 1 (2002): 1–33, quote on 5.
93. Ibid., 2.
94. Ibid., 20.
95. Matsuyama Iwao, *Uwasa no enkinpō*, rev. ed. (Tokyo: Kōdansha, 1997), 4.
96. Ibid., 246–82.
97. Ralph L. Rosnow, "Rumor as Communication: A Contextualist Approach," *Journal of Communication* 38, no. 1 (1988): 12–28, quote on 16. Rosnow is summarizing the work of sociologist Tamotsu Shibutani.
98. "1-i wa Misora Hibari 'Kawa no nagare no yō ni': Kokoro ni nokoru uta 1000-man tōhyō," *Asahi shinbun*, January 23, 1998, evening ed., 7.
99. "Uta no tabibito: Kawa no nagare no yō ni; 'donchō' wo orosu tame ni. . . ." *Asahi shinbun*, April 5, 2008, weekend suppl., 10.
100. You can hear the leap past G in the song's chorus in the ascent between "no" and "na," and again in the descent from that "na" to "ga," in the title phrase "kawa no nagare no yō ni," but G appears not only in the chord structure to the song but also in the melody line near the end of the chorus and in the song's coda. Moreover, the stressed "yō" here is a C, the seventh step in the D-major scale. For the musical score for the song, see Matsuyama Yūshi, ed., *Misora Hibari meikyoku zenshū* (Tokyo: Doremi, 2003), 250–51.

3. MYSTERY PLANE

1. On the Nichigeki Western Carnivals and the introduction of rockabilly into Japan, see Billy Morokawa, *Shōwa roman rokabirī: Kikikaki; Jazu kissa kara Uesutan Kānibaru e* (Tokyo: Heibonsha, 2005), 51–58; and Kitanaka Masakazu, *Nihon no uta: Sengo kayōkyoku shi*, rev. ed. (Tokyo: Heibonsha, 2003), 97–105.
2. On Taiyō-zoku and the new youth culture, see Ann Sherif, "The Aesthetics of Speed and the Illogicality of Politics: Ishihara Shintarō's Literary Debut," *Japan Forum* 17, no. 2 (2005): 185–211.

3. "Rittoru Dahring," *Time*, April 14, 1958, 30.

4. George Lipsitz, *Dangerous Crossroads: Popular Music, Postmodernism and the Poetics of Place* (London: Verso, 1994), 160–61.

5. Greil Marcus, *Mystery Train: Images of America in Rock 'n' Roll Music*, 4th rev. ed. (1975; repr., New York: Plume, 1997).

6. Paul Gilroy, *The Black Atlantic: Modernity and Double Consciousness* (Cambridge, Mass.: Harvard University Press, 1993), 4.

7. The transnational career of rockabilly is clearly a symptom of Paul Virilio's "dromological" power, whereby speed itself becomes the central form of domination in contemporary society, as discussed in *Speed and Politics*, trans. Mark Polizzotti (New York: Semiotext[e], 1977). But, as I hope to demonstrate here, this is not (à la Virilio) solely a matter of the erasure of territory but also simultaneously and necessarily one of reterritorialization.

8. Jeffrey T. Schnapp, "Propeller Talk," *Modernism/Modernity* 1, no. 3 (1994): 153–78.

9. John Torpey, *The Invention of the Passport: Surveillance, Citizenship and the State* (Cambridge: Cambridge University Press, 2000).

10. Peter Guralnick, *Careless Love: The Unmaking of Elvis Presley* (Boston: Little, Brown, 1999), 91–119.

11. Sakamoto's fellow rockabilly singer Kamayatsu Hiroshi writes in his autobiography of a childhood spent watching air battles between B-29s and Zero fighters over the skies of Tokyo: *Musshu!* (Tokyo: Nikkei BP-sha, 2002), 22–23.

12. Ei Rokusuke, *Sakamoto Kyū monogatari: Roku-hachi-kyū no kyū* (Tokyo: Chūō kōron sha, 1990), 165–68.

13. WVTR, the predecessor to Armed Forces Radio's FEN Japan network, began broadcasting in September 1945. Its lineup included a weekly Saturday night hit parade program that introduced the latest in American pop music not only to GIs but also to any Japanese who wanted to tune in. It became an important source of information for Japanese musicians and music fans. See Tōya Mamoru, *Shinchūgun kurabu kara kayōkyoku e: Sengo Nihon popyurā ongaku no reimeiki* (Tokyo: Misuzu shobō, 2005), 22, 51.

14. R. E. G. Davies, *Airlines of Asia Since 1920* (London: Putnam, 1997), 425–514. On the rise of air travel and international tourism, and the role that Asia played in it, in 1950s America, see Christina Klein, *Cold War Orientalism: Asia in the Middlebrow Imagination, 1945–1961* (Berkeley: University of California Press, 2003), 103–9.

15. Ei, *Sakamoto Kyū monogatari*, 121. Fellow rockabilly singer Kamayatsu Hiroshi (who reappears in the next chapter) also yearned to be a pilot as a teenager and even applied unsuccessfully to join the Air Self-Defense Force in hopes of achieving that dream. See Kamayatsu, *Musshu!*, 50.

16. Klein, *Cold War Orientalism*, esp. 93.

17. Keith Lovegrove, *Airline: Identity, Design and Culture* (New York: teNeues, 2000). See also Christine R. Yano, *Airborne Dreams: "Nisei" Stewardesses and Pan American World Airways* (Durham, N.C.: Duke University Press, 2011).

18. Naoki Sakai, *Voices of the Past: The Status of Language in Eighteenth-Century Japanese Discourse* (Ithaca, N.Y.: Cornell University Press, 1991).

19. Naoki Sakai, *Translation and Subjectivity: On "Japan" and Cultural Nationalism* (Minneapolis: University of Minnesota Press, 1997), 2 (italics in original).

20. Lee Yeounsuk, *The Ideology of Kokugo: Nationalizing Language in Modern Japan*, trans. Maki Hirano Hubbard (Honolulu: University of Hawai'i Press, 2009).

21. Peter Guralnick describes the reaction of Sam Phillips, head of Sun Records, to the first successful studio session with Elvis, when his debut single "That's All Right (Mama)" was recorded:

> [Phillips] knew that something was in the wind. He knew from his experience recording blues, and from his fascination with black culture, that there was something intrinsic to the music that could translate, that did translate. "It got so you could sell a half million copies of a rhythm and blues record," Sam told a Memphis reporter in 1959, reminiscing about his overnight success. "These records appealed to white youngsters just as Uncle Silas [Payne's] songs and stories used to appeal to me. . . . But there was something in many of those youngsters that resisted buying this music. The Southern ones especially felt a resistance that even they probably didn't quite understand. They liked the music, but they weren't sure whether they ought to like it our not. So I got to thinking how many records you could sell if you could find white performers who could play and sing in this same exciting, alive way." (*Last Train to Memphis: The Rise of Elvis Presley* [Boston: Little, Brown, 1994], 96)

22. I'm indebted to Loren Kajikawa for these observations.

23. Japanese-language cover versions of "Wooden Heart" were recorded by Sasaki Isao and Kamayatsu Hiroshi.

24. Quoted in Guralnick, *Last Train to Memphis*, 134–35 (italics in original).

25. Simon Frith, *Sound Effects: Youth, Leisure, and the Politics of Rock 'n' Roll* (New York: Pantheon, 1981), 19.

26. There are other instances in the early history of rock and roll of "literal reading" as a means of effecting a distinction between mainstream and peripheral culture—comedians, for example, who would parse the lyrics to rock-and-roll songs as if they were difficult grammar exercises. This strategy for enforcing hierarchies in the speech community apparently has a long history. In E. M.

Forster's *A Room With a View*, for example, we encounter Mrs. Honeychurch, "who hoped to cure her children of slang by taking it literally" ([1908; repr., New York: Vintage Books, n.d.], 95).

27. Morokawa, *Shōwa roman rokabirī*, 112–20. Morokawa lists Sakamoto among the candidates but ultimately prefers Hirao Masaaki as the real "Japanese Elvis."

28. The German references remain in the Japanese lyrics in the versions of "G.I. Blues" recorded by Sasaki Isao and Mickey Curtis but not in the version by Kamayatsu Hiroshi.

29. For a useful account of the 1960 protests against the renewal of the Security Treaty and the impact of those protests on early-1960s Japanese culture, see David Desser, *Eros Plus Massacre: An Introduction to the Japanese New Wave Cinema* (Bloomington: Indiana University Press, 1988), 13–38.

30. Morokawa, *Shōwa roman rokabirī*, 230.

31. Watanabe Productions, Sakamoto's management firm and one of the most important players in Japanese popular music during the 1950s and 1960s, began life as a booking agency providing Japanese musicians for U.S. military-base clubs. The enormous impact of the bases on postwar Japanese popular music can hardly be overstated. For a detailed history, see Tōya, *Shinchūgun kurabu kara kayōkyoku e*. See also Carolyn S. Stevens, *Japanese Popular Music: Culture, Authenticity, and Power* (London: Routledge, 2008), 72–74.

32. Although most of Sakamoto's early singles in Japan were covers of American pop hits, only two were included among the twelve songs on his U.S. album, *Sukiyaki and Other Hits* (Capitol Records, 1963): "Good Timing" and "Good-bye Joe." The lyrics for both were translated into Japanese, and neither was released as a single in the United States.

33. "Rittoru Dahring."

34. Henri Bergson, *Laughter: An Essay on the Meaning of the Comic*, trans. Cloudesley Brereton and Fred Rothwell (New York: Macmillan, 1911).

35. Gilroy, *Black Atlantic*, 85.

36. Wanda Jackson, who appeared as an opening act on a number of Elvis's early concerts, was a rare exception, though she considered herself more a country western singer than a rockabilly queen. Her 1959 visit to Japan (she, too, arrived on a Pan American jet), after her "Fujiyama Mama" unexpectedly became a hit there, created a sensation among Japanese rockabilly fans. For contemporary coverage of her visit, see Kurosawa Susumu, ed., *Roots of Japanese Pops, 1955–1970* (Tokyo: Shinkō Music, 1995), 68–71.

37. Take Hideki, *Yomu J-pop: 1945–1999 shiteki zenshi* (Tokyo: Tokuma shoten, 1999), 54–65.

38. Ei Rokusuke, the song's lyricist, discusses this aspect of the song as one key to its subsequent international popularity in *Ue wo muite utaō: Shōwa kayō no jibun shi* (Tokyo: Asuka shinsha, 2006), 59–60.

39. Aikura Hisato, "Sukiyaki songu de zenbei wo sekken shita Sakamoto Kyū," *Bungei shunjū*, October 1981, 179–81.

40. Mark Schilling, "Kyu Sakamoto," in *The Encyclopedia of Japanese Pop Culture* (New York: Weatherhill, 1997), 215–17.

41. Kurosawa, *Roots of Japanese Pops*, 237; Ed Hogan, "Kyu Sakamoto," in Allmusic, http://www.allmusic.com/artist/kyu-sakamoto-p111600 (accessed May 10, 2011).

42. "Kyū-chan hoshi wo mitsuketa," *Mainichi gurafu*, July 14, 1963, 22–27.

43. "Kangei ni kimo tsubusu: Amerika de no Kyūchan," *Asahi shinbun*, August 20, 1963, evening ed., 5. Sakamoto also hoped to meet Audrey Hepburn but was told that she likewise was too busy. His third request, to visit Disneyland, was fulfilled. Sakamoto's visit to Los Angeles in 1963 was ignored by the *Los Angeles Times* but received heavy coverage in the local Japanese-American newspaper, the *Rafu Shimpo*, in both its English and Japanese language sections.

44. "Rising Son," *Newsweek*, July 1, 1963, 64.

45. Sakamoto's version of "Shina no yoru" was released in the United States on August 3, 1963. The song, from a film of the same name, had been a wartime hit for both Watanabe Hamako and the film's star, Ri Kōran (Yamaguchi Yoshiko, known in Hollywood in the 1950s as Shirley Yamaguchi), a Japanese actress who masqueraded as a Japanophilic Chinese in a series of wartime films. On Ri Kōran, who is also discussed in chapter 2, see Miriam Silverberg, "Remembering Pearl Harbor, Forgetting Charlie Chaplin, and the Case of the Disappearing Western Woman: A Picture Story," *positions* 1, no. 1 (1993): 24–76.

46. "Kyū-chan Amerika wo seifuku su," *Shūkan josei*, September 4, 1963, 120–22.

47. According to Ishioka Ritsuko, "Probably to give the image of 'Japan,' it has been given its new title, which bears no relation whatsoever to the song's original title in Japanese" ("Kongetsu no supotto: Kyu Sakamoto," *Music Life*, September 1963, reprinted in Kurosawa, *Roots of Japanese Pops*, 246–47). Following its success abroad, in late 1963 the song was rereleased by Toshiba in Japan under the title "Sukiyaki," whereupon it reentered the Japanese hit charts.

48. Ei Rokusuke, "Rokusuke Amerika noshiaruki," *Fujin kōron*, May 1963, 244–50.

49. Robert Walser, *Running with the Devil: Power, Gender, and Madness in Heavy Metal Music* (Hanover, N.H.: University Press of New England / Wesleyan University Press, 1993), 113.

50. Satō Yoshiaki has argued that the song became a hit worldwide because it inadvertently exploited a similarity in scales that were emerging in Japanese and Anglo-American popular music at this time, in *J-pop shinkaron: "Yosahoi bushi" kara "Automatic" e* (Tokyo: Heibonsha, 1999), 106–27. The scale stressed melodies ending on a major second interval and thereby allowed for connections to African American and Japanese folk scales.

51. These two cover versions also exploit the shared proclivity toward pentatonic melodies that characterizes both Japanese popular songs and American rhythm and blues.

52. Gilroy, *Black Atlantic*, 99.

53. On orientalist exoticism in Japan-related popular music, see Shuhei Hosokawa, "Martin Denny and the Development of Musical Exotica" and "Soy Sauce Music: Haruomi Hosono and Japanese Self-Orientalism," both in *Widening the Horizon: Exoticism in Post-War Popular Music*, ed. Philip Hayward (Sydney: Libbey, 1999), 72–93, 114–44.

54. Sakai, *Translation and Subjectivity*, 6 (italics in original).

55. According to Sakai, "Even in its praise of 'extraordinary cultural achievements by other civilizations,' the narcissism of the West seeks only to find in other cultures and civilizations what distinguishes the West from the rest of the world, and continually expects the others to respond to its narcissistic demand for acknowledgement of its distinction" (ibid., 70–71).

56. For a discussion on how the practice and rhetoric of adoption helped produce the structure of feeling required for the Cold War culture of integration of the free world, see Klein, *Cold War Orientalism*, 143–90.

57. Tejaswini Niranjana, *Siting Translation: History, Post-Structuralism, and the Colonial Context* (Berkeley: University of California Press, 1992).

58. I have in mind here the notion of "strategic anti-essentialism" and the notion that popular music can provide "a form of camouflage" that enables musicians "to satisfy those in power while subtly conveying oppositional messages at the same time" (Lipsitz, *Dangerous Crossroads*, 103).

59. Other singers from the late 1950s rockabilly boom, including Mickey Curtis and Kamayatsu Hiroshi, would retain "rock" credibility through the turbulent 1960s and 1970s and beyond. They, though, never enjoyed anything like the international success accorded Sakamoto, although their 1960s bands, the Spiders (Kamayatsu) and Samurai (Curtis), would tour in the West.

60. Lipsitz, *Dangerous Crossroads*, 165.

61. Lydia H. Liu, *Translingual Practice: Literature, National Culture, and Translated Modernity; China, 1900–1937* (Stanford, Calif.: Stanford University Press, 1995).

62. Quoted in Ei, *Sakamoto Kyū monogatari*, 10.

63. Davies, *Airlines of Asia Since 1920*, 476–84.

64. Kashiwagi Yukiko, *Ue wo muite arukō* (Tokyo: Fuji Terebi shuppan, 1986), 161.

65. Aikura, "Sukiyaki songu."

66. Klein, *Cold War Orientalism*, 243–52.

4. WORKING WITHIN THE SYSTEM

1. "Taigāsu ga ōhaba na imēji chēnji," *Shūkan heibon*, August 15, 1968, 56–57. Like Sakamoto Kyū, the Tigers were managed by Watanabe Productions. The core of the group was made up of high school friends from Kyoto who began playing together in 1965. In early 1966, they added lead singer Sawada Kenji ("Julie") and built up a large fan base through live gigs. They made their national debut at the Nichigeki Western Carnival in 1967 and released their first record shortly thereafter. The Tigers played their farewell concert in January 1971.

2. On the break between "teenage culture" and "youth culture," see Simon Frith, *Sound Effects: Youth, Leisure, and the Politics of Rock 'n' Roll* (New York: Pantheon, 1981), esp. 181–201.

3. The Tigers' management insisted at the time that the band members had engaged in "no antisocial behavior" and noted that the members had dressed conservatively in suits and ties for the taping of the canceled NHK show, refuting claims that their long hair and image represented forms of rebellion. See "Za Taigāsu NHK kara shimedashi!" *Shūkan heibon*, November 23, 1967, 26–30. On the incident, see also Julian Cope, *Japrocksampler: How the Post-War Japanese Blew Their Minds on Rock 'n' Roll* (London: Bloomsbury, 2007), 99–100; and Kitanaka Masakazu, *Nihon no uta: Sengo kayōkyoku shi*, rev. ed. (Tokyo: Heibonsha, 2003), 148.

4. William Marotti, "Japan 1968: The Performance of Violence and the Theater of Protest," *American Historical Review* 114, no. 1 (2009): 97–135, quote on 98.

5. Between 1955 and 1965, the number of high school students in Japan increased from 2.59 million to 5.07 million, while the number of college students increased from 600,000 to 1.08 million. See Kitanaka, *Nihon no uta*, 122.

6. John W. Dower, "Peace and Democracy in Two Systems: External Policy and Internal Conflict," in *Postwar Japan as History*, ed. Andrew Gordon (Berkeley: University of California Press, 1993), 3–33; and Matthew Penney, "Nationalism and Anti-Americanism in Japan: Manga Wars, Aso, Tamogami, and Progressive Alternatives," *Asia-Pacific Journal: Japan Focus*, April 2009, http://www.japanfocus.org/-Matthew-Penney/3116.

7. Marilyn Ivy, "Formations of Mass Culture," and Laura Hein, "Growth versus Success: Japan's Economic Policy in Historical Perspective," both in Gordon, *Postwar Japan as History*, 239–58, 99–122.

8. Koichi Hamada, "Japan 1968: A Reflection Point During the Era of the Economic Miracle," Center Discussion Paper, no. 764 (August 1996), Economic Growth Center, Yale University, http://www.econ.yale.edu/growth_pdf /cdp764.pdf.

9. Marotti, "Japan 1968," 102.

10. Kitanaka, *Nihon no uta*, 147.

11. Frith, *Sound Effects*, 69–70.

12. Minamida Katsuya, *Rokku myūjikku no shakaigaku* (Tokyo: Seikyūsha, 2001), esp. 10–39.

13. On the romanticization of rock, see Theodore Gracyk, *Rhythm and Noise: An Aesthetics of Rock* (Durham, N.C.: Duke University Press, 1996), esp. 175–206.

14. Frith, *Sound Effects*, 11.

15. Pierre Bourdieu, *Distinction: A Social Critique of the Judgement of Taste*, trans. Richard Nice (Cambridge, Mass.: Harvard University Press, 1984).

16. Frith, *Sound Effects*, 122.

17. Ibid., 225–28. For a theoretical explication of the gendered ethics of guitar playing, see Reginald Jackson, "Gender, Race, and the Ethical Praxis of Slide Guitar," *Women & Performance: A Journal of Feminist Theory* 17, no. 2 (2007): 139–69.

18. Frith, *Sound Effects*, 21.

19. "GS būmu kara mūdo kōrasu jidai e," *Shūkan heibon*, September 12, 1968, 126–30.

20. In 1967, likewise, *Kawara-ban*, an underground journal devoted to covering the incipient folk scene, began publication in the Kansai region. See Maeda Yoshitake and Hirahara Kōji, *Nihon no fōku & rokku no jidai 1: 60-nendai fōku no jidai* (Tokyo: Shinkō Music, 1993), 83.

21. Robert Walser, *Running with the Devil: Power, Gender, and Madness in Heavy Metal Music* (Hanover, N.H.: University Press of New England / Wesleyan University Press, 1993), 42.

22. Jacques Attali, *Noise: The Political Economy of Music*, trans. Brian Massumi (1977; repr., Minneapolis: University of Minnesota Press, 1985), 6.

23. Ibid., 6.

24. Ibid., 14.

25. Ibid., 11.

26. Ibid., 33 (italics added).

27. You can feel band members Kishibe Osami and Kishibe "Shirō" struggle palpably to find a new role for the Tigers in a 1970 interview. Osami speaks of his

desire to cut through the accumulated image of the Tigers as a cute band and to find an audience outside the fifteen- and sixteen-year-olds who attended Nichigeki Western Carnival showcases, while Shirō speaks of his recent seven-month sojourn in the United States, where he attended performances by Jimi Hendrix, Cream, Donovan, and Santana. See "Ningen hōmon," *Music Life*, March 1970, 154–55.

28. "'Jurī shineitai' gonin no sono ato," *Yangu redi*, November 16 and 23, 1970 (double issue), 150–53.

29. "Za Taigāsu ga jijitsujō no kaisan," *Yangu redi*, December 21, 1970, 28–30.

30. "Konnichi no poppu shiin: Taigāsu no iyoku arubamu," *Music Life*, December 1968, 173.

31. The latter clearly alludes to Jimi Hendrix throughout.

32. Narumo Shigeru, "Nihon no gurūpu wa minna kaisan shiyō!" *Music Life*, January 1970, 152–53.

33. Sawada, still using the nickname "Julie," had numerous hits in the 1970s, mostly sentimental ballads. His image from this later period trades on a flamboyant glam-rock look, with a stress on partying and outrageous costumes and gender-bending makeup (in some ways a continuation of the image he had with the Tigers). Kishibe, though, retired from music in 1975. Some of his subsequent film roles refer playfully back to his days as a Group Sounds superstar, including *Seishun dendekedekedeke* (1992) and *GS Wonderland* (2008).

34. "Hitomi Minoru / Ren'ai mo dekinakatta: Kyōki no 4-nenkan," *Yangu redi*, December 28, 1970, 26–29. Hitomi made good on his vow, becoming a respected Chinese teacher and scholar of Chinese, declining even to participate in a series of Tigers reunion events that began in 1981.

35. Kurosawa Susumu, *Nihon rokku ki GS hen konpurīto: Psychedelia in Japan, 1966–1969: The Ultimate "Group Sounds" (Japanese Garage / Psych) Record Guide* (Tokyo: Shinkō Music, 2007), 14. The archival work and critical writings of Kurosawa Susumu (1954–2007) laid the foundation for all subsequent studies of Group Sounds, as well as of other genres of 1960s and 1970s Japanese popular music. My account of the history of Group Sounds is based on *Nihon rokku ki*, as well as on Kurosawa's *Nihon no 60-nendai rokku no subete complete* (Tokyo: Shinkō Music, 2008). See also Kitanaka, *Nihon no uta*, 141–55; and Cope, *Japrocksampler*, esp. 87–103.

36. See, for example, "Gurūpu saunzu no subete," *Yangu redi*, September 16, 1967, 49–56.

37. Kurosawa, *Nihon rokku ki*, 34–35.

38. On the *ereki būmu*, see ibid., 5–13; Kurosawa, *Nihon no 60-nendai rokku*, 144–84; Kitanaka, *Nihon no uta*, 128–33; and Cope, *Japrocksampler*, 73–83.

39. For a history of Japanese electric-guitar production during this period, see Hiroyuki Noguchi, "Japanese Guitars," in *Fuzz & Feedback: Classic Guitar Music of the '60s*, ed. Tony Bacon (San Francisco: Miller Freeman, 2000), 64–69.

40. The Japanese college folk music scene was inspired, in part, by the ongoing folk revival in the United States. Japanese tours by the Kingston Trio (1961), Pete Seeger (1963), and Peter, Paul, and Mary (1964) brought the sound of the Newport Folk Festival directly to audiences in Japan. More intellectual than *ereki*, it would morph into protest folk, which I touch on again in the following chapter. Another difference from *ereki*: the early 1960s college folk boom was entirely divorced from the lively music scene at U.S. military-base clubs. See Kitanaka, *Nihon no uta*, 122–28; and Maeda and Hirahara, *Nihon no fōku & rokku no jidai*.

41. Kurosawa, *Nihon rokku ki*, 4.

42. Kitanaka, *Nihon no uta*, 143.

43. Satō Yoshiaki, *J-pop shinkaron: "Yosahoi bushi" kara "Automatic" e* (Tokyo: Heibonsha, 1999), 130.

44. "Gurūpu saunzu no subete," 50.

45. Other British Invasion groups had performed in Japan before the Beatles, including the Animals, Manfred Mann's Earth Band, Herman's Hermits, the Honeycombs, and Peter and Gordon. In late 1964, the Liverpool Five, a group of musicians from London, began an extended residence at the Shinjuku ACB club, which instantly became a Mecca for Japanese rock and rollers eager to access the "real thing" in person: not just the musicians but also their Vox amps and AKG mikes.

46. The rebellious nature and sound of the Golden Cups is brilliantly captured in a documentary film, *The Golden Cups: One More Time!* (dir. San Ma Meng, 2004). Their 1968 cover version of "Hey Joe," featuring Louis Louise Kabe's astonishing bass playing, surely represents one of the high points of Japanese psychedelic rock.

47. Kurosawa, *Nihon rokku ki*, 15, 64–65.

48. "Asa made matenai" remains a worldwide cult classic among devotees of 1960s garage rock—though I am also partial to another of the band's early recordings, the equally fuzz-toned "I Am Just a Mops" from their LP *Psychedelic Sound in Japan* (1968). I'm not alone in this preference: an early, sympathetic but largely negative ("lacking in power") review of the band's debut album also singles out this track for praise. See "Moppusu," *Music Life*, June 1968, 163.

49. For a review of the concert, see "Gurūpu saunzu to dabutta koten ongaku," *Music Life*, July 1968, 162. Organizer Ichiyanagi Toshi is interviewed after the event in "Sakkyokuka Ichiyanagi Toshi: Poppusu wa kagirinai kanōsei

wo hisometa atarashii geijutsu da," *Music Life*, September 1968, 165. See also Kurosawa Susumu, "Hoshi Katsu za Moppusu: Karuto GS intavyū 2," *Rokku gahō*, September 2002, 24–27.

50. "Wasei gurūpu saunzu wa kore kara ittai nani wo shite ikeba ii darō? Suzuki Hiromitsu (za Moppusu) ni kiku," *Music Life*, October 1969, 162–63. The interviewer also asks Suzuki about the apparent split between what I am calling the second- and third-generation GS bands. Suzuki acknowledges the gap but continues in language that reveals his own take on the issue of "authenticity": "In fact, there is little difference between what they [the two different factions of GS] are doing. None of the groups perform with any real understanding of the blues." He laments that current Japanese bands are only feeble copies of Western groups, which he says is an inevitable result given the shallow history of rock in Japan.

51. The Golden Cups played their last concert in Okinawa in January 1972 (after the concert hall in which they were playing caught fire midshow, destroying all their equipment), while the Mops held out until 1974.

52. Frith, *Sound Effects*, 18.

53. Gracyk, *Rhythm and Noise*, 99 (italics in original).

54. Steve Waksman, "The Turn to Noise: Rock Guitar from the 1950s to the 1970s," in *The Cambridge Companion to the Guitar*, ed. Victor Anand Coelho (Cambridge: Cambridge University Press, 2003), 109–21, quote on 110.

55. Michael Ross, *Getting Great Guitar Sounds*, rev. ed. (Milwaukee: Leonard, 1998), 39.

56. Gracyk, *Rhythm and Noise*, 109–14. See also Michael Lydon, "The Electric Guitar," in *Boogie Lightning: How Music Became Electric*, ed. Michael Lydon and Ellen Mandel (New York: Da Capo, 1974), 145–58.

57. Tony Bacon, "Beatle Guitars," in Bacon, *Fuzz & Feedback*, 56. The Beatles included "I Feel Fine" in their 1966 live performances at the Budōkan in Tokyo, including the opening feedback effect.

58. Robert Palmer, "The Church of the Sonic Guitar," *South Atlantic Quarterly* 90, no. 4 (1991): 649–73, quote on 673.

59. Gracyk, *Rhythm and Noise*, 109–10.

60. Ibid., 122–23. See also Palmer, "Church of the Sonic Guitar," 658–59.

61. Waksman, "Turn to Noise."

62. Frith, *Sound Effects*, 51.

63. At least one critic has argued that rock is distinguished from other musical genres precisely by the centrality of the recording process to the form: "Rock is a tradition of popular music whose creation and dissemination centers on recording technology. . . . In rock the musical work is less typically a song than an arrangement of recorded sounds" (Gracyk, *Rhythm and Noise*, 1).

64. Ibid., 123–24.
65. Kurosawa, *Nihon rokku ki*, 14.
66. Ibid.
67. Kurosawa, "Hoshi katsu za Moppusu," 24–27.
68. Inoue Takayuki, *Supaidāsu arigatō!* (Tokyo: Shufu to seikatsu sha, 2004), 75.
69. The Jacks' first LP was called *Vacant World* in English but *Jakkusu no sekai* (*The World of the Jacks*) in Japanese. Whereas the debut single was released on the relatively minor Takuto label, the album was released on Express, a side label owned by the major Toshiba Corporation.
70. Kurosawa, *Nihon rokku ki*, 102–5. See also Hayakawa Yoshio, *Rabu zenerēshon* (Tokyo: Jiyū kokuminsha, 1972), 10–28; and Maeda and Hirahara, *Nihon no fōku & rokku no jidai*, 132–38.
71. "Tadaima LP seisaku chū," *Music Life*, July 1968, 162.
72. "Kongetsu no shinguru," *Music Life*, July 1968, 164.
73. "Kongetsu no arubamu," *Music Life*, October 1968, 170.
74. Ibid.
75. Hayakawa, *Rabu zenerēshon*, 2, 3.
76. Cope, *Japrocksampler*, esp. 163–76.
77. Ibid., 169.
78. Marotti, "Japan 1968," 99–100.
79. "Kore ga yume no ōru sutā saunzu da!" *Shūkan heibon*, June 15, 1967, 44–47.
80. "Gurūpu saunzu no subete," 54.
81. Narumo, "Nihon no gurūpu."
82. Cope, *Japrocksampler*, 145–46, 238.
83. Terauchi Takeshi, *Teketeke-den: Terry's Special Electric Life* (Tokyo: Kōdansha, 2000), 16. See also "Furusato Tsuchiura de konsāto: 'Ereki no kamisama' Terauchi Takeshi-san," *Asahi shinbun*, August 31, 2004, Tochigi ed., 31. Terauchi claims that his youthful experimentation produced the world's first electric guitar, but guitarists were already using electrically amplified guitars before his birth.
84. Terauchi, *Teketeke-den*, 17–18.
85. Kurosawa, *Nihon no 60-nendai rokku*, 40–41.
86. Kamayatsu Hiroshi, *Musshu!* (Tokyo: Nikkei BP-sha, 2002), 36.
87. Terauchi, *Teketeke-den*, 35–36.
88. Kurosawa, *Nihon no 60-nendai rokku*, 182.
89. Kurosawa, *Nihon rokku ki*, 40–41.
90. Ibid., 108–9.
91. Cope, *Japrocksampler*, 92.
92. Quoted in Gracyk, *Rhythm and Noise*, 9.
93. Terauchi, *Teketeke-den*, 182–214.

94. "Terauchi Takeshi-san: Kotoba koeru ereki no sekai / Tochigi," *Asahi shinbun*, Tochigi ed., May 12, 1996.

95. Satō, *J-pop shinkaron*, 128.

96. Mickey Curtis, "Nyū rokku no kopī nante nansensu," *Music Life*, December 1970, 96–97.

97. Terauchi, *Teketeke-den*, 4.

98. One the Spiders' career, see Inoue, *Supaidāsu arigatō!*; Kamayatsu, *Musshu!*; and Kurosawa, *Nihon rokku ki*, 78–83.

99. Saeki Kenzō, "Ribapūru saundo no jidaitte jitsu wa odotteru yatsu ga inakatta: Musshu Kamayatsu intavyū," *Rokku gahō*, April 2001, 22–26. See also Inoue, *Supaidāsu arigatō!*, 54–57; and Kamayatsu, *Musshu!*, 76–88.

100. Kamayatsu, *Musshu!*, 88–89. See also Kurosawa, *Nihon rokku ki*, 12; and Kitanaka, *Nihon no uta*, 142.

101. Kamayatsu, *Musshu!*, 106; Inoue, *Supaidāsu arigatō!*, 70–72. A number of Japanese bands opened the bill for the Beatles' shows, including Jackie Yoshikawa and the Blue Comets and Terauchi Takeshi and Blue Jeans.

102. "Za Supaidāsu Yōroppa nagurikomi," *Shūkan heibon*, October 27, 1966, 86–87.

103. "Kinpatsu onna wo horesaseru zo," *Shūkan heibon*, November 10, 1966, 100–103.

104. "Za Supaidāsu ga Amerika honkoku ni tekizen jōriku," *Shūkan heibon*, June 22, 1967, 32–35. See also Inoue, *Supaidāsu arigatō!*, 106–11.

105. Quoted in Inoue, *Supaidāsu arigatō!*, 128.

106. Miyagi Chikako, "Mitsu soroi no Eikoku-chō de shōbu shimasu!," *Shūkan heibon*, November 30, 1967, 68–71.

107. "Gurūpu saunzu no subete," 51.

108. "Meiji hyaku-nen, Supaidāsu shichi-nen," *Music Life*, February 1969, 171.

109. See, for example, the laudatory description of the album in Shibata Shūhei, ed., *Rokku kuronikuru Japan*, vol. 1, *1968–1980* (Tokyo: Ongaku shuppansha, 1999), 101.

110. Kamayatsu, *Musshu!*, 20.

111. Ibid., 27–37.

112. Ibid., 39–40.

113. Ibid., 46.

114. Yuasa Manabu, "Aoreru saundo wo rekōdo de hyōgen shita Bītoruzu wa soko de 'kachi' datta ne: Terauchi Takeshita intavyū," *Rokku gahō*, April 2001, 12–15.

115. Kamayatsu, *Musshu!*, 107.

116. Ibid., 120

117. Ibid., 121–33.

118. Ibid., 136.

119. Ibid., 138–40.

120. Ibid., 146–53.

121. Ibid., 195.

122. Kamayatsu Hiroshi, "Mitōshi akarui Nihon no rokku kai," *Music Life*, September 1970, 149–50.

123. Kodama Tsunetochi, "Kamayatsu Hiroshi Monsieur," in Shibata, *Rokku kuronikuru Japan*, 105.

124. Satō, *J-pop shinkaron*, 161.

125. Kitanaka, *Nihon no uta*, 147.

126. Hagiwara Ken'ichi, *Shōken* (Tokyo: Kōdansha, 2008), 14.

127. Kamayatsu, *Musshu!*, 113.

128. Inoue, *Supaidāsu arigatō!*, 91–92.

129. Ibid.

130. "Za Tenputāzu no kaishingeki," *Shūkan heibon*, February 29, 1968, 42–45.

131. For contemporary reportage on the band's popularity rivaling that of the Tigers, see "Za Tenputāzu to isshūkan," *Shūkan heibon*, May 2, 1968, 64–68.

132. Hagiwara, *Shōken*, 19.

133. "Tenputāzu," *Music Life*, August 1968, 162–63.

134. "Za Tenputāzu to gonin no hahaoya no kangeki," *Shūkan heibon*, September 19, 1968, 98–100. The occasion for this article surveying the members' mothers was the Tempters' release of the sentimental ballad "Mother" (Okāsan).

135. Kurosawa, *Nihon rokku ki*, 87.

136. Ibid., 88.

137. American musicians who participated in the sessions included guitarist Charlie Freeman, drummer Sammy Creason, bassist Tommy McClure, and keyboardists Jim Dickinson and Mike Utley, the same studio musicians who backed Aretha Franklin on her classic album *Spirit in the Dark*. Dickinson would go on to work with such groups as Big Star (he produced their third album) and the Rolling Stones. The backing singers on *The Tempters in Memphis* were Mary Holladay and Ginger Holladay, who backed Elvis Presley on many of his classic Memphis recordings, and Allen Reynolds, who would go on to become a celebrated producer in country music, working with such figures as Garth Brooks, Crystal Gayle, and Don Williams.

138. "Nyū arubamu: Tenputāzu in Menfisu," *Music Life*, January 1970, 161–62.

139. Kamayatsu, *Musshu!*, 130.

140. Alan Merrill, e-mail message to author, March 2, 2005.

141. Inoue, *Supaidāsu arigatō!*, 137.

142. Ibid., 138–39.

143. Ibid.

144. Kitanaka Masakazu, "GS ni kodawaru," *New Music Magazine*, March 1970, 81–82.

145. Hagiwara, *Shōken*, 28.

146. Inoue, *Supaidāsu arigatō!*, 140; Cope, *Japrocksampler*, 191.

147. "Aran Meriru: Gaijin GS intavyū," *Rokku gahō*, September 2002, 44–47.

148. "Vodka Collins [Alan Merrill]," *Strange Days*, October 2004, 102–4.

149. Dave Thompson, "Footnote Archives: Belly Up to Vodka Collins," *Goldmine*, November 26, 2004, 20.

150. Kurosawa, "Hoshi katsu za Moppusu," 24–27.

151. Gracyk, *Rhythm and Noise*, 74.

152. Hayakawa Yoshio, *Tamashii no basho* (Tokyo: Shōbunsha, 2002), 12.

153. Hayakawa, *Rabu zenerēshon*, 1.

154. Satō, *J-pop shinkaron*, 157–59.

155. Frith, *Sound Effects*, 214.

156. Ibid., 241.

157. Ibid., 144. At the same point, the United States accounted for 40 percent and the United Kingdom, 6 percent.

158. Lawrence Grossberg, *We Gotta Get Out of This Place: Popular Conservatism and Postmodern Culture* (New York: Routledge, 1992), 296, 300.

159. Attali, *Noise*, 9, 109.

160. Yoshikuni Igarashi, "Dead Bodies and Living Guns: The United Red Army and Its Deadly Pursuit of Revolution, 1971–1972," *Japanese Studies* 27, no. 2 (2007): 119–37, quote on 121.

5. NEW MUSIC AND THE NEGATION OF THE NEGATION

1. The Kingston Trio toured Japan in 1961, the Brothers Four in 1962, Pete Seeger in 1963, Peter, Paul, and Mary in 1964, and Odetta in 1965. Two important precursors to campus folk were booms in Russian folk songs and labor songs that spread across Japan in the 1950s and early 1960s. See Maeda Yoshitake and Hirahara Kōji, *Nihon no fōku & rokku no jidai 1: 60-nendai fōku no jidai* (Tokyo: Shinkō Music, 1993), 23.

2. Kitanaka Masakazu, *Nihon no uta: Sengo kayōkyoku shi*, rev. ed. (Tokyo: Heibonsha, 2003), 125–27.

3. Ibid., 156–57.

4. Maeda and Hirahara, *Nihon no fōku & rokku no jidai*, 1:35, 52–53.

5. David W. Hughes, *Traditional Folk Song in Modern Japan: Sources, Sentiment and Society* (Folkestone, Eng.: Global Oriental, 2008), 8–45; William P. Malm, *Traditional Japanese Music and Musical Instruments*, rev. ed. (Tokyo: Kodansha International, 2000), esp. 261–73.

6. On Tsugaru-jamisen master Takahashi, see Hughes, *Traditional Folk Song in Modern Japan*, 84–85. On *shakuhachi* master Yamaguchi's career as performer

and teacher, see Christopher Yohmei Blasdel, *The Single Tone: A Personal Journey into Shakuhachi Music* (Tokyo: Printed Matter, 2005).

7. Koizumi's work was enormously influential not just among musicologists but also among practitioners. For a summary in English, see Shunsuke Tsurumi, *A Cultural History of Postwar Japan, 1945–1980* (London: Kegan Paul, 1987), 79–102.

8. Maeda and Hirahara, *Nihon no fōku & rokku no jidai*, 1:44. Hughes stresses the barrier between *min'yō* and *fōku* in *Traditional Folk Song in Modern Japan*, 39–42. But live and studio recordings by *fōku* musicians from the period show substantial crossover.

9. Maeda and Hirahara, *Nihon no fōku & rokku no jidai*, 1:145–52.

10. Ibid., 161–62, 196–201.

11. Ibid., 49.

12. Ibid., 122–23.

13. Maeda Yoshitake and Hirahara Kōji, *Nihon no fōku & rokku no jidai 2: Nyū myūjikku no jidai* (Tokyo: Shinkō Music, 1993), 29–32.

14. Maeda and Hirahara, *Nihon no fōku & rokku no jidai*, 1:176–77.

15. Maeda and Hirahara, *Nihon no fōku & rokku no jidai*, 2:6.

16. Ibid., 70–72.

17. Satō Yoshiaki, *J-pop shinkaron: "Yosahoi bushi" kara "Automatic" e* (Tokyo: Heibonsha, 1999), 157–59.

18. Maeda and Hirahara, *Nihon no fōku & rokku no jidai*, esp. 2:27, 74.

19. Ibid., 156–61.

20. Unsigned introductory statement, "Bokura ni totte no dentō no mondai," *New Music Magazine*, December 1971, 16.

21. Yoshikuni Igarashi, *Bodies of Memory: Narratives of Postwar Japanese Culture, 1945–1970* (Princeton, N.J.: Princeton University Press, 2000).

22. Muro Kenji, "Nakatsugawa de kanjita watashi no fuman," *New Music Magazine*, October 1971, 24–27, quote on 25.

23. The most comprehensive sources on Happy End are Hagiwara Kenta, *Happī Endo no densetsu* (Tokyo: Hachiyōsha, 1983); and Kimura Yutaka, ed., *Happī Endo Book* (Tokyo: Shinkō Music, 2004). See also the following special issues of music magazines devoted to the band: "Happī Endo no kaze ga fuita jidai," special issue, *Rekōdo korekutāzu*, August 2000; and "20 seiki saigo no Happī Endo tokushū," special issues, *Rokku gahō*, June and October 2000. In English, I have relied on Mark Anderson, "Happy Endo," in *Encyclopedia of Contemporary Japanese Culture*, ed. Sandra Buckley (London: Routledge, 2002), 185; and Shuhei Hosokawa, "Soy Sauce Music: Haruomi Hosono and Japanese Self-Orientalism," in *Widening the Horizon: Exoticism in Post-War Popular Music*, ed. Philip Hayward (London: Libbey, 1999), 114–44.

24. K. T., "Nyū gurūpu: Eipuriru Fūru [April Fool]," *Music Life*, September 1969, 162–63. See also Hagiwara, *Happī Endo no densetsu*, 24–36.

25. Unlike its predecessor, however, *Kazemachi roman* finished in only fourth place for the *New Music Magazine* Record Award in 1972 It's worth noting, though, that members of Happy End acted as session men or producers and arrangers for the albums that finished first (Endō Kenji's *Manzoku dekiru ka na*) and second (Kosaka Chū's *Arigatō*) that year. See Maeda and Hirahara, *Nihon no fōku & rokku no jidai*, 2:36.

26. Lawrence Olsen, *Ambivalent Moderns: Portraits of Japanese Cultural Identity* (Savage, Md.: Rowman & Littlefield, 1992).

27. Takashi Fujitani, "*Minshūshi* as Critique of Orientalist Knowledges," *positions* 6, no. 2 (1998): 303–22; Carol Gluck, "The People in History: Recent Trends in Japanese Historiography," *Journal of Asian Studies* 38, no. 1 (1978): 25–50.

28. Murai Osamu, *Nantō ideorogī no hassei*, rev. ed. (Tokyo: Ōta shuppan, 1995).

29. Igarashi, *Bodies of Memory*, 166.

30. Eiji Oguma, *A Genealogy of "Japanese" Self-Images*, trans. David Askew (Melbourne: Trans Pacific, 2002).

31. Hagiwara, *Happī Endo no densetsu*, 96–109; Hosokawa, "Soy Sauce Music"; David Toop, *Exotica: Fabricated Soundscapes in a Real World* (London: Serpent's Tail, 1999), 219–24.

32. Lisa Yoneyama, *Hiroshima Traces: Time, Space, and the Dialectics of Memory* (Berkeley: University of California Press, 1999), 5.

33. Eric L. Santner, *Stranded Objects: Mourning, Memory, and Film in Postwar Germany* (Ithaca, N.Y.: Cornell University Press, 1993); Marilyn Ivy, *Discourses of the Vanishing: Modernity Phantasm Japan* (Chicago: University of Chicago Press, 1995), 13–15; Yoneyama, *Hiroshima Traces*, 26–33.

34. Anderson, "Happy Endo." On melodrama in postwar popular culture in Japan, see Igarashi, *Bodies of Memory*, as well as chapter 6 this volume.

35. On the ideologies of the sincere voice in American folk, see Simon Frith, *Sound Effects: Youth, Leisure, and the Politics of Rock 'n' Roll* (New York: Pantheon, 1981), 27–32.

36. Ivy, *Discourses of the Vanishing*, 20.

37. Maeda and Hirahara, *Nihon no fōku & rokku no jidai*, esp. 1:84–85.

38. See, for example, E. Taylor Atkins, *Blue Nippon: Authenticating Jazz in Japan* (Durham, N.C.: Duke University Press, 2001).

39. Maeda and Hirahara, *Nihon no fōku & rokku no jidai*, 1:170.

40. Hayashi Hikaru, "Katakana-kotoba no uta sekai: Watashitachi no nijū gengo teikoku," *New Music Magazine*, November 1971, 18–22. Hayashi also argues, however, that contemporary Japanese popular culture is a "dual-language empire" (*nijū gengo teikoku*), in which a native Japanese strain coexists with

a *katakana* strain, which provides a kind of buffer zone that eases the shock when Japanese encounter foreign cultural productions. This, he suggests, may in the future lead to new forms of music arising from this double structure.

41. Fukamachi Jun, "Bokutachi jishin no Nihongo no uta wo tsukurō," *New Music Magazine*, November 1971, 30–34.

42. Nakamura Tōyō, "Wareware ni 'naniwabushi' wa sonzai suru ka," *New Music Magazine*, December 1971, 18–23.

43. Matsumoto Takashi, "Happī Endo no kinjitō *Kazemachi roman*," in *Bessatsu taiyō: Nihon no rokku 50's–90's*, ed. Takahashi Yōji (Tokyo: Heibonsha, 1993), 82.

44. K. T., review of album *Happī Endo*, in *Roots of Japanese Pops, 1955–1970*, ed. Kurosawa Susumu (Tokyo: Shinkō Music, 1995), 387.

45. Quoted in Take Hideki, *Yomu J-pop: 1945–1999 shiteki zenshi* (Tokyo: Tokuma shoten, 1999), 134.

46. Matsumoto Takashi, "Bokura no 'Nihon' o mitsukeyō," *New Music Magazine*, December 1971, 33.

47. Matsumoto Takashi, "Gendai no rokku wa hōrō kara umareru," *Music Life*, August 1970, 150–51.

48. Hosokawa, "Soy Sauce Music," 119 (italics in original).

49. Satō, *J-pop shinkaron*, 144–87.

50. Shida Ayumu, "Haru yo koi," *Rekōdo korekutāzu*, August 2000, 101–17.

51. Frith, *Sound Effects*, 35–38.

52. Uchida Yūya, Matsumoto Takashi, Ōtaki Eiichi, et al., "Cross Talk: Nihon no rokku jōkyō wa doko made kita ka," reprinted in *Music Magazine*, December 1994, 123–25.

53. Jennifer Robinson, "It Takes a Village: Internationalization and Nostalgia in Postwar Japan," in *Mirror of Modernity: Invented Traditions of Modern Japan*, ed. Stephen Vlastos (Berkeley: University of California Press, 1998), 110–29.

54. Homi K. Bhabha, *The Location of Culture* (London: Routledge, 1994), 40, 45, 65.

55. On the wildly popular late 1960s folk song "Children Who Don't Know War" (Sensō o shiranai kodomotachi), see Igarashi, *Bodies of Memory*, 197–98.

56. Maeda and Hirahara, *Nihon no fōku & rokku no jidai*, 1:153–57, 208–10. By the end of their career, Happy End was releasing their albums on Bellwood, a specialty label initially owned by King Records, which had acquired the URC catalog and its roster of artists. Bellwood became an independent label in 1973.

57. Ibid., 200.

58. Matsumoto, "Happī Endo no kinjitō *Kazemachi roman*."

59. Hosokawa, "Soy Sauce Music," 120.

60. Naoki Sakai, *Translation and Subjectivity: On "Japan" and Cultural Nationalism* (Minneapolis: University of Minnesota Press, 1997), 170.

61. Katō Norihiro, *Haisengo ron* (Tokyo: Kōdansha, 1997). See also Igarashi, *Bodies of Memory*, 207–10.

62. Susan Stewart, *On Longing: Narratives of the Miniature, the Gigantic, the Souvenir, the Collection* (Durham, N.C.: Duke University Press, 1993), 23.

63. Quoted in Hagiwara, *Happī Endo no densetsu*, 104

64. Matsutōya Yumi, *Rūju no dengon* (Tokyo: Kadokawa shoten, 1983), 44–46.

65. Ibid., 57–59.

66. "Ninki batsugun fōku-kai no joō Arai Yumi," *Heibon panchi*, January 12, 1976, 50–51.

67. A number of popular appreciations of Yuming's music have been published in Japan, including Gotō Wataru, ed., *Matsutōya Yumi: Yuming* (Tokyo: Tōkyō FM shuppan, 2003); Fukami Haruka, *Yūmin no toiki: Metoroporisu no kataribe* (Tokyo: Mirion shuppan, 1989); Ochiai Shinji, *Yūmin: Ren'ai fūkei ron* (Tokyo: Seikyūsha, 1993); Fukami Haruka, *Yuming World: Matsutōya Yumi no sekai* (Tokyo: Zest, 1998); and Tsuta Kiui, *Yūmin "ai" no chirigaku* (Tokyo: Kawade shobō, 2006).

68. For Yuming's own explication of her status as a genius, see Matsutōya, *Rūju no dengon*, 6–39.

69. On Yuming's role as pioneer for a more assertive kind of female voice in Japanese popular song that emerged in the 1990s, see James Stanlaw, "Open Your File, Open Your Mind: Women, English, and Changing Roles and Voices in Japanese Pop Music," in *Japan Pop! Inside the World of Japanese Popular Culture*, ed. Timothy J. Craig (Armonk, N.Y.: Sharpe, 2000), 75–100. See also Mark Anderson, "Matsutoya Yumi," in Buckley, *Encyclopedia of Contemporary Japanese Culture*, 340.

70. Apparently, though, in live performance with her stage band Daddy Oh (not Caramel Mama), the hard-rock sound returned to the song. See the description of a live performance in Kitanaka Masakazu, "Karumen Maki, Arai Yumi nado josei shingā no katsuyaku buri," *New Music Magazine*, December 1974, 56–59.

71. Gotō, *Matsutōya Yumi*, 20–21.

72. Dan Ikuma, "Nippon no uta 48," *Shūkan yomiuri*, March 6, 1976, 100–101.

73. On the relationship between the Procol Harum song and Bach's compositions, see Richard Middleton, *Studying Popular Music* (Philadelphia: Open University Press, 1990), esp. 30–31. The chord progressions in Arai Yumi's single "The Darkening Room" (Kageriyuku heya, 1976) likewise recall eighteenth-century classical music, especially hymns—an allusion hammered home with the use of a pipe organ and chorus in the recording.

74. Maeda and Hirahara, *Nihon no fōku & rokku no jidai*, 2:10–12.

75. Ibid., 89–90.

76. Aono Motoo, "Nyū myūjikku no kishutachi," *Sandē Mainichi*, March 7, 1976, 123–25.

77. The article reporting this laments that the previous year's winner, idol singer Yamaguchi Momoe, had dropped to number 5 in the 1975 results. The 1975 male winner was singer Fuse Akira. See "Momoe-chan wa furui Yumi-chan no jidai," *Shūkan Yomiuri*, December 20, 1975, 31.

78. Tomisawa Issei, "Arai Yumi no ongaku seikatsu hakusho," *Heibon panchi*, February 16, 1976, 24–28.

79. Frith, *Sound Effects*, 134.

80. For example, Aono, "Nyū myūjikku no kishutachi," 123.

81. Tomisawa Issei, "Yūmin daihyakka," *Heibon panchi*, April 5, 1976, 87–94, quote on 87–88.

82. Tanaka Yasuo, *Nantonaku kurisutaru* (Tokyo: Shinchōsha, 1985), 71.

83. Carolyn S. Stevens, *Japanese Popular Music: Culture, Authenticity and Power* (London: Routlege, 2008), esp. 47–49.

84. Tomisawa, "Yūmin daihyakka," 88.

85. Maeda and Hirahara, *Nihon no fōku & rokku no jidai*, 2:24–32, 68–69.

86. Gotō, *Matsutōya Yumi*, 161.

87. Kitanaka, "Karumen Maki," 59.

88. Dan Ikuma, "Nippon no uta 66," *Shūkan Yomiuri*, July 10, 1976, 70–71.

89. The allergy to television appearances among new-music performers actually amounted to a refusal to appear on certain kinds of television programs, especially those associated with *enka* and other older forms of pop. The launch in 1978 of *The Best Ten* (TBS network) and similar new-music shows created a new, hipper venue for television appearances, and many new-music artists would take advantage of it. See Maeda and Hirahara, *Nihon no fōku & rokku no jidai*, 2:138, 142, 159–61. See also Stevens, *Japanese Popular Music*, 91–98.

90. On Hosono's solo albums, see Hosokawa, "Soy Sauce Music."

91. On Sakamoto's musical training, see Brian Currid, " 'Finally, I Reach to Africa': Ryuichi Sakamoto and Sounding Japan(ese)," in *Contemporary Japan and Popular Culture*, ed. John Whittier Treat (Honolulu: University of Hawai'i Press, 1996), 69–102.

92. Maeda and Hirahara, *Nihon no fōku & rokku no jidai*, 2:178.

93. On YMO's history as a band, see Endō Toshiaki, *YMO konpurekkusu: The YMO Complex; Take Me to Techno's Limit* (Tokyo: Heibonsha, 2003); Yoshimura Eiichi, ed., *Compact YMO* (Tokyo: Tokuma shoten, 1998); Tayama Miki, ed., *Nice Age: YMO to sono jidai, 1978–1984* (Tokyo: Shinkō Music Entertainment, 2007); and *YMO: Yellow Magic Orchestra* (Tokyo: Asupekuto, 2007). In English, see Hosokawa, "Soy Sauce Music"; and Currid, "Finally, I Reach to Africa."

94. Maeda and Hirahara, *Nihon no fōku & rokku no jidai*, 2:178.
95. Yoshimura, *Compact YMO*, 117.
96. Sakamoto Ryūichi's composition "Behind the Mask" was originally intended to be used in a television commercial, according to *YMO: Yellow Magic Orchestra*, [304]. The song's title alludes in part to Mishima Yukio's classic novel *Confessions of a Mask* (*Kamen no kokuhaku*, 1948). Sakamoto's father was Mishima's editor on the book. See Endō, *YMO konpurekkusu*, 35.
97. Endō, *YMO konpurekkusu*, 50–51.
98. Karatani Kōjin, "Rizumu, merodī, konseputo," in *Sai toshite no basho* (Tokyo: Kōdansha, 1996), 286–90.
99. Endō, *YMO konpurekkusu*, 14–18.
100. My argument is based on ibid., 13
101. Currid, "Finally, I Reach to Africa," 75.
102. Endō, *YMO konpurekkusu*, 31.
103. *YMO: Yellow Magic Orchestra*, [304].
104. Ibid., [302].
105. Endō, *YMO konpurekkusu*, 76–87.
106. Carl Cassegard, "From Withdrawal to Resistance. The Rhetoric of Exit in Yoshimoto Takaaki and Karatani Kojin," *Asia-Pacific Journal: Japan Focus*, March 4, 2008, http://www.japanfocus.org/-Carl-Cassegard/2684.
107. Quoted in Toop, *Exotica*, 221–24.

6. THE JAPAN THAT CAN "SAY YES"

1. "Season of the Sun" was first published in the July 1955 issue of the journal *Bungakkai*. It has been reprinted in numerous collections, including *Shōwa bungaku zenshū*, ed. Ishihara Shintarō et al. (Tokyo: Shōgakkan, 1986–1990), 29:7–30. The story is available in translation as "Season of Violence," in Shintaro Ishihara, *Season of Violence*, trans. John G. Mills, Toshie Takahama, and Ken Tremayne (Rutland, Vt.: Tuttle, 1966).
2. On Ishihara's relation to postwar youth culture and mass media, as well as for a survey of the critical reception of his early fiction, see Ann Sherif, "The Aesthetics of Speed and the Illogicality of Politics: Ishihara Shintarō's Literary Debut," *Japan Forum* 17, no. 2 (2005): 185–211.
3. Michael Raine, "Ishihara Yūjirō: Youth, Celebrity, and the Male Body in Late-1950s Japan," in *World and Image in Japanese Cinema*, ed. Dennis Washburn and Carole Cavanaugh (Cambridge: Cambridge University Press, 2001), 202–25; Mark Schilling, "Ishihara Yujiro," in *The Encyclopedia of Japanese Pop Culture* (New York: Weatherhill, 1997), 70–76. On the *taiyōzoku* genre of films, see David Desser, *Eros Plus Massacre: An Introduction to Japanese New Wave*

Cinema (Bloomington: Indiana University Press, 1988). For a discussion of Yūjirō's hit film *The Man Who Called Up a Storm* (*Arashi o yobu otoko*, 1957) and the music in it, see also Michael Molasky, *Sengo Nihon no jazu bunka: Eiga, bungaku, angora* (Tokyo: Seidōsha, 2005), 73–87.

4. Honda Yasuhiro, *"Sengo": Misora Hibari to sono jidai* (Tokyo: Kōdansha, 1989), 155–56.

5. In the film *Crazed Fruit*, this is addressed more directly: the song is used as background to a scene in which Yūjirō's character forcibly makes his move on the heroine, his brother's girlfriend, whom Yūjirō has learned is actually married to an American man: a revenge rape fantasy in which once again a woman serves as the object through which two brothers (and two nations) define their relation. Also, to link the 1950s Japanese Hawaiian boom to American pop culture is not to say that Japan did not have its own earlier tropical-island fixation, including prewar popular Hawaiian songs. See Shuhei Hosokawa, "East of Honolulu: Hawaiian Music in Japan from the 1920s to the 1940s," *Perfect Beat* 2, no. 1 (1994): 51–68. See also the discussion of the images of colonial females in prewar Japan in Miriam Silverberg, "Remembering Pearl Harbor, Forgetting Charlie Chaplin, and the Case of the Disappearing Western Woman: A Picture Story," *positions* 1, no. 1 (1993): 24—76.

6. Christine R. Yano, *Tears of Longing: Nostalgia and the Nation in Japanese Popular Song* (Cambridge, Mass.: Harvard University Asia Center, 2002). For an account of a similar process of Japanese self-exoticization in the realm of tourism, of the production of a nostalgia for nostalgia, see Marilyn Ivy, *Discourses of the Vanishing: Modernity, Phantasm, Japan* (Chicago: Chicago University Press, 1995).

7. For a discussion about how the 1960s saw a major restructuring of the Japanese music industry through which *enka* emerged as a distinct, somewhat marginalized genre as a result of these processes, see chapter 2.

8. The four books are Ishihara Shintarō and Morita Akio, *"No" to ieru Nihon* (Tokyo: Kōbunsha, 1989); Ishihara Shintarō, Watanabe Shōichi, and Ogawa Kazuhiko, *Soredemo "No" to ieru Nihon* (Tokyo: Kōbunsha, 1990); Ishihara Shintarō and Etō Jun, *Danko "No" to ieru Nihon* (Tokyo: Kōbunsha, 1991); and Ishihara Shintarō and Mahathir bin Mohamad, *"No" to ieru Ajia* (Tokyo: Kōbunsha, 1994). Following the panicked reaction in Washington to the first volume, an unauthorized translation was widely circulated. In response, an authorized translation was published, dropping the sections of the book written by Morita and adding sections written especially by Ishihara for his English-language readers: Shintaro Ishihara, *The Japan That Can Say No*, trans. Frank Baldwin (New York: Simon and Schuster, 1991). A translation of the

fourth volume is also available: Mahathir Mohamad and Shintaro Ishihara, *The Voice of Asia: Two Leaders Discuss the Coming Century*, trans. Frank Baldwin (Tokyo: Kodansha, 1995). Because of Ishihara's justified sensitivity to unauthorized translation, I quote wherever possible from these authorized English versions; all other translations of Japanese-language materials are mine.

9. James L. Smith, *Melodrama* (London: Methuen, 1973), 10.

10. Peter Brooks, *The Melodramatic Imagination: Balzac, Henry James, Melodrama, and the Mode of Excess* (New Haven, Conn.: Yale University Press, 1976), 15.

11. Elaine Hadley, *Melodramatic Tactics: Theatricalized Dissent in the English Marketplace, 1800–1885* (Stanford, Calif.: Stanford University Press, 1995). See also Mark Anderson, *Japan and the Specter of Imperialism* (New York: Palgrave Macmillan, 2009), esp. 24–25.

12. See, for example, E. Ann Kaplan, *Motherhood and Representation: The Mother in Popular Culture and Melodrama* (London: Routledge, 1992); and Angela Partington, "Melodrama's Gendered Audience," in *Off-Centre: Feminism and Cultural Studies*, ed. Sarah Franklin, Celia Lury, and Jackie Stacey (London: HarperCollins, 1991), 49–68. For accounts of how melodrama functions in East Asia, see Wimal Dissanayake, ed., *Melodrama and Asian Cinema* (Cambridge: Cambridge University Press, 1993); and Joseph Murphy, "Approaching Japanese Melodrama," *East-West Film Journal* 7, no. 2 (1993): 1–38. In the interest of pursuing my critique of Ishihara's claims for an essential Japanese difference from the West, I am ignoring the question of whether a putatively "Western" category like "melodrama" can apply to a putatively "non-Western" culture like Japan: to accept those cultural categories unproblematically would be to buy into the terms of Ishihara's argument.

13. Ishihara likewise argues that market forces will destroy national unity in Russia and China, leaving Japan the sole superpower national culture not crushed by the forces of capitalism, in Ishihara and Etō, *Danko "No" to ieru Nihon*, 190.

14. Ibid., 157.

15. Ishihara, *Japan That Can Say No*, 118. Note the allusion to popular music. The Japanese version of this passage (from one of the new chapters that Ishihara wrote for the English translation) appears in the second volume in the series: Ishihara, Watanabe, and Ogawa, *Soredemo "No" to ieru Nihon*, 220–21.

16. Ishihara, *Japan That Can Say No*, 76.

17. Perhaps the clearest statement of this global political vision is in Ishihara, Watanabe, and Ogawa, *Soredemo "No" to ieru Nihon*, 225–26.

18. Yoshikuni Igarashi, *Bodies of Memory: Narratives of War in Postwar Japanese Culture, 1945–1970* (Princeton, N.J.: Princeton University Press, 2000).

19. Ishihara, *Japan That Can Say No*, 106. The Japanese citation of *The King and I* (one of the new chapters that Ishihara wrote for the English translation) appears in the second volume in the series: Ishihara, Watanabe, and Ogawa, *Soredemo "No" to ieru Nihon*, 223–24.

20. On the history of the *Madame Butterfly* narrative, see Anderson, *Japan and the Specter of Imperialism*, 15–45; and Jonathan Wisenthal, Sherrill Grace, Melinda Boyd, Brian McIlroy, and Vera Nicznik, eds., *A Vision of the Orient: Texts, Intertexts, and Contexts of Madame Butterfly* (Toronto: University of Toronto Press, 2006).

21. Ishihara and Etō, *Danko "No" to ieru Nihon*, 159, 163.

22. The poleless world order is described in ibid., 189; the tripolar world order, in Ishihara, Watanabe, and Ogawa, *Soredemo "No" to ieru Nihon*, 216.

23. In the second volume, coauthor Watanabe cites Spengler on the inevitable collapse of European civilization but maintains that Japanese culture will persist eternally: "In contrast to Western civilization, based on a desire for limitless conquest, Japan's simple, unadorned [*kinari*] culture is Nature in itself, and so unlike the West it has no concept of eschatology, it does not lose its power suddenly when it comes up against the concept of entropy, and in short as long as the earth continues to exist, the fundamental images of Japanese culture will be able to exist eternally in harmony with it" (Ishihara, Watanabe, and Ogawa, *Soredemo "No" to ieru Nihon*, 130).

24. For a discussion of how postmodern theories in Japan have been transformed into a conservative discourse through a process of dehistoricization and depoliticization, see Mitsuhiro Yoshimoto, "Melodrama, Postmodernism, and Japanese Cinema," in Dissanayake, *Melodrama and Asian Cinema*, 102–26.

25. For a survey of how modern intellectuals have reinflected the gender politics of Motoori Norinaga, see Tomiko Yoda, *Gender and National Literature: Heian Texts in the Constructions of Japanese Modernity* (Durham, N.C.: Duke University Press, 2004).

26. Ueno Chizuko, "Are the Japanese Feminine? Some Problems of Japanese Feminism in Its Cultural Context," in *Broken Silence: Voices of Japanese Feminism*, ed. Sandra Buckley (Berkeley: University of California Press, 1997), 293–301. Another discussion of the status of feminism in Japan, including the need to overcome "nationalistic feminism," can be found in Kanai Yoshiko, "Issues for Japanese Feminism," in *Voices from the Japanese Women's Movement*, ed. AMPO–*Japan Asia Quarterly Review* (Armonk, N.Y.: Sharpe, 1996), 3–22.

27. Watanabe (Ishihara, Watanabe, and Ogawa, *Soredemo "No" to ieru Nihon*, 124–25) and Etō (Ishihara and Etō, *Danko "No" to ieru Nihon*, 173–74) take up Western feminism, while Mahathir (Mahathir and Ishihara, *Voice of Asia*, 24–25) cites gay and lesbian marriages as markers of decline in the West.

28. Ueno, "Are the Japanese Feminine?," 300.

29. Schilling, *Encyclopedia of Japanese Pop Culture*, 274.

30. Fuji Television, "Fuji Terebi jōhō pakku," press release, no. 91-46 (September 18, 1991).

31. Koichi Iwabuchi, *Recentering Globalization: Popular Culture and Japanese Transnationalism* (Durham, N.C.: Duke University Press, 2002), 146.

32. Brooks, *Melodramatic Imagination*, 20.

33. "Fuji kaibutsu bangumi: 36.7%," *Sankei supōtsu*, September 18, 1991, 22.

34. On wartime and postwar films in Japan that portray World War II in terms of a feminized Japanese victimization, a strategy that helps evade responsibility for Japanese aggression in the war and inculcates the patriarchal order of the "family state" proposed by the Japanese state to both its domestic and colonial audiences, see Marie Thorsten Morimoto, "The 'Peace Dividend' in Japanese Cinema: Metaphors of a Demilitarized Nation," in *Colonialism and Nationalism in Asian Cinema*, ed. Wimal Dissanayake (Bloomington: Indiana University Press, 1994), 11–29.

35. Maurizia Boscagli, "A Moving Story: Masculine Tears and the Humanity of Televised Emotions," *Discourse* 15, no. 2 (1992–1993): 64–79.

36. Ibid., 75.

37. For a discussion of ideological reproduction and resistance, see Douglas Kellner, *Media Culture: Cultural Studies, Identity and Politics Between the Modern and the Postmodern* (London: Routledge, 1995).

38. Christopher Small, *Musicking: The Meanings of Performing and Listening* (Hanover, N.H.: University Press of New England / Wesleyan University Press, 1998).

39. My sources of information on C&A include the following books: Ren'ai Kajin Kenkyū-kai, *Mr. Asia: Chage & Aska no nazo* (Tokyo: Seikokusha, 1996); Chage & Asuka Project, *Pride: Chage & Aska 10-nen no fukuzatsu*, 2 vols. (Tokyo: Hachiyōsha, 1989); Yamaguchi Miruko and Nagasaki Setsuko, eds., *Chage & Aska Document: Asian tour no shinjitsu* (Tokyo: Gentōsha, 1996); Ishihara Shin'ichi, *Keredo sora wa ao: Asuka Ryō-ron* (Tokyo: Hachiyōsha, 1990); Chage, *Tsuki ga iiwake o shiteru: The Moon Says "Excuse Me"* (Tokyo: Gentōsha, 1994); and Asuka Ryō, *Interview* (Tokyo: Gentōsha, 1996). C&A have also been covered extensively by tabloid newspapers and popular magazines, in particular those published by the Fuji-Sankei group (parent company to both Fuji Television and Pony Canyon, C&A's record label). Among the most important journalistic articles on C&A are the twelve-part series "Futari de hitotsu no 13-nen," *Sankei shinbun*, July 11–24, 1992, evening ed.; the three-part series "Million Sellers: Hit Maker Shinjidai," *Nikkan supōtsu*, March 30–April 1, 1993; and the special section "Chage & Aska," *Gekkan Kadokawa*, June 1996, 18–71.

40. On the importance of local regional scenes in 1970s new music (contests, radio stations, etc.), see Maeda Yoshitake and Hirahara Kōji, *Nihon no fōku & rokku no jidai 2: Nyū myūjikku no jidai* (Tokyo: Shinkō Music, 1993), 98–122.

41. Even as they speak openly about their ambitions for international success, however, C&A frequently insist that their music is specifically Japanese in nature. See, for example, the assertions by Chage that the rhythm of their music is rooted in the *taiko* drumming that he learned as a child attending local festivals, in "Futari de hitotsu no 13-nen: 7," *Sankei shinbun*, July 18, 1992, evening ed., 2.

42. The album sold more than 1 million copies on its first day of release. A tabloid article reporting this compares the breakthrough that C&A have achieved with Hoshino's winning of Kaoru in *The 101st Proposal*; in both cases, it demonstrates that *yasashisa* (gentleness) has won the day: "It appears that the current age demands the '*yasashisa*' of these two, that it needs their music" ("Chage & Aska Album *Tree*: 100 manmai chō-ōure," *Sankei supōtsu*, October 11, 1991, 24). On the same page are photographs of Asano Atsuko, the actress who played Kaoru, acting as "an ordinary mom" attending a sports festival at her son's elementary school.

43. I am indebted to Loren Kajikawa for pointing this out, as well as for helping me understand other aspects of the structure of this song.

44. Susan McClary, *Feminine Endings: Music, Gender, and Sexuality* (Minneapolis: University of Minnesota Press, 1991), 156.

45. Robert Walser, *Running with the Devil: Power, Gender, and Madness in Heavy Metal Music* (Hanover, N.H.: University Press of New England / Wesleyan University Press, 1993), 30.

46. Rey Chow, "Listening Otherwise, Music Miniaturized," in *Writing Diaspora: Tactics of Intervention in Contemporary Cultural Studies* (Bloomington: Indiana University Press, 1993), 144–64. My reading here is greatly influenced by this essay as well as by Lawrence Grossman, *Dancing in Spite of Myself: Essays on Popular Culture* (Durham, N.C.: Duke University Press, 1997), especially his notion of "indifference." But see also Theodor Adorno, "On Popular Music," in *Essays on Music*, ed. Richard Leppert (Berkeley: University of California Press, 2002), 437–69, especially on "inattention" (459) as a contrasting concept to Grossberg's "indifference."

47. Walser, *Running with the Devil*, 31.

48. Small, *Musicking*, 10 (italics in original).

49. Ibid., 169.

50. Walser, *Running with the Devil*, 132 (italics in original). Walser cites Sue Wise, "Sexing Elvis," in *On Record: Rock, Pop, and the Written Word*, ed. Simon Frith and Andrew Goodwin (New York: Pantheon, 1990), 390–98.

51. The mean age of first marriage for Japanese women increased from 24.7 years (1975) to 25.5 (1985) and to 26.3 (1995). The figures for Japanese men show a less-pronounced increase in age. During the same twenty-year period, the average household size in Japan shrank from 3.28 members to 2.82 members. See Government of Japan, Bureau of Statistics, http://www.stat.go.jp/english/data/handbook/c02cont.htm#cha2_4 (accessed May 28, 2010).

52. Chow, "Listening Otherwise," 163.

53. On the spread of Japanese television programming across Asia in the 1990s, see Iwabuchi, *Recentering Globalization*. A Korean remake of *The 101st Proposal* aired in South Korea in 2006.

54. "Asuka Ryō: Utaidashita totan okyakusan ga kaette shimatta koto ga arimasu," *Shūkan bunshun*, August 1, 1996, 50–54.

55. C&A have also expressed an interest in performing in Malaysia and China. A planned Chinese concert in 1996 was canceled due to the crisis that arose when China conducted naval exercises off the coast of Taiwan. C&A also had ambitions beyond Asia: they hoped to use their success in Asia to break into the Western pop market. They were especially active in England, in 1996 releasing *One Voice*, a tribute album featuring Western artists such as Lisa Stansfield and Boy George covering C&A songs. C&A were also active in Hollywood sound tracks, contributing (either as a duo or as solo artists) songs to the sound tracks of the films *Street Fighter II* (1995) and *Judge Dredd* (1995).

56. In this light, it is important to remember the central role that the working through of traumatic memories (Kaoru's need to forget her dead fiancé) plays in *The 101st Proposal*. On the one hand, Kaoru's traumatic loss three years earlier is nearly synchronized to the bursting of the economic bubble; on the other, another historical time line is invoked in the phrase from the series' dialogue that was widely used in promotional materials—Hoshino's "I swear that I will love you in fifty years the same as I do now" (used, for example, as a blurb in boldface on the cover of the novelization of the series). The year 1991, of course, marked the fiftieth anniversary of Japan's expansion of its war with China into Southeast Asia. See the advertising flyleaf on Nojima Shinji, *101 kaime no puropōzu* (Tokyo: Ōta shuppan, 1991). For another working through of Japan's orientalist relations to its Asian neighbors, see Dorinne Kondo, *About Face: Performing Race in Fashion and Theater* (London: Routledge, 1997), esp. 85–95.

57. For evidence of how a similar ideology of romance was used during the 1930s and 1940s to represent Japan's relation to its colonies, see Silverberg, "Remembering Pearl Harbor."

58. Chage & Aska, *Document: Asian Tour no shinjitsu*, 97.

59. "The duo's record label, Pony Canyon Records, opened its Shanghai offices in October, resolved to begin opening the Chinese market. It seems inevitable

that local radio stations, centered in that city, will play C&A's songs more frequently. With a population of 1.2 billion, it is possible that China could have hit songs registering sales in the range of 10 million copies, a figure that spurs on the duo's enthusiasm" ("Chūgoku shinshutsu," *Sankei supōtsu*, August 15, 1995, 20). This initial enthusiasm quickly faded, however, and Pony Canyon and other Japanese labels had shut down most of their Asian branch offices by the late 1990s, according to Iwabuchi, *Recentering Globalization*, 107.

60. Iwabuchi, *Recentering Globalization*, 66. The Taiwan concert video is reported to have sold 100,000 copies during the first two weeks of its release in Japan. See "Chage-Asu ni 'kōeishō,'" *Sankei supōtsu*, April 6, 1996, 22. A similar video was released following their first concert appearance in Korea in 2000.

61. The phrase comes from Yao Souchou, "The Romance of Asian Capitalism: Geography, Desire and Chinese Business," in *The Rise of East Asia: Critical Visions of the Pacific Century*, ed. Mark T. Berger and Douglas A. Borer (London: Routledge, 1997), 221–40.

62. Iwabuchi, *Recentering Globalization*, 39.

63. Ibid., 28.

64. Simon Frith, *Sound Effects: Youth, Leisure, and the Politics of Rock 'n' Roll* (New York: Pantheon, 1981), 129.

65. For a discussion of "the ambiguous, multilayered, and, at times, irrelevant responses" of Taiwanese consumers to the commodities of what is ostensibly "Japanese" popular culture, see Leo Ching, "Imaginings in the Empires of the Sun: Japanese Mass Culture in Asia," *Boundary 2* 21, no. 1 (1994): 198–219. On the ways that Asian indigenization of Japanese popular culture forms hybridizes those forms, undermining any simple notions of authenticity or originality, see also Iwabuchi, *Recentering Globalization*, esp. 105–6.

66. "Sekai no Chage-Asu," *Sankei supōtsu*, February 10, 1994, 24.

67. Bernard Gendron, "Theodor Adorno Meets the Cadillacs," in *Studies in Entertainment: Critical Approaches to Mass Culture*, ed. Tania Modleski (Bloomington: Indiana University Press, 1986), 18–36, quote on 35.

68. On the history of the term *J-pop*, see Ugaya Hiromichi, *J-poppu to wa nani ka: Kyodaika suru ongaku sangyō* (Tokyo: Iwanami, 2005), esp. 4–7.

CODA

1. Ugaya Hiromichi, *J-poppu to wa nani ka: Kyodaika suru ongaku sangyō* (Tokyo: Iwanami, 2005), 28–29. Sales of music CDs reached a peak in Japan in 1998, going into steady decline in the years after that. See Carolyn S. Stevens, *Japanese Popular Music: Culture, Authenticity and Power* (London: Routledge, 2008), 83–84.

2. On the origin and dissemination of the term *J-pop*, see Ugaya, *J-poppu to wa nani ka*, 2–24.

3. On the integration of Japanese, European, and African American elements into contemporary J-pop, see Satō Yoshiaki, *J-pop shinkaron: "Yosahoi bushi" kara "Automatic" e* (Tokyo: Heibonsha, 1999), esp. 10–28, 190–213.

4. Koichi Iwabuchi, *Recentering Globalization: Popular Culture and Japanese Transnationalism* (Durham, N.C.: Duke University Press, 2002), esp. 112–18.

5. Quoted in ibid., 161.

6. Ugaya, *J-poppu to wa nani ka*, 41–44. See also Stevens, *Japanese Popular Music*, esp. 101–31.

7. Ian Condry, *Hip-Hop Japan: Rap and the Paths of Cultural Globalization* (Durham, N.C.: Duke University Press, 2006), 115, 195.

8. On the rise of rap music in Japan, see ibid., esp. 61–86.

9. Jennifer Matsue, *Making Music in Japan's Underground: The Tokyo Hardcore Scene* (New York: Routledge, 2009); David Novak, "Japan Noise: Global Media Circulation and the Transpacific Circuits of Experimental Music" (Ph.D. diss., Columbia University, 2006).

10. Marvin D. Starling, *Babylon East: Performing Dancehall, Roots Reggae, and Rastafari in Japan* (Durham, N.C.: Duke University Press, 2010).

11. James Roberson, "'Doing Our Thing': Identity and Colonial Modernity in Okinawan Rock Music," *Popular Music and Society* (forthcoming).

12. Stevens, *Japanese Popular Music*, 25–27.

13. Jim Frederick, "Rinngo's [*sic*] a Star: On the Cookie-Cutter Pop Scene, One Singer Goes for the Unique," *Time* (Asian ed.), August 11, 2003, http://www.time.com/time/asia/2003/cool_japan/rinngo.html (accessed June 15, 2010).

INDEX

9 780231 158756